FOCUS ON

IELTS

NEW EDITION

SUE O'CONNELL

Map of the book

► The IELTS Test: overview

Introduction

IELTS stands for *International English Language Testing System*. The test consists of four modules – Listening, Speaking, Reading and Writing – and takes two hours and 45 minutes to complete.

This book provides preparation for the Listening and Speaking modules, which all candidates take, and also for the Academic Reading and Writing modules, which are normally taken by candidates intending to use English for study purposes. General Training versions of these modules are also available and, while much of the material in the book would provide useful practice, there is no specific exam preparation for these modules.

The test result is published in the form of a report, which places candidates on a scale of one to nine according to language ability (see page 7). There is a score for each of the four modules and also an overall score. Most universities and colleges require an IELTS score of 6.0 or more, but it's important to check the specific requirement for your intended course of study.

IELTS can be taken at test centres in over 100 countries. Test dates are fixed, and tests are normally available throughout the year in most areas. Further information and a list of local centres is available on the IELTS website – www.ielts.org

IELTS modules in brief

Listening   Time: 30 minutes

There are four sections and a total of 40 questions, testing different listening skills. You will hear a variety of recorded texts, including monologues and dialogues. Texts and tasks become more difficult as the test progresses. The recording is played **only once,** but you are allowed time to read the questions beforehand. There is an **extra ten minutes** at the end for you to transfer your answers to the answer sheet.

Academic Reading   Time: 60 minutes

There are three reading passages and a total of 40 questions, which test a range of reading skills. Passages come from magazines, journals, books and newspapers, and the topics are of general interest. Texts and tasks become more difficult as the test progresses. There is **no extra time** for transferring your answers to the answer sheet.

Academic Writing   Time: 60 minutes

There are two tasks, one of at least 150 words and the other of at least 250 words. In **Task 1**, you have to look at a diagram or data of some kind and present the information in your own words. In **Task 2**, you have to discuss a current issue, present and justify an opinion or analyse and assess a development or problem.

Speaking   Time: 11–14 minutes

This interview between the candidate and an examiner has three main parts. In **Part 1**, you are asked general questions about yourself, your home or family, your job or studies, etc. In **Part 2**, you are given a topic and allowed one minute to prepare. You then have to talk on the topic for between one and two minutes. **Part 3** is a discussion of more abstract issues related to the topic in Part 2.

IELTS modules: details

Listening

The first two sections are concerned with social needs. In **Section 1**, you will hear a conversation in a social situation, for example, two friends discussing holiday plans or an interview at an accommodation agency. In **Section 2**, you will hear a monologue on a general subject, for example, a short talk on healthy eating or tourist information.

The last two sections are concerned with educational or training contexts. In **Section 3**, you will hear a conversation between up to four people, for example, a tutorial discussion between tutor and student, or several students discussing an assignment. In **Section 4**, you will hear a monologue, for example, a lecture or talk of general academic interest.

The recordings may include a range of accents including British, American or Australian English. For this reason, different accents are used on the recordings accompanying this course, and you can also help yourself further by listening to as wide a variety of English as possible, on the radio or television, for example.

QUESTIONS

Questions include multiple choice, short-answer questions, completion and matching tasks, and diagram labelling. Each one requires a specific approach and specific skills, and these are outlined in the **Exam briefing** boxes and **Task approach** sections in the book.

You are allowed an extra ten minutes at the end of the test to transfer your answers onto the answer sheet.

NB Take care when transferring your answers – you will lose marks if you make spelling or grammar mistakes.

MARKING

One mark is awarded for each of the 40 questions, and the result is translated into a score on the IELTS nine-band scale (see page 7).

Reading

The three reading passages contain up to 2,700 words, which means that you will need to read efficiently, using appropriate reading skills for each task, in order to complete the paper in the time allowed. The course includes a varied selection of reading texts, and you can help yourself further by reading from as wide a range of sources as possible, such as newspapers, magazines and journals.

QUESTIONS

Questions include multiple choice, short-answer questions, completion and matching tasks, and Yes/No/Not Given or True/False/Not Given. Each one requires a specific approach and specific skills, and these are outlined in the **Exam briefing** boxes and **Task approach** sections in this book.

You must write your answers on an answer sheet, but there is no extra time for this.

NB Take care when transferring your answers – you will lose marks if you make spelling or grammar mistakes.

MARKING

One mark is awarded for each of the 40 questions, and the result is translated into a score on the IELTS nine-band scale (see page 7).

Writing

There are two tasks. The instructions specify the minimum number of words for each task and also recommend the amount of time you should spend on each one. It's important to follow these guidelines, because Task 2 carries more weight in marking than Task 1, and you will need to give the appropriate time to each part in order to get good marks. Answers must be written on the answer sheet. They must be written in full, not in note form.

Task 1: You are given a diagram or data of some kind and you have to present the information in your own words. For example, you may have to consider a set of statistics and then write a description outlining the key features; you may have to study a diagram of a machine and explain how it works; or you may have to look at a flow chart and describe the main stages in a process.

You have to write at least **150 words** for Task 1 and you are recommended to spend **20 minutes** on it.

Task 2: You are given brief details of an opinion, an argument or a problem, and you have to write an essay in response. For example, you may have to consider an opinion in relation to evidence, or weigh up the pros and cons of an argument before presenting your own view on the matter. You may also have to discuss various aspects of a problem and then outline your ideas for solving it.

You have to write at least **250 words** for Task 2 and you are recommended to spend **40 minutes** on it.

NB You will lose marks if you write less than the required number of words.

MARKING

Scripts are assessed according to the following criteria:

- **Task Achievement (Task 1):** Have you satisfied all the requirements of the task? Have you presented a clear, accurate and relevant description of the information?

- **Task Response (Task 2):** Have you discussed all parts of the task? Have you developed and supported relevant ideas and arguments, and made your position clear?

- **Coherence and Cohesion (Tasks 1 & 2):** Is your writing well-organized? Is there a clear progression of information and ideas? Are sentences and paragraphs logically linked?

- **Lexical Resource (Tasks 1 & 2):** Have you used a good variety of appropriate vocabulary? Is your spelling and word formation reasonably accurate?
- **Grammatical Range and Accuracy (Tasks 1 & 2):** Have you used a good variety of structures? Is your grammar and punctuation reasonably accurate?

The overall result is translated into a score on the IELTS nine-band scale (see right).

Speaking

The interview is in three parts.

Part 1 Introduction and interview (4–5 minutes)
In the first part, the examiner will ask a number of general questions. Be prepared to introduce yourself, to say where you come from and to talk about such topics as your family or home, your country or city, your job or studies, your interests or hobbies.

Part 2 Individual long turn (3–4 minutes)
In this part, you are given a card outlining a particular topic and asked to talk about the topic for one to two minutes. You have one minute to prepare and make notes if you wish. Be prepared to describe people, places or events and to explain their significance to you.

Part 3 Two-way discussion (4–5 minutes)
In the last part, the examiner asks questions linked to the topic in Part 2 and develops a discussion of more abstract issues. Be prepared to listen carefully and respond appropriately, to express opinions and preferences and give reasons.

MARKING

Performance is assessed on the following criteria:

- **Fluency and Coherence:** Do you express ideas and opinions clearly and coherently, without long hesitations?
- **Lexical Resource:** Do you use a wide range of vocabulary?
- **Grammatical Range and Accuracy:** Do you use a wide range of structures and make only a few minor mistakes?
- **Pronunciation:** Are you easy to understand? Do you use English pronunciation features naturally?

The overall result is translated into a score on the IELTS nine-band scale (see right). All scores are reported in whole and half bands.

CEFR	B1	B2	C1	C2
Cambridge ESOL Exams	PET	FCE	CAE	CPE
IELTS	3.5–4.5	5.0–6.0	6.5–7.0	7.5+

THE IELTS NINE-BAND SCALE

Band 9 – Expert User
Has fully operational command of the language: appropriate, accurate and fluent with complete understanding.

Band 8 – Very Good User
Has fully operational command of the language with only occasional unsystematic inaccuracies and inappropriacies. Misunderstandings may occur in unfamiliar situations. Handles complex detailed argumentation well.

Band 7 – Good User
Has operational command of the language, though with occasional inaccuracies, inappropriacies and misunderstandings in some situations. Generally handles complex language well and understands detailed reasoning.

Band 6 – Competent User
Has generally effective command of the language despite some inaccuracies, inappropriacies and misunderstandings. Can use and understand fairly complex language, particularly in familiar situations.

Band 5 – Modest User
Has partial command of the language, coping with overall meaning in most situations, though is likely to make many mistakes. Should be able to handle basic communication in own field.

Band 4 – Limited User
Basic competence is limited to familiar situations. Has frequent problems in understanding and expression. Is not able to use complex language.

Band 3 – Extremely Limited User
Conveys and understands only general meaning in very familiar situations. Frequent breakdowns in communication occur.

Band 2 – Intermittent User
No real communication is possible except for the most basic information using isolated words or short formulae in familiar situations and to meet immediate needs. Has great difficulty in understanding spoken and written English.

Band 1 – Non User
Essentially has no ability to use the language beyond possibly a few isolated words.

Band 0 – Did not attempt the test
No assessable information provided.

1 ▶ Health's 'magic bullet'

magic bullet *n* [C] **1** a drug or treatment that can cure an illness quickly and easily **2** *informal* something that solves a difficult problem in an easy way: *There's no magic bullet for school reform.* (Longman Exams Dictionary)

In this unit you will practise
- Talking about personal interests; comparing/contrasting
- Skimming, scanning; reading for detail
- Reading and answering global multiple-choice questions; paragraph headings; short-answer questions; True/False /Not Given
- Dealing with unknown vocabulary

Key Language
Grammatical terms

Exam Focus
Speaking: Parts 1–3
Reading skills

Lead-in

1 Work with a partner to complete each statement below by choosing a pair of figures A–E from the box.

A 90 : 31	B 120 : 420	C 30 : 1	D 3 : 3	E 5 : 40

1 The minimum daily amount of physical activity recommended for adults is … minutes and for children … hour(s).

2 Less than … per cent of children and … per cent of adults in the UK achieve this.

3 … per cent of children walked or cycled to school 50 years ago. Only … per cent do so today.

4 It takes about … months of regular exercise to become fit and … week(s) of inactivity to lose fitness.

5 Watching football for 1 hour burns … calories, while playing football burns … .

2 Check your answers on page 253 and then discuss these questions.

1 Do any of the facts surprise you? Which ones, and why?

2 Why is exercise good for you? List as many benefits as you can.

3 Why are many people inactive nowadays? List as many reasons as you can.

Focus on speaking 1 *Talking about personal interests*

> ► **EXAM BRIEFING** **Speaking: introduction**
>
> The test has three parts. In Part 1, you answer short questions about familiar topics such as your home or family. In Part 2, you speak for 1–2 minutes on a topic. In Part 3, you have a discussion with the examiner on more general topics related to the subject of your Part 2 talk.

Parts 1 and 2: Interview and long turn

► *Focus on Academic Skills for IELTS* pages 16–17

> **EXAM TIP:** Use fluency markers in the Speaking test to help you 'buy time' before you answer.

Work with a partner. Take turns asking and answering these questions. Before you begin, look at the *Useful language* box below.

What kind of exercise …

* do you do regularly? (Where and when?)
* do you enjoy least? (Say why.)
* should you do more often? (Say why.)

> **Useful language**
>
> | | |
> |---|---|
> | (*Well*) I jog / I go jogging
I swim at the local pool | on a regular basis / most days / three times a week, etc. |
> | The thing I (*really*) hate is …
(*I'm afraid*) I (*just*) can't stand … | because I find it so *boring / monotonous*, etc. |
> | (*Actually*) I ought to walk more | but I always take the bus because … |
> | I should play tennis more often | but I'm always making excuses not to play. |

Notice the expressions in italics: *Well, I'm afraid, Actually,* etc. These fluency markers are important to learn and use because they help a speaker to sound more fluent and natural.

Focus on reading 1 *Text types*

Texts have different features of style depending on their purpose and the audience they were written for. For example, a newspaper article written for a general audience is likely to have shorter paragraphs, simpler sentence structure and more informal language than a report in an academic journal written for experts.

EXAM TIP: Recognising a text type quickly helps you read more efficiently in the exam.

1 Match each extract A–D to one of the sources below. Compare your answers with another student and discuss which texts you found a) easiest and b) hardest to read and understand, and why.

1 Newspaper/magazine   2 Academic journal
3 Advertisement   4 Online encyclopaedia

A **Physical exercise** is a bodily activity that develops and maintains physical fitness and overall health. It is often practised to strengthen muscles and the cardiovascular system, and to enhance athletic skills. Regular physical exercise boosts the immune system and helps prevent such conditions as heart disease, Type 2 diabetes and obesity. It also improves mental health and helps prevent depression.

B The present study was conducted among 92 adolescents living in two rural and two urban areas, with particular focus on the availability of walking trails and cycling tracks. Results revealed that both rural and urban adolescents spent more time engaged in sedentary activities such as watching TV/video and playing TV/data games than on regular physical activity. No differences were observed between the two groups with regard to activity patterns. However, the average distance the urban adolescents walked …

C After years of studying numerous nutritional and lifestyle factors for lifetime fitness, researchers at the Harvard School of Public Health have come up with a result. It's the single thing that comes close to a magic bullet in terms of strong and universal health benefits.

Quite simply, it is exercise!

D Have you ever wished that you could work out in the comfort of your own home, without having to go to the gym? With **Leapfrog** you can. **Leapfrog** is the most technologically advanced home sports equipment available. Every product is the result of millions of dollars of university-based research. Engineering excellence and top quality components mean that Leapfrog equipment needs virtually no maintenance, while each product is fully backed by a 5-year warranty.

2 Discuss these questions about the purpose of each extract.

1 Which one is designed to make the reader want to do something? (persuasion)
2 Which **two** report on the results of research? (evidence and conclusions)
3 Which one sets out to explain a particular expression? (definition)
4 Which one compares two groups? (comparison and contrast)

The terms in brackets are examples of language functions. For more information see *Academic Style 1*, page 16.

3 Which text A–D contains:

    1 the shortest paragraph?
    2 the shortest sentence?
    3 two examples of the passive voice?
    4 fairly simple sentences with frequent use of the linking word 'and'?
    5 a direct question?
    6 the most formal vocabulary?

4 Look at extract B again and complete the following description of academic English. Delete the incorrect answer in each case.

> Academic English is characterised by fairly **1** *formal / informal* grammar and vocabulary. It normally **2** *avoids / includes* colloquial expressions, contractions such as 'isn't' or 'don't' and direct questions. The style is generally **3** *personal / impersonal*, with **4** *few / many* personal pronouns such as 'I' or 'we' and **5** *frequent / infrequent* use of the passive voice. Facts and figures are stated very **6** *precisely / generally*. The organisation is logical and clear.

For more information see *Academic Style 2*, page 36.

Focus on speaking 2 *Comparing and contrasting*

Part 3: Discussion

▶ *Focus on Academic Skills for IELTS* pages 28–29

1 **In Part 3 of the Speaking test you may have to compare two things, for example life in your home town and in another place. Study the *Useful language* below, then work in pairs to do the practice tasks that follow.**

> **Useful language**
> They're **both** …
> **But / On the other hand,** …
> The **main difference** is that X is … **while / whereas** Y is …
> **Also / Another thing** is (that) X is … **er / more** … **than** Y

2 **Complete the following dialogue using *Useful language* from the box.**
    A: Examiner **B:** Candidate
    A: How does using an exercise bike compare with riding a real bike?
    B: Well, they're **1** .... good forms of exercise and you use the same technique on each. **2** .... there are also some differences.
    A: Such as?
    B: I think the **3** .... one is that an exercise bike is static **4** .... you can actually go somewhere on a real bike! **5** .... using an exercise bike is safer **6** .... cycling on the road.

3 **Discuss these exam topics using the *Useful language* from the box above.**
    1 How does travelling by plane compare to travelling by train?
    2 Which is better: watching a sporting event on TV or attending the event?
    3 What is the difference between school and university?

Focus on reading 2 *The walking school bus*

> ▶ **EXAM BRIEFING** Academic reading tasks
>
> There are three reading passages and your reading skills will be tested through a variety of tasks including **completion**, **labelling**, and **True/False/Not Given**. The questions are always in the same order as the information in the passage.

1 To answer exam questions efficiently, you need to use the right reading skills for each task.

Skimming means reading fairly quickly for a general idea of the kind of writing, the overall topic and the main subject of each paragraph. The global multiple choice and paragraph headings exam tasks below test skimming.

Scanning is also reading fairly quickly but in this case to find a specific fact, such as a name, date or place. The short answers exam task below tests scanning.

Reading for detail means careful study of the text so that you understand exactly what the author is saying. Exam tasks like the True/False/Not Given exam task below test reading for detail.

RECOGNISING TEXT TYPES **2** **Skim the text opposite, then say whether it's:**

1 a news item from a local newspaper.
2 part of an advertising leaflet.
3 an extract from a serious journal or website.
4 an entertaining article from a popular newspaper.

INTRODUCING EXAM TASKS **3** In this task you have to identify the main topic in each paragraph by choosing
Paragraph headings suitable headings. In the exam, there are more headings than paragraphs but to make this introductory task easier, there are no extra headings. One answer has been given as an example. Begin by underlining one or two key words in each heading i–vii. Then look for matching ideas in the text.

▶ *Focus on Academic Skills*
for IELTS page 34

The reading passage has seven paragraphs, **A–G.**
Choose the correct heading for each paragraph from the list of headings below.
*Write the correct number, **i–vii** in the spaces provided.*

List of headings

i	Benefiting the local environment	1	Paragraph A ..iv..
ii	The development of the walking school bus	2	Paragraph B ..vi..
iii	Allowing children to communicate	3	Paragraph C ..ii..
iv	~~The aim of the walking school bus~~	4	Paragraph D ....
v	Providing healthy daily exercise	5	Paragraph E ..iii..
vi	How the walking school bus works	6	Paragraph F ..i..
vii	Playing a part in the community	7	Paragraph G ..vii..

The Walking School Bus

A In recent years there has been a significant decline in the number of school children who walk to school each day, compared with previous generations. In an attempt to alter this trend, a healthy and environmentally-conscious movement called the walking school bus has been developed and promoted in some school districts. The main goal is to have students walk to school, under the guidance of adults, and thus enjoy the benefits of physical activity.

B On a walking school bus, a 'driver' (adult) calls at specific stops along a set route to collect 'passengers' (children) and they walk together to school. At the end of the school day, all of the walking school bus riders and drivers congregate at a designated school location and begin the walking journey to each passenger's home, simply reversing their earlier route. It has been suggested that, for safety purposes, a driver should be at the front of the 'bus' and a conductor should walk at the rear (Kearns, Collins and Neuwelt, 2003). Families can depend on the consistency of the walking school bus, which operates to a regular timetable, regardless of the weather.

C The walking school bus concept originated in 1998 in St Alban's, England, as a result of parental concerns over speeding vehicles and children's safety. The idea spread through Britain and was adopted quickly in Australia, New Zealand and Canada. Because of the social and physical benefits of the walking school bus, the number of such programs has continued to grow in these locations. In the United States, however, walking school bus programs have not caught on as quickly. Hopefully the number of such programs there will multiply as people recognize their numerous advantages.

D Perhaps the greatest advantage of the walking school bus is the health benefits of regular physical exercise. With the rise of childhood obesity, this is a significant factor. Studies show that approximately 14 per cent of young people are not physically active (Nelson 2004) while approximately 10 per cent of children aged 2 to 6, and 15 per cent of children aged 6 to 19 in the United States are considered overweight (Ogden, Flegal, Carol and Johnson, 2002). The implementation of the walking school bus may support efforts to reduce these substantial percentages.

E The 15 to 20-minute walk each morning and afternoon also provides children with time to socialize before and after their school day. Sarah, a 2nd grader, was asked whether or not she enjoyed 'riding the bus' each morning and afternoon and she responded, "The best part about the bus is that I get to talk to my friends." Having the opportunities to chat with friends was a recurring theme among those children interviewed.

F Furthermore, as increasing numbers of children participate in the walking bus program, fewer parents are driving their children to and from school, which improves the quality of the urban environment by reducing traffic congestion and pollution in the area. The school authorities in Auckland, New Zealand, analyzed traffic problems outside an elementary school before and after implementation of the walking bus and it was reported that there were on average 19.5 fewer cars during drop off and pick up times.

G Finally, the walking school bus helps create a positive school image in the local community. In addition to providing children with physical exercise, safety and socialization, the image of young learners walking to and from school affects all those who witness it. From dog walkers to car drivers, members of the entire community enjoy watching 'the bus' go by, and may be reminded of their own personal school experiences. The program is now a feature in many cities and can be seen as part of a broader international movement to encourage childhood health and improve the environment.

Short-answer questions

4 These questions require short factual answers such as a date, a place or a name, which you can find by scanning the passage. The instructions tell you the maximum number of words you can use. In this introductory task, you will find one answer in each paragraph, B, C and D.

*Choose **NO MORE THAN THREE WORDS AND/OR A NUMBER** from the passage for each answer.*

1 Who should walk at the back of the walking school bus? .... *CONDUCTOR*
2 When did the idea of the walking school bus begin? *1998*
3 In which country are ten per cent of young children overweight? .... *UNITED STATES*

True/False/Not Given

> **▶ EXAM BRIEFING**   **Academic Reading: True/False/Not Given and Yes/No/Not Given**
>
> These are the same as True/False tasks but with an additional option, Not Given, which is used when there is no information in the text. The only difference between the two versions is that True/False/Not Given focuses on facts, while Yes/No/Not Given focuses on the writers' opinion. The questions are always passage order.

5 This practice task is based on paragraphs A–C. There are two TRUE answers, two FALSE answers and just one NOT GIVEN. Note: this information is designed to make this introductory task easier. It is <u>not</u> given in the exam.

TASK APPROACH

- Read each statement and underline key words.
- Find the relevant part of the text and study the information carefully.
- Look for expressions which mean the same as words in the statement.
- Only write **True** if the statement exactly matches information in the text.

Do the following statements agree with the information in the reading passage?

Write

TRUE	*if the statement agrees with the information*
FALSE	*if the statement contradicts the information*
NOT GIVEN	*if there is no information on this*

1 Fewer children walk to school now than in the past. *T*
2 The walking school bus does not run when it is raining. *NG F*
3 The idea of the walking school bus comes from the US. *T*
4 One of the advantages of the walking school bus is that it doesn't cost any money. *NG*
5 The walking bus proved popular in Australia. *T*

Global multiple choice

6 This task asks you to identify the main topic of the passage. Be careful to choose a topic which applies to the passage as a whole, not just one section.

*Choose the correct answer, **A**, **B**, **C** or **D**.*

What is the text about?
A the history of the walking school bus
B the benefits of the walking school bus
C how to set up a walking school bus
D where walking school bus schemes operate

Focus on vocabulary *Dealing with unknown vocabulary*

EXAM TIP knowing which words are important to understand is a key exam skill.

▶*Focus on Academic Skills for IELTS* page **8**

1 You can expect to meet unknown words in IELTS reading texts. Some will be important to your understanding but some will not, and can safely be ignored. Read the following advice.

- Study the questions and identify the parts of the text with relevant information.
- Ignore unknown vocabulary in other parts of the text.
- Try to rough guess the meaning of important vocabulary by identifying the **part of speech** and by looking for **clues in the context**.
- Specialised technical terms are often explained in a footnote at the end of the text.

KEY LANGUAGE
Grammatical terms
▶ p. 210, ex.1

2 Underline the word 'originated' in paragraph C of the text. The form and context should tell you that it's a verb in the past tense (*-ed*), with the general meaning 'began'.

Underline the word 'substantial' in paragraph D. What part of speech is it and what is the general meaning?

3 Work out the meaning of the following words from the Walking School Bus text.

1 Find each one and study how it is used in the text.
2 Circle the correct part of speech. (The first one has been done for you.)
3 Choose a general meaning from the box below.

a) decline (para A)	(noun)	verb	adjective	adverb
b) alter (A)	noun	verb	adjective	adverb
c) goal (A)	noun	verb	adjective	adverb
d) benefit (A)	noun	verb	adjective	adverb
e) specific (B)	noun	verb	adjective	adverb
f) approximately (D)	noun	verb	adjective	adverb
g) theme (E)	noun	verb	adjective	adverb
h) positive (G)	noun	verb	adjective	adverb

decrease	*change*	*aim*	*advantage*	*good or useful*
topic	*roughly*	*particular*		

The words a)–h) come from the *Academic Word List* (AWL). For more information see page 208.

Academic Style I *Functions*

Introduction

Functions are a basic feature of any text and a helpful way of approaching academic writing. They represent the writer's purpose, for example to describe something or express an opinion.

Recognising functions enables you to understand the relationship between ideas in a text and so read more effectively. It will also help to improve your own academic writing.

1 Texts often have more than one function. Look at the advertisement and match sections 1–3 with the correct function A–C:

A **comparison** (pointing out similarities and differences between things)

B **description** (saying what something is like)

C **persuasion** (encouraging someone to do something)

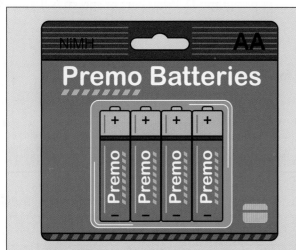

Functional language

Each function is expressed through specific language. For example, in the advert in exercise 1, **comparison** is expressed through the structure *-er ... than*. Other typical comparative language includes expressions such as *Both ... and or while, whereas*. Page references for relevant language are shown in brackets in the following list.

List of key functions

- **Describing an object** (pages 75, 204)
- **Describing a process** (pages 102, 162, 242–244)
- **Definition** (page 162)
- **Comparison and Contrast** (pages 11, 235, 237, 238, 250)
- **Cause and Effect** (pages 64, 99, 224)
- **Change and Development** (page 212)
- **Problem and Solution** (pages 236)
- **Argument and Persuasion** (pages 63, 122, 239)

2 a Match each of the following extracts to one of the functions in the list above.

b Say what the main tense is in each case and underline key language which expresses the main function of the extract. The first one has been done as an example.

A *Change and Development (**main tense:** present progressive; **key language:** trend)*

Complaints about advertisements <u>are increasing</u> rapidly, according to the Advertising Standards Agency. Each year the ASA <u>is receiving</u> growing numbers of complaints about direct mail in particular, and <u>this trend</u> <u>seems likely to</u> continue.

B ....

A **BLOG** refers to a private webpage containing words, pictures or both, which functions as a personal journal or diary. **Blogs** are commonly used to provide a commentary on topics which are of interest to the **blogger** (i.e. the author). Many **blogs** have an interactive facility which allows visitors to post comments.

C ....

A recent survey reports that the average British woman spends two days a year, or five months in a lifetime, vacuum-cleaning the house. By contrast, in a typical lifetime men spend just over a month vacuuming, less than a quarter the time spent by women. Both sexes typically clean four rooms each time ...

D ....

First, green coffee beans are heated to between 180 and 240 degrees C for 8–15 minutes, depending on the degree of roast required. During the roasting process moisture is lost and a chemical reaction takes place. Starches are converted into sugar, proteins are broken down and ...

Academic Vocabulary 1

Introduction

In these sections you will meet important vocabulary that you need to understand and learn. All the words come from the *Academic Word List* (AWL), a list of the most common words in academic texts (see pages 208–209). Once your answers have been checked, correct any mistakes so you can use this page as a reference point for revision.

Knowing a word

There is more to 'knowing' a word than just understanding the meaning. For example, you need to be aware of how it fits into a sentence (**Grammar**), and which other words it often combines with (**Word partners**). To know a word well, you need to meet it several times and pay attention to different aspects of its meaning and use.

Meaning

1 Academic vocabulary is generally fairly formal. Match the common AWL verbs 1–5 to less formal verbs with the same meaning a)–e).

   1 **demonstrate** The graph **demonstrates** a decrease in smoking.
   2 **obtain** It is not easy to **obtain** research funding.
   3 **occur** Most accidents **occur** between 8 and 10 am.
   4 **purchase** Textbooks can be **purchased** online.
   5 **respond** We cannot **respond** to this email.

a) get/receive	b) reply	c) show
d) buy	e) happen	

Grammar: *Parts of speech*

2 Identifying the part of speech is helpful in working out the meaning of a word. Study the way the academic words in bold are used in the examples and write the correct part of speech, noun (N), verb (Vb), adjective (Adj) or adverb (Adv) for each one.

   1 *The walking school bus **concept** originated in 1998.* ....
   2 *The present study was **conducted** ...* ....
   3 *... in two rural and two urban **locations** ....*
   4 *... compared with **previous** generations ....*
   5 *Results **revealed** that ...* ....

3 For each academic word in exercise 2 suggest a less formal word with the same meaning.

Word building: *Nouns*

4 Try to learn the other family members of each new academic word. What nouns can be formed from the verbs and adjectives below?

1	available	3	demonstrate	5	respond
2	maintain	4	participate	6	significant

Word partners

5 It's important to learn the word partners which often occur with an academic word. Fill in the missing prepositions in these phrases.

   1 a decline ..... population
   2 as demonstrated ..... research
   3 to focus ..... a subject
   4 to participate ..... events
   5 to respond ..... a question

6 In each sentence ONE of the words in brackets cannot be used. Cross out the incorrect word in each group.

   1 There has been an expansion of (road/rail/ship) transport.
   2 The country's transport (method/system/network) needs modernisation.
   3 The price rise is due to increased transport (costs/money/charges).

Spot the error: *Spelling*

7 Make sure you record new vocabulary accurately. There are five spelling mistakes in the following extract. Underline the mistakes and correct them.

   > Exercise has many benefitts. Reserch has shown that it is a good way of maintaining phisical fitness and overal health. It also improves mental health and helps to prevent depresion.

8 Choose five academic words from this page to learn, and write personal examples to help you remember them.

   1 ....
   2 ....
   3 ....
   4 ....
   5 ....

2 ▶ Food for thought

> **food for thought** something that makes you think carefully: *The teacher's advice certainly gave me food for thought.* (Longman Exams Dictionary)

In this unit you will practise	Key Language	Exam Focus
• Talking about diet and eating habits • Listening and answering multiple-choice questions; completing forms • Interpreting and presenting data from graphs • Paragraphing: cohesion; logical and grammatical links	Names of tenses Adjectives describing change Reporting tenses	**Speaking:** Part 1 **Listening:** Sections 1, 2 **Writing:** Tasks 1, 2

Lead-in

1 Who eats more healthily: men or women? Look at the following table which compares eating habits for men and women in England, and then discuss these questions with another student.

1 Which of the eating habits are healthy? Which ones are unhealthy? Why?
2 Which group has a healthier diet, men or women? Why?

Check your answers to question 1 on page 253.

Eating Habits

ENGLAND	Percentages	
	Women	Men
a) Eat vegetables or salad at least daily	70	64
b) Add salt in cooking	68	67
c) Usually drink skimmed/semi-skimmed milk	66	60
d) Eat fruit at least daily	54	44
e) Eat high-fibre cereal	44	37
f) Take sugar in coffee	31	48
g) Take sugar in tea	27	46
h) Usually eat wholemeal bread	27	21
i) Eat confectionery at least daily	17	19
j) Use solid cooking fat	13	14

Source: Social Focus on Men and Woman, Crown copyright

Focus on writing 1 *Interpreting data*

KEY LANGUAGE
Names of tenses
▶ p. 211, ex. 2

> **EXAM BRIEFING** Academic writing: introduction
>
> There are two tasks. In Task 1 you have to look at a graph, chart or diagram and write a 150-word summary of the information. Task 2 is a discursive essay, which will be introduced in more detail in Unit 4.

GRAPHS
Task 1

Graphs A and B below show trends in two activities in Britain.

consumption of fruit and vegetables (vegetables v fruit)
cigarette smoking (male vs female)

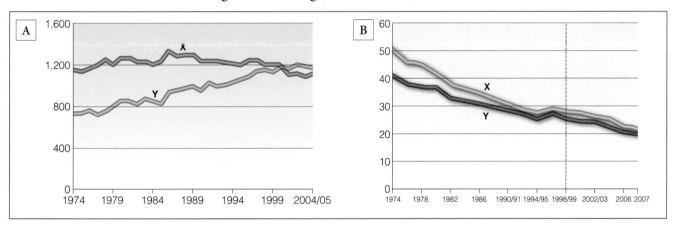

1   Fill in the chart by matching Graphs A and B to the following short paragraphs. Then say which activities you think each graph represents.

   1   There was **a steady downward trend** in both X and Y **between 1974 and 1994**. Both activities then **levelled out** briefly before continuing to **fall**.

   2   Activity X **remained** fairly **steady over the period, reaching a** small **peak** in about 1986. Meanwhile there was an **increase in** Activity Y, which **exceeded** Activity X for the first time in 2000.

Graph	Paragraph	Activity
A		
B		

Make sure you can match each expression in bold to features on the graphs.

2 a Read through the language in the *Useful language* box and check any expressions you don't know.

b Find another way of saying the following.

1	a very small increase	4	to rise quickly
2	from 2000 until 2003	5	to reach a maximum
3	a steep decline	6	to stop falling

▶ *Focus on Academic Skills for IELTS* pages 11–13

> **KEY LANGUAGE**
> Adjectives describing change
> ▶ p.212, ex. 3

Useful language: Describing data

	Adjectives	**Nouns**
a	slight steady / gradual sharp / steep / rapid marked / significant	increase / rise (in) decrease / decline / fall / (in) upward/downward trend (n) recovery

	Verbs	**Adverbs**
to	rise / increase fall / decline / decrease be at / reach a peak level out remain steady exceed	slightly / steadily / gradually sharply / steeply / significantly / rapidly

Time expressions

in 2000 / recent years, etc.

since (point of time) July / 2000, etc.

for (period of time) several months / ten years, etc.

during /over the year / the period 1999 to 2009, etc.

between May and December / 1999 and 2009, etc.

House prices have fallen steadily since the beginning of 2008.

Car sales reached a peak during the month of June.

There was a slight increase in the cost of living between 2005 and 2007.

3 Complete the description of Graph C using terms from the *Useful langauge* box. When you've finished, compare your answers with another student.

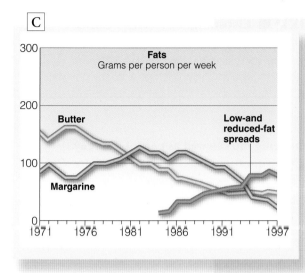

Over the period 1971 to 1997 as a whole, there was
1 .... in the consumption of butter and margarine and a 2 .... in the consumption of low-fat spreads. Butter was the most popular fat at the beginning of the period, and consumption 3 .... of about 150 grams per person per week in about 1975. Since then, there has been 4 .... In 1981, the consumption of margarine 5 .... that of butter for the first time, but since 1987 there has been 6 .... in the consumption of margarine, which seems set to continue. Low-fat spreads were introduced 7 .... and there has been 8 .... in their consumption since then, so that by about 9 .... they were more popular than either butter or margarine.

KEY LANGUAGE
Reporting tenses
▶ p.212, ex. 4

▶ *Focus on Academic Skills for IELTS* page 19

4 Now write five sentences describing Graph D (see page 253).

Focus on speaking *Eating habits*

Part 1: Interview

In the Interview, it's important to notice the **tense or verb form** in the examiner's questions as this can help to guide your reply.

1 Answer the questions below.

1 What tense and/or particular verb form would you be likely to use in replying to questions beginning:

a) What do you usually …? e) Where would you …?
b) When did you last …? f) How long ago …?
c) Do you enjoy …? g) How interested are you in …?
d) How long have you …? h) When you finish your studies, …?

2 Complete each question in a suitable way and then ask and answer in pairs.

2 Work in pairs to discuss the following questions.

1 What are your favourite and least favourite foods?
2 What did you eat the last time you invited a friend for a meal?
3 Do you prefer eating at home or in a restaurant? Why?
4 What special dish from your country would you recommend to a visitor?

▶ *Focus on Academic Skills for IELTS* pages 16–17

Focus on listening 1 *Students' Union survey*

Section 1: Multiple choice; form completion

You are going to hear a student being interviewed as part of a survey. Before you listen, look through the questions carefully. For questions 2 and 3, study the drawings and think of words to describe them.

Questions 1–7
*Choose the correct letter, **A, B** or **C**.*

> *Example*   What is the survey about?
> **A** study methods
> **B** leisure activities
> **Ⓒ** eating habits

1 What is the Students' Union planning to produce?

A a report

B a leaflet

C a newsletter

2 What is the student's favourite food?

A   **B**   **C**

3 What is his least favourite food?

A   **B**   **C**

4 Which meals does he eat in a day?

A just breakfast

B just lunch

C just dinner

5 How many eggs does he eat a week?

A none   **B** one   **C** two

6 How often does he eat fresh fruit?

A never   **B** very rarely   **C** regularly

7 What's his opinion of organic food?

A He thinks it's a waste of money.

B He thinks it's poor quality.

C He would eat it if he could afford it.

Questions 8–10
*Complete the form below. Write **NO MORE THAN THREE WORDS AND/OR A NUMBER** for each answer.*

Name (Optional): *Jamie*	**8** _____
Course:	**9** _____
Faculty:	*Business Studies*
Year:	**10** _____

Focus on listening 2 *Healthy eating*

> ▶ **EXAM BRIEFING** Listening: completion tasks
>
> In a completion task, you have to fill in missing information in **notes**, **sentences**, a **summary**, a **table** or a **flow-chart**. You can use up to three words/or a number in your answer and correct spelling is essential. Occasionally you have to choose the correct letter A, B, etc. from a box of answers.

Section 2: Note completion

You will hear a short talk about healthy eating and you have to complete a set of notes. Before you start, read the *Task Approach* below.

TASK APPROACH

- Read the **instructions** carefully. Notice how many words you can write.
- Identify the **topic** by looking quickly at the heading (if there is one) and the questions.
- Study the first few questions. Underline **key words** and think about **possible answers**. This will help you 'tune into' the topic so that you listen more effectively.
- Remember to check your **spelling**.

Before you listen, work with another student to guess the answer to each question. Fill in your guesses in pencil.

▶ *Focus on Academic Skills for IELTS pages 14–15*

While you listen, check your answers. If your guess was correct, put a tick (✓) next to it. If not, write in the correct answer.

Questions 1–10
Complete the notes below. Use **NO MORE THAN THREE WORDS AND/OR A NUMBER** *for each answer.*

Healthy Eating

Very important to eat a **1** .... *diet*

People in Europe and the US eat **2** .... *more sugar now than in 1800*

Try to eat plenty of fresh fruit and veg – **3** .... *servings a day, if poss.*

Avoid foods containing a lot of sugar, especially **4** .... *drinks*

Cut down on fat – eat lean meat, poultry, fish and low-fat **5** ....

Eat no more than **6** .... *eggs a week*

In cooking, use lemon juice instead of **7** ....

Try to eat **8** .... *a day*

Most nutritious fruit is **9** ....

  contains: • *165 calories per 100g*

  • **10** .... *protein as milk*

  • *more vitamins A, B and C than milk*

Focus on writing 2 *Paragraphing*

Task 2
WHAT IS A PARAGRAPH?

1 a Divide the following text into three paragraphs.

> Almost all food, with the exception of water and salt, provides some energy, and this is measured in calories. About half the calories we consume are used for physical activity and half for growth, breathing, digestion and other bodily processes. The reason people put on weight is simple – they consume more energy than they use up in daily activities. Any excess energy is stored as body fat for later use. Too much body fat puts a strain on the heart and can cause pain in the back and joints. Surveys show that although our energy intake has decreased by about a third over the past 40 years, we're still getting heavier. That's because our energy expenditure is lower than ever; we drive to the shops, use lifts and escalators, and have increasingly sedentary jobs.

b Compare your answer with another student and discuss these questions.

1 What kind of text should be divided into paragraphs, and why?
2 How do you decide when to begin a new paragraph?

COHESION

2 Which of the two following paragraphs is preferable? Why?

A
> Pizza is made with flour, yeast, salt and water. Pizza can be compared with Greek and Middle Eastern flat breads. Pizza is most firmly associated with Naples in Italy.

B
> Pizza, which is made with flour, yeast, salt and water, can be compared with Greek and Middle Eastern flat breads, but it is most firmly associated with Naples in Italy.

> **EXAM TIP** Good linking between sentences is essential for successful writing in the IELTS writing test.

Well-written texts are *cohesive*. This means that ideas are connected using *reference links*, which can be logical or grammatical.

LOGICAL LINKS

3 Logical links include:

Addition	*and, in addition, as well as*
Cause/Result	*because, since, due to, therefore*
Contrast	*while, whereas, on the other hand*
Concession	*but, despite, however*
Purpose	*so, so as to, to, in order to*
Time	*when, before, while, during*

Underline five logical links in Texts A and B.

A The diet of the earliest humans, although simple, contained all the things that nutritionists say are best to eat. Moreover, according to scientists, emulating primitive diets would improve modern health.

B Because hunter-gatherer societies do not grow and store crops, there are bound to be times of short supply. To survive such occasions, humans can build up a cushion of fat. When there are no shortages, fat continues to build, creating its own health problems.

GRAMMATICAL LINKS

> KEY LANGUAGE
> Cohesion: reference links
> ▶ p. 217, ex. 10

▶ *Focus on Academic Skills for IELTS* page 45

4 Study the following *Useful language.*

> **Useful language: Grammatical links**
>
> | | |
> |---|---|
> | **Personal pronouns** | e.g. *it, they, this, that, these, her, him, us* |
> | **Relative pronouns** | e.g. *who, which, that, where* |
> | **Other substitutions** | e.g. *so, such, thus, there, then* |
> | **Articles** | e.g. *Evidence was found …* <u>the</u> *evidence suggested …* |

Underline eight grammatical links in Texts C and D.

C Plants have only been cultivated for food in the last 30,000 years. Before that, hunter-gatherer societies dominated the earth. A few such societies, including the Kalahari bushmen of southern Africa, still exist. These communities live primarily in warm inland climates, similar to those prevailing when man first evolved. They rely for food on wild nuts and berries, and meat from wild animals.

D Although meat accounts for between 30% and 80% of primitive diets, the meat eaten is different from that found in today's butchers' shops. Wild animals have five times less fat than domestic livestock, which are specially bred to satisfy the modern taste for tender meat.

5 Rewrite the following paragraphs using logical links and grammatical links to connect the ideas.

A We know that pizzas were eaten in ancient Pompeii. Brick pizza ovens have been uncovered in Pompeii by archaeologists. Early pizzas would have lacked one of their main modern ingredients. The first tomato seeds were not brought to Europe from Peru until 1,500 years later.

B Tomatoes were held in low esteem by most Europeans. The poor people of Naples added tomatoes to their yeast dough. The people of Naples created the first modern pizza. By the 17th century, pizza was popular with visitors. Visitors would go to poor neighbourhoods to taste pizza. Pizza was a peasant dish. Pizzas were made by men called pizzaioli.

SPOT THE ERROR

6 The following phrases and sentences contain common errors. Identify and correct the errors.

Errors	Corrected version
1 Prices remained steady between 2001 to 2005.	between 2001 <u>and</u> 2005
2 I only had statistics which they were out of date.	....
3 The graph shows an increase of expenditure.	....
4 The rate of inflation was fallen last year.	....
5 Accident rates have been rising since ten years.	....
6 Sales of MP3s have raised in recent years.	....
7 We often go for swimming together.	....
8 There was a slightly decrease in sales in May.	....

Check your answers by referring to the *Useful language* on page 20 and/or the *Error Hit List* on page 26.

ERROR HIT LIST

do/play/go

✗	✔
He makes several sports.	He <u>does</u> several sports.
You should make more exercise.	You should <u>do/take</u> more exercise.
I play a lot of sport.	I <u>do</u> a lot of sport.
We often do swimming.	We often <u>go</u> swimming.

- Use the verb **do** with the general word *sport*.
- **Play** can be used when the actual sport is named, e.g. *I play a lot of tennis*.
- Use the verb **go** before sports ending in *-ing*.
- Use the verbs **do** or **take** with *exercise*.

which

✗	✔
Pizza, which it was invented in Italy,	Pizza, which i̶t̶ was invented in Italy,

- When **which** is a relative pronoun, don't use another pronoun after it.

increase/decrease

✗	✔
A decrease of the consumption of fish …	A decrease <u>in</u> the consumption …
Standards of living have increased.	Standards of living have <u>risen</u>.
The number of accidents has been increased.	The number of accidents has b̶e̶e̶n̶ increased.

- As nouns, **increase** and **decrease** normally take the preposition *in*. For specific figures we can say: *an increase of 10%*.
- As verbs, they may take various prepositions, e.g. *Houses increased **in** value; Prices increased **from** $2 **to** $3 / **by** 20%*, etc.
- Don't use the verbs **increase** or **decrease** to refer to the level or standard of something. Use *go up/rise* or *fall*, e.g. *The level of crime has **gone up***.
- The verbs **increase** and **decrease** don't normally occur in the passive form.

rise/raise/fall

✗	✔
There has been a fall of spending on books.	… a fall <u>in</u> spending …
The cost of living raised by 5% last year.	The cost of living <u>rose</u> …

- The nouns **rise** and **fall**, when referring to amount, rate, standard, etc., normally take the preposition *in*. For specific figures we can say: *a rise of 10%*.
- As verbs, **rise** and **fall** may take various prepositions, e.g. *Houses have fallen **in** value; Prices rose **from** $2 **to** $3 / **by** 20%*, etc.
- Don't confuse the verbs **rise** (become more) with **raise** (make something rise), e.g. *Interest rates are set to **rise**. The Bank of England has **raised** the interest rate.*

Reflective Learning 1 *What is reflective learning?*

What is reflective learning

Reflective learning means giving careful attention to the way you study. It includes noticing tasks which you do well and less well, and thinking about the reasons, as well as trying new approaches to study and assessing the results.

Reflective learning will help you prepare for the IELTS test more effectively by becoming a more independent learner. In the longer term, it will enable you to go on learning after the course has finished, and prepare you for success in academic study.

Good learning habits

1 Work in pairs to study the list below.
Put a tick (✓) after the learning habits which are characteristic of a good learner. Discuss why the remaining habits may be less helpful.

1	Is afraid to make mistakes	
2	Relies on the teacher to set learning goals for them	
3	Is willing to experiment with new learning techniques	
4	Tries to analyse and correct mistakes	
5	Doesn't like making guesses about meaning	
6	Looks for opportunities for extra practice outside class	
7	Is more interested in an overall mark for written work than in the teacher's comments	
8	Monitors their own progress	
9	Prefers working alone to working with fellow students	
10	Plans how to do a task and reviews it carefully afterwards.	

Ideas for Reflective Learning

Try to get into the habit of reviewing your learning experiences on a regular basis. This will help you develop a more focused approach to learning.

---

2 Look through the guidelines below, then use them to discuss recent learning experiences with another student.

Successful learning

- Think of some new language you have learnt in the last week and ask yourself:
  - How will this help me? (e.g. in the exam/in my work/for general communication)
  - What factors helped me to learn? (e.g. something I/my teacher/my fellow students did)
  - What do I need to do in future to consolidate this learning? (e.g. check/revise/use the new language)

Learning in progress

- Think of something you have not fully learnt yet, or find difficult, and ask:
  - Is there something which is preventing me from learning this?
  - What have I done so far to help myself learn this?
  - What steps could I take in future to help myself learn this?

Feelings

- For each of the following, think about reasons for your feelings. Is there a way of changing negative feelings?
  - a classroom activity that you find particularly enjoyable or useful
  - a classroom activity that you particularly dislike
  - an aspect of English or the IELTS exam that you are concerned about

Setting goals

3 On the basis of exercises 1 and 2, consider how much you reflect on your learning at present and give yourself a score out of 10. Aim to continue doing what you already do well but write down <u>three</u> things you can do to help yourself learn more effectively.

1 ………………………..………………………..……......

2 ………………………..………………………..……......

3 ………………………..………………………..……......

Reviewing goals

Having set goals for yourself, it's essential that you review progress on a regular basis. This is called a **Plan/Do/Review** cycle. Each Reflective Learning section in this book will give you the opportunity to review progress in the goals you set.

3 ▶ Location is everything

"The three most important factors in choosing a home are location, location, location." (Anon)

In this unit you will practise	Key Language	Exam Focus
• Discussing the development of cities / population concerns • Describing a place • Reading and identifying topic and text structure; using parallel expressions and grammar clues • Reading and matching; sentence completion	The passive Geographical positions	**Speaking:** Parts 1–3 **Reading skills**

Lead-in

1 Work in pairs to discuss which of the following cities:

1 is the most highly populated now, in the 21ˢᵗ century.
2 was the most highly populated in the first century.
3 is a city and also an independent country.
4 is the highest above sea level.
5 has the highest average temperature.
6 has the greatest number of skyscrapers.

Amsterdam	*Bangkok*	*Hong Kong*	*London*	*Los Angeles*
Mexico City	*New York*	*Rome*	*Shanghai*	*Singapore*
Sydney	*Tokyo*			

2 Use the maps and descriptions below to identify four of the cities from the box.

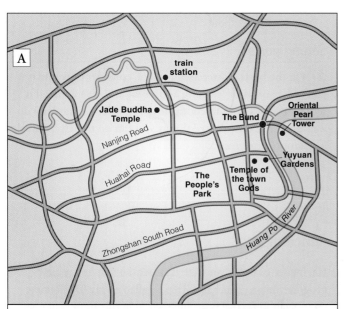

This city is the industrial, financial and commercial centre of its country, though not the capital, and one of the fastest growing cities in the world. It lies on the east coast and has an important cargo port. Among its tourist sights are the historic Bund area and the 468m-high Oriental Pearl Tower, both of which are located on the Huang Po River.

The city is situated on the largest natural harbour in the world and is a popular tourist destination. Its two most famous landmarks are the modern Opera House and the Harbour Bridge. Around a third of the population were born overseas, making this one of the most multicultural cities in the world.

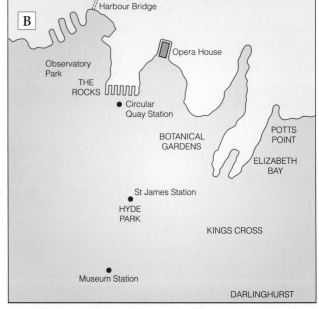

This city has roughly the same population as London but covers an area almost three times as large. It has the highest level of car ownership in the world, and two-thirds of its land area is devoted to roads and parking. Not surprisingly, it suffers from serious environmental pollution.

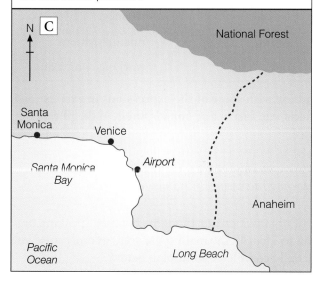

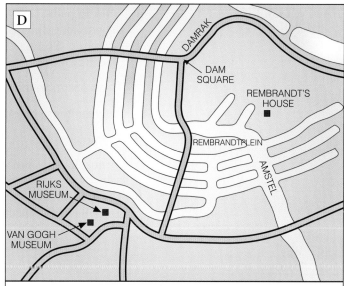

This is the capital and largest city in the country and is known for its extensive system of canals. It has a number of important art galleries as well as the oldest stock exchange in the world. With an estimated 1 million bicycles and many bike paths, it is one of the most bicycle-friendly cities in the world.

> **KEY LANGUAGE**
> **The Passive**
> ▶ p. 212, ex. 5
> e.g. *The city is situated on the … harbour.*

You can check your answers to questions 1 and 2 on page 253.

3 Underline useful words and phrases in texts A–D, then practice using them to describe other cities you know about.

Focus on speaking 1 *Urban problems*

Part 3: Discussion

1 What is the problem described in text C above? In pairs, discuss the following questions.

1 What are the reasons for this problem?
2 Why should citizens be concerned about this problem?
3 What can be done about it?

2 The sentences below describe some of the most pressing problems facing world cities. With your partner, select the most likely answer to complete each sentence.

1 Sixty-five million people move to cities every *month / year / decade.*
2 One-third of the world's population are under the age of *15 / 20 / 30.*
3 The population increases by over four people every *second / minute / hour.*
4 There are currently around *five / twelve / twenty* megacities (cities with over ten million people) in the world.

▶ *Focus on Academic Skills for IELTS* pages 28–29

You can check your answers on page 253.

TOPIC VOCABULARY

3 a Work in pairs. Divide the following words and phrases into five groups and suggest a heading for each group.

child labour	medical staff	textbooks
prescription drugs	overcrowding	toxic waste
greenhouse gases	pollution	truancy
homelessness	slums	unemployment
hospital equipment	teachers	working conditions

b These adjectives can combine with some of the expressions in exercise 3a to describe problem situations, e.g. *increasing homelessness*. Make phrases using each adjective at least once.

(in)sufficient/(in)adequate   (in)appropriate   poor   serious
severe   damaging   growing/increasing   trained/qualified

MINDPLAN

4 Mindplans are a useful way of organising your thoughts before a speaking or writing task. They enable you to identify the main topic areas and organise your ideas clearly. Look at the partially completed mindplan below.

a Work in pairs to write a few more examples for each heading. Then, using ideas from exercise 3 add three more headings with examples.

b Tell your partner about the effect of one or two of these problems in your country.

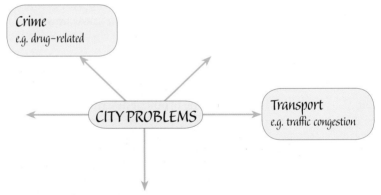

Focus on reading *Location is everything*

IDENTIFYING THE TOPIC

1 Always study the title of a reading passage, and the subheading if there is one. These can give useful information about the topic and style.

a Read the title and subheading on page 31. What is the topic?

b Skim the first few paragraphs to confirm or correct your guess.

TEXT STRUCTURE

2 When forming a general picture, it's important to think about text structure. Look through the passage and say whether the information is presented:

1 by geographic region
2 in chronological order
3 by type of city layout

Location is everything

The estate agent's advice dates back to 3500BC when the first city of trade took off

Our distant ancestors led pretty simple lives. Until around 10,000BC, all humans were hunter-gatherers and lived a nomadic life, searching endlessly for food. It was the development of agriculture that enabled humans to settle down and live, first as farmers and then as villagers. Around 3500BC, small towns began appearing in Mesopotamia, surrounded by defensive high walls and irrigated fields that fed the town's population.

In the thousand years that followed, when agriculture had become more of a science and crop yields had risen, fewer people were needed to produce food. People took other jobs, became wealthier and more and more chose to live in towns close to shops and markets. This worked well for centuries. Towns flourished and eventually one of the grandest, Rome, became the world's first city of more than one million people around 100AD.

Although the fertile lands surrounding Rome could have adequately fed the city, the Roman people began importing food and became reliant on long supply chains. When Gaiseric the Vandal began withholding vital North African grain supplies from Rome in 455AD, the city's power went into steep decline. The Dark Ages that ensued saw people deserting cities across Europe and returning to the countryside.

Make it accessible

It was not until 1200AD that people began flocking back to the cities, a trend encouraged by the growth of iron technology and further improvements in agriculture. Cities and towns began to spring up across Europe and Asia.

The main factor which determined where a city was founded, according to Derek Keene, Director of the Centre for Metropolitan History at the University of London's Institute of Historical Research, was simple geography. "Was it accessible to people who wished to trade there or bring in supplies?"

However, there were other important considerations. "A city might be successfully founded in a desert if there was a need for a staging post or an interchange on a trade route," he says. Then there were the simple demands of a ruler's ego, or a need to defend people against invaders. Finally, there was one other major motivating force: religion. "A sacred site attracts many visitors who require service," Keene says.

In medieval times, cities grew to exploit trade routes. Bruges in Belgium became rich by weaving wool from Britain. Florence, too, prospered from its wool industry until banking came to dominate its economy.

Constantinople became by far Europe's largest city and premiere trading centre, the true heir to the Roman legacy during the Middle Ages. The gateway between the Eastern Mediterranean, India and Africa on one side and Europe on the other, Constantinople played a crucial role in the trade of Eastern riches for Western wool and heavy iron products.

At the same time, Venice was prospering thanks to trade, its proximity to the sea, Africa and the treasures of Persia. The city-state traded luxury goods such as precious stones, spices, silks and ivory.

Cities that broke the rules

The lure of trading riches has encouraged the growth of cities in unlikely locations. When the East India Trading Company needed a base with good access to the Ganges Valley, it founded Calcutta on swamp land. The site was the furthest inland point that could be reached by ocean-going ships, and the city has grown to a population of 15.5 million today.

The most ludicrously located city has to be St Petersburg, built as the capital of a vast empire by Peter the Great. Thousands of slave labourers died during its construction, and he had to force people to live there.

Other major world capitals had no such problems. London, founded in 50AD, grew steadily and is the least planned world city, with snobbery playing a large part in determining its layout. Mainline stations are dotted around the periphery of inner London, as wealthy 19th-century residents refused construction of a giant central London rail terminal.

By the 1930s, US architect, Frank Lloyd Wright, was arguing that city size should be limited. But as Wright's treatise was published, New York was becoming the world's first city with a population of ten million, and cities have since grown at an astonishing rate – Mexico City is home to 16.5 million people and 26.9 million now live in Tokyo.

▶ EXAM BRIEFING   Academic reading: matching

In these tasks you have to match statements (1, 2, 3, etc.) to items in a box (A, B, C, etc.). Typical IELTS tasks involve matching Opinions and People, or Causes and Effects. There is only one correct answer for each question, but you can use a letter more than once.

- Study the instructions and example (if there is one) so you know exactly what to do.
- Check information in the relevant section of text. Don't rely on guesswork.

Matching

TASK APPROACH

▶ *Focus on Academic Skills for IELTS* page 22

3 **In this task, you have to match cities to their descriptions.**

- Circle or highlight the cities A–I in the text so they are easy to find. NB The cities are in passage order.
- Underline key words in statements 1–8. NB these are not in passage order.
- Study the information about each city in the text looking for expressions which match words and phrases in the statements.

Questions 1–8

Look at the following descriptions (1–8) and the list of cities below.
Match each statement with the correct city (A–I).

NOTES

Example	*Answer*
grew into a successful trading city because of its location close to the sea.	**E**

1 became an important centre for banking

2 was the largest city in the world in the 1930s

3 was important for weaving in the Middle Ages

4 was built on unsuitable land but has developed into a major world city

5 was Europe's most powerful city in the Middle Ages

6 has inconvenient rail connections

7 lost its power and influence rapidly when it suffered food shortages

8 cost many lives to build

List of Cities

A Rome	**D** Constantinople	**G** St Petersburg
B Bruges	**E** Venice	**H** London
C Florence	**F** Calcutta	**I** New York

▶ *Focus on Academic Skills for IELTS* page 20

EXAM BRIEFING	Academic reading: sentence completion

There are two versions of this task. In the first you complete sentences by choosing the best ending from a list of options, as in the task below. In the second you select words from the passage. In both cases, the answers are in passage order so it's best to answer them in sequence.

Sentence completion
TASK APPROACH

4 **Read the following advice.**

- Study each unfinished sentence and underline the key words or phrases. (These are in italics in the questions on page 34.)
- Locate the relevant section of text and look for parallel expressions.
- Choose the best answer from the list of endings, checking again for parallel expressions.
- Make sure your answer fits both **logically** and **grammatically**.

PARALLEL EXPRESSIONS

5 **Instead of using exactly the same words as the text, questions often substitute expressions with the same meaning.**

The following words and phrases come from the text on page 31. Find two parallel expressions for each in the box below.

1 population (line 13)	6 began to spring up (line 41– 42)	
2 became reliant on (line 29)	7 accessible (line 49)	
3 ensued (line 34)	8 ludicrously (line 95)	
4 deserting (line 34)	9 vast (line 97)	
5 flocking back (line 38)		

leaving	*started developing*	*enormous*
depended on	*citizens*	*convenient to get to*
ridiculously	*came afterwards*	*returning*
huge	*easy to reach*	*appeared*
followed	*foolishly*	*couldn't manage without*
migrating back	*inhabitants*	*abandoning*

NB In the sentence completion task which follows, some of the words and phrases in the questions are in italics. Look for parallel expressions from the text to help you identify the correct answer.

GRAMMATICAL CLUES

6 **When deciding which phrase best completes a sentence, you may be able to eliminate any answers which are grammatically impossible.**

Read the incomplete sentences 9–14 on page 34 and answer these questions.

1 Which three must be followed by phrases beginning with **verbs**?
2 Which three must be followed by phrases beginning with **nouns** or *-ing* forms?

7 Now complete the exam task below.

Questions 9–14

*Complete each of the following sentences with the correct ending, **A–I** from the box below.*

Example	*Answer*
As *farming* became more scientific, *not so many* people	**F**

9 As a result of the development of *farming*, people ....
10 The design of the earliest towns was for ....
11 Towns first *began to grow and prosper* when people ....
12 Rome finally *lost its power* because of ....
13 Cities were usually *established* in places which ....
14 One reason for people to visit a city was ....

A were *convenient* for trade.
B the growth of the population.
C the *protection* of the inhabitants.
D *its dependence on* imported supplies.
E the presence of a *religious* site.
F *were required* to work on the land.
G *made money* and left the countryside.
H were unable to grow their own food.
I were able to *live permanently in one place.*

Focus on speaking 2 *Describing places*

Parts 1 and 2: Interview
and long turn

▶ EXAM BRIEFING Speaking: Parts 1 and 2

In Part 1 of the interview, the examiner may ask you general questions about your home, your town/city, or your country. In Part 2, you may be asked to describe one of these places in more detail.

1 Work in pairs to ask and answer the following questions.

1 Which town or city do you come from?
2 What's the best thing about living there?
3 Is there anything you don't like?
4 Which places would you recommend a tourist to visit?

2 Use information from the maps to help you complete the description of a city.

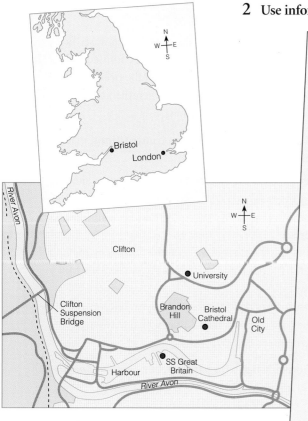

> I live in the city of Bristol, which is 1 .... of my country, about 200 kilometres from the capital, London. It has a 2 .... of about half a million.
>
> Bristol 3 .... the River Avon, and in the past it was an important port. Nowadays, that's all finished, and the harbour is mainly used by pleasure boats. The main industries are financial services, which 4 .... things like banks and insurance companies, and also engineering and micro-electronics.
>
> There's an open space 5 .... Brandon Hill 6 .... centre of town and 7 .... of that is a district called Clifton, which has beautiful 18th-century houses. It's a nice place to visit, but unfortunately it's too expensive for me to live there!
>
> There are quite a lot of things to see in Bristol. For example, there's a beautiful 16th-century cathedral and several other 8 .... like the Clifton Suspension Bridge and the SS Great Britain, which is one of the earliest iron ships.
>
> We've got two universities and also several colleges, so there are lots of students and plenty of 9 .... like bookshops and cinemas and restaurants. It's a good place to live!

3 Use the following headings to make notes about your own home town or city in the form of a mindplan. Include any relevant information.

Location	Size/Population	History	Business/Industry
Layout	Attractions	Amenities	

KEY LANGUAGE
Geographical positions
▶ p. 213–214, ex. 6
e.g. *north/northern; in the north/to the north; northernmost, etc.*

4 When you've finished, work in groups and describe your city to one or two other students. Try to include one or two personal impressions, as in the example.

SPOT THE ERROR

5 This exercise practices on of the good learning habits from *Reflective Learning 1*, page 27. Most of these sentences contain common errors. Identify and correct the errors.

1 The city has spent a big amount of money on crime prevention.
2 A number of cities has more than ten million inhabitants.
3 A large proportion of people commute to work by car.
4 The major cities have a large level of unemployment.
5 A number of surveys has been carried out.
6 Only a small percentage of the houses has electricity.
7 The number of private cars is increasing rapidly.
8 People are now enjoying a higher level of living.
9 The food supply is not proportion about the size of the country.
10 Comparing with other countries, Libya spends a high percentage of income on education.

Check your answers by referring to the *Error Hit List* on page 46.

Academic Style 2 *Formality*

Introduction

Academic writing is fairly formal and impersonal. The main emphasis is generally on the argument you want to put forward, or the information you want to convey, rather than on the writer personally. This section looks at some of the basic features of a formal style.

Formal v. Informal

1 **The following texts convey the same information but in different styles. Compare these two texts. What differences do you notice in length and in style?**

Academic English

It has been found that faulty interpretation of forensic evidence has contributed to approximately half of all wrongful convictions in the US in recent years.

Spoken English

I heard they've been looking into cases in the States where someone has gone to prison for a crime they didn't actually commit. And what they've found is that about half of all those cases were down to people making mistakes with forensic evidence. How shocking is that?

What to avoid

In formal and academic English, it's best to avoid:

- informal words/expressions, e.g. *the States, down to, telly*
- abbreviations and contactions, e.g. *they've, i.e.*
- phrasal verbs (when formal alternatives are available), e.g. *look into, locked up*
- overuse of the pronoun *I*, and the phrases, *I think* and *In my opinion*.
- questions to the reader, e.g. *"How shocking is that?"*

2 **Examples of language which is not formal enough for academic writing have been underlined in the following text. Choose expressions from the list below to replace the underlined sections.**

> The popularity of camera phones, has made it <u>more and more tricky</u> to prevent people from <u>taking photos of things</u> they <u>shouldn't</u> record, <u>e.g.</u> military equipment. <u>But</u> now <u>there's</u> a system that can <u>find out</u> any camera phones and <u>send out</u> rays of light to <u>mess up</u> any <u>pictures</u> they take.

detect	emit	images	should not
difficult	for example	increasingly	subjects
distort	however	photographing	there is

The passive

Passive forms occur in 25 per cent of all verb phrases in academic English, reflecting the focus on actions and processes rather than on the agents. Passives avoid the need to use a general word like *People* or *Someone* when the identity of the agent isn't known or isn't important.

3 **Rewrite the following as passive constructions, making any changes necessary.**

e.g. People used the North Star as a navigation aid. <u>The North Star was used</u> (formal English)

1 <u>You can even see Venus</u> in the middle of the day. Venus …
2 They outlawed smoking in public places in 2003.
3 Someone has found a new galaxy circling the Milky Way.
4 Researchers repeated the tests a year later.
5 They are testing a nasal spray which may cure Alzheimer's disease.

For more practice with passive forms, see *Key Language*, page 212, exercise 5.

It-constructions

The use of an it-construction with the passive voice is a common way of making a statement more impersonal.

e.g. *what <u>they've found</u> is …* ➤ <u>*It has been found that*</u>. (formal English).

4 **Change the following phrases to passive constructions with it-.**

e.g. Most people agree that … <u>It is generally agreed</u> that …

1 Scientists think that volcanic eruptions may have destroyed the dinosaurs.
2 Nowadays we know that exercise can reverse many symptoms of ageing.
3 Researchers have found that sun bathing is addictive.
4 In the past, people used to think that bed rest was good for people with weak hearts.
5 Some people might argue that sending young offenders to jail is counterproductive.

Common verbs used in *it*-constructions in academic English include:

accept	*suggest*	*say*	*consider*
believe	*agree*	*think*	*show*
find	*claim*	*argue*	*understand*

Academic Vocabulary 2

Meaning

1 Replace the underlined part of each sentence using suitable academic words from the list below. Make changes and/or add extra words as necessary.

adequate	alter	community	component
goal	positive	promote	site	specific
trend			

1 The village shop was a valuable amenity for <u>all the local people</u>. *community*
2 No-one agrees about the best <u>area of ground</u> for the new airport. *site*
3 <u>What I hope to achieve</u> in life is to run my own company *goal*
4 The Internet has <u>changed</u> our lives dramatically. *altered*
5 The campaign is designed to <u>encourage</u> healthy eating. *promote*
6 The current <u>general tendency</u> is towards retiring later. *trend*
7 The factory makes <u>parts</u> for computers. *component*
8 We are hoping for a <u>good or useful</u> outcome to the talks. *positive*
9 The games are designed for three <u>particular</u> age-groups. *specific*
10 The station does not have <u>good enough</u> parking facilities. *adequate*

Grammar

2 Rewrite the following sentences using the academic words in brackets, so that the meaning is the same. Do not change the form of the word in brackets.

Example The data is not correct (**error**)

There is an error in the data.

1 With a longer runway larger planes could land. (**enable**)
2 The company has been in existence since 1822. (**founded**)
3 There are about 1 million bicycles in Amsterdam. (**estimated**)
4 Thousands of labourers died while the city was being built. (**construction**)
5 It's an advantage to have work experience in another country. (**overseas**)
6 Manufacturing output has fallen. (**a decline**)

Word building: *Adjectives ending in -al*

3 Think of adjectives ending in *-al* which have a meaning connected with the following:

Example politics: <u>political</u>
1 the mind *mental*
2 the body *physical*
3 money *financial*
4 the law *legal*
5 the ability to see *visual*
6 the treatment of disease *medical*
7 a particular area of a country *regional*
8 the smallest number or amount *minimal*
9 the whole world *global*
10 the air, land and water on Earth *environmental*

> **Language Fact**
> Adjectives ending in *-al* are extremely common, particularly in academic English.

Word partners

4 Only ONE of the words in brackets combines with the academic word in bold. Underline the correct answer in each case.

1 The country (suffers from/bears/enjoys) severe **environmental** problems.
2 The economy (went/began/came) into a **decline**.
3 Poverty may be the (main/big/top) **factor** in crime.
4 Fish farming (plays/makes/takes) a crucial **role** in the economy.
5 The city (covers/spreads/contains) a vast **area**.

Spot the error: *Spelling*

5 Five of the words below, which all featured in *Academic Vocabulary 1*, are spelt wrongly. Underline the mistakes and correct them.

1	availible	5	maintainance
2	comence	6	ocur
3	concept	7	purchas
4	demonstrate	8	significant

6 Choose five academic words from this page to learn, and write personal examples to help you remember them.

1 ....
2 ....
3 ....
4 ....
5 ....

4 ▶ Haves and have-nots

haves / hævz / *n* [U] the rich people in a country or society OPP **have-nots**: *the widening gap between the* **haves** *and the* **have-nots** (Longman Exams Dictionary)

In this unit you will practise	Key Language	Exam Focus
• Comparing living standards in different countries • Interpreting and comparing data from diagrams and tables • Paragraph structure; presenting the solution to a problem • Listening and labelling a diagram; completing a table; short answers • Listening and completing notes and a diagram	Comparison 1, 2 **Writing Practice** Task 1: Comparing data Task 2: Problem/ solution	**Speaking skills** **Writing:** Tasks 1, 2 **Listening:** Sections 3, 4

Lead-in

1 Read the following information and then discuss the questions below.

World Population Milestones
- 1 billion in 1804
- 2 billion in 1927 (123 years later)
- 3 billion in 1960 (33 years later)
- 4 billion in 1974 (14 years later)
- 5 billion in 1987 (13 years later)
- 6 billion in 1999 (12 years later)
- 7 billion in 2013 (14 years later)

life expectancy *n* [C] **1** the length of time that a person or animal is expected to live **2** the length of time that something is expected to continue to work, be useful, etc.

standard of living *n* [C usually singular] the amount of wealth, comfort, and other things that a particular person, group, country, etc. has; **high/low standard of living**: *a nation with a high standard of living*

the poverty line/level the income below which a person or a family is officially considered to be very poor and in need of help: *20% of American families now live below the poverty line.*

Source: LDOCE

1 What is most significant about the figures for world population growth?

2 One factor affecting life expectancy is the availability of clean water. What other factors can you think of?

3 What criteria might be used in measuring a country's wealth and 'comfort'?

2 The following quiz is based on information in a UN report. Work in pairs to answer the questions. (Key on page 253).

World Quiz

For questions 1–4, choose the best answer A, B or C.

1 What is the average life expectancy worldwide?

   A 54   B 67   C 74

2 Which figure is closest to the percentage of the world population living in developing countries?

   A 50%   B 65%   C 80%

3 Which figure is closest to the percentage of people living below the poverty line?

   A 10%   B 18%   C 25%

4 How many wealthy people own half of all the property in the world?

   A 358   B 1,204   C 10,389

For questions 5–8, choose from the list of countries in the box below.

5 Which two countries enjoy the highest standard of living in the world?

6 Which country has the highest percentage of students in tertiary education?

7 The citizens of which country have the highest life expectancy in the world?

8 In which country do people work most hours?

| Australia Brazil Canada China Egypt France |
| Germany Greece Iceland India Japan |
| Norway South Korea Spain Sweden Thailand |
| UK USA |

Focus on Speaking *Standards of living*

Part 3: Discussion

1   Many discussion topics in the exam require you to express a personal opinion. Try to use a variety of expressions to do this. Study the *Useful language* below.

> **Useful language: Expressing an opinion**
>
> I think / I believe (that) …
>
> It seems to me that …
>
> In my opinion, / In my view, …
>
> Do NOT say "According to me" or "According to my opinion".

2   Work in pairs to discuss these questions.

1   What other factors, apart from standard of living, can make a country a good place to live?

2   What do you think is the point of assessing the quality of life in different countries?

3   What can be done to help people who are living in poverty?

4   Do you think that wealthy countries have a responsibility to help poorer ones? If so, how?

5   What are the implications for a country whose citizens have a high life expectancy?

Focus on writing 1 *Interpreting and comparing data*

BAR CHARTS, PIE CHARTS

Task 1

1   Before you look at the data, discuss these questions with another student.

1   Who can expect to live longer: an American or an Australian?

2   Which continent has the highest percentage of people who can read and write: Europe or America?

3   In which country should you be able to see a doctor most quickly: UAE or Latvia?

4   Where did most of the world's population live in 1990: city or country?

5   Where will most of the world's population live by 2025: city or country?

2   Turn to diagrams A–D on page 40 and use the information from the data to answer these questions. Choose the correct heading for each diagram as quickly as possible.

1   Healthcare   …….

2   Adult Literacy Rates   …….

3   City vs Country   …….

4   Life Expectancy   …….

3 **Study the data more carefully to answer these questions.**

A 1 What do the figures at the top of the chart (41, 42, etc.) represent?
2 Who lives the longest of all, men or women, and where?

B 3 How many 'slices' of the pie chart are there? What do they represent?
4 What do the figures (20,000, etc.) represent?
5 In which country is a doctor responsible for the fewest patients?

C 6 What does the bar chart compare?
7 What do the letters F and M represent?
8 What do the figures at the top of the chart (38.5, 61.7, etc.) represent?

D 9 What proportion of the world is described as 'developing' in 1990?
10 What proportion of the world is predicted to be 'developing' in 2025?

4 **Now use the information in the data to check your answers to exercise 1.**

A

The chart shows the average age to which men and women are expected to live.

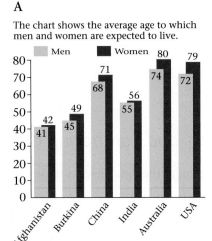

B

The chart shows how many people there are per doctor in each country

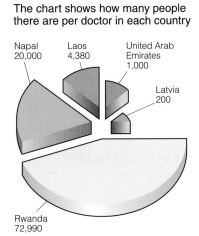

C

The chart shows the per centage of each region's male and female population aged over fifteen who can read and write.

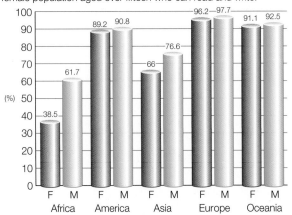

D

These pie charts show the proportion of the world's population living in urban and rural areas in 1990 and the forecast for 2025.

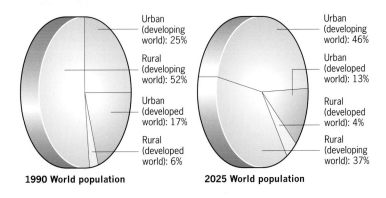

5 Complete the following descriptions using information from the diagrams on page 40. If you need help, there is a list of useful expressions below.

A 1 Life expectancy for men and women in India is almost ....

   2 An Australian woman can be expected to live almost .... as long as an Afghan woman.

   3 The country with .... difference in life expectancy between men and women is the USA.

B 4 Doctors in Nepal have .... as many patients as doctors in the UAE.

C 5 There is a .... literacy rate for women in Asia than in Oceania.

   6 In America, Europe and Oceania, there is .... difference in literacy rates for men and women.

D 7 In 1990, ... of the population of the developing world lived in urban areas.

   8 By 2025, ... the population of the developing world will live in cities.

► *Focus on Academic Skills for IELTS* page 25

almost	*exactly*	*a quarter / 25%*	*half / 50%*
much lower/higher		*twice* *X times*	*(very) little*
identical	*the greatest/smallest*		

6 Write three more sentences comparing the following.

1 male/female literacy rates in Africa

2 patients per doctor in Nepal/Latvia

3 the proportion of the world's population living in rural areas in 1990/2025

TABLES

7 In the table below, five of the world's largest cities are compared according to criteria including population, air and noise pollution and traffic congestion.

a According to the figures, which city:

1 is the noisiest?

2 has the worst air pollution?

3 has the heaviest traffic congestion?

4 is the safest to live in?

5 has the fewest inhabitants?

6 is best supplied with basic services?

	Los Angeles	London	Shanghai	Mexico City	Tokyo
Population (millions)	12.5	13	13.6	16.9	27.2
% Homes with water/electricity	94	100	95	94	100
Murders per 100,000 people	12.4	2.5	2.5	27.6	1.4
% Children in secondary school	90	58	94	62	97
Levels of ambient noise (1–10)	6	8	5	6	4
Traffic/km per hour in rush hour	30.4	16.6	24.5	12.8	44.8
Clean air (score out of ten)	3	7	7	2	7

► *Focus on Academic Skills*
for IELTS page 85

b In pairs, study the information in the table on page 41 and discuss the following questions.

1 If you had to live in Shanghai or Los Angeles, which would you choose, and why?
2 Which of the five cities would you prefer to live in? Why?

c Write two paragraphs.

Paragraph 1: Compare Shanghai and Los Angeles.

- Don't try to describe every detail. Identify the most significant information.

Paragraph 2: Say which of the five cities provides the best environment overall, and why.

- Present the various factors in order of priority and try to describe them in your own words, rather than using the descriptions in the table.

WRITING PRACTICE
Comparing data (example answer)
► p. 235, ex. 1

Focus on listening 1 *Wasting energy*

► **EXAM BRIEFING** Listening: Sections 3 and 4

In Sections 3 and 4, you will hear about topics related to study or education. Section 3 is a discussion among up to four speakers, while Section 4 is a lecture or talk by one speaker.

Section 3: Labelling a diagram; table completion; short-answer questions

TASK APPROACH

Notice that there are three different task types in the following task. Before you begin, read the advice on labelling a diagram below.

- Study the graph including key features such as the unit of measurement and Key.
- Notice questions 1 and 2. Try to describe those parts of the graph.

Listen to two students giving a presentation and answer Questions 1–10.

WASTING ENERGY

Questions 1 and 2
Label the two bars identified on the graph below.
*Choose two answers from the box and write the letters **A–E** next to questions **1–2**.*

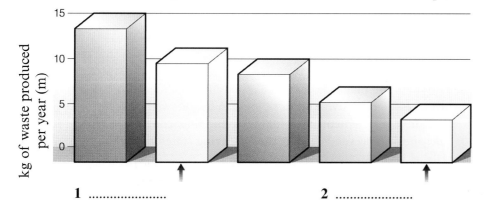

List of Cities
A Calcutta
B Los Angeles
C Mexico City
D New York
E Tokyo

1 ....

2 ....

Questions 3–7
Complete the table.
*Write **NO MORE THAN ONE WORD AND/OR A NUMBER** for each answer.*

Material	Time to biodegrade	Notes
Food (bread)	**3**	
Paper	3–12 months	Needs **4** .... conditions
Metal	1–10 years	Excluding aluminium (used in **5** ....% of soft-drink cans)
6	100 years (estimated)	
Glass	**7** .... (minimum)	

Questions 8–10
List three factors which affect the speed of decay.
*Write **ONE WORD ONLY** for each answer.*

8 ....

9 ....

10 ....

Focus on writing 2 *Paragraphing*

PARAGRAPH STRUCTURE

1 A typical paragraph contains a main or topic statement, with supporting points. The topic statement is usually, but not always, in the first sentence of the paragraph.

> Since the invention of the internal combustion engine, cities have been shaped by the car and by their inhabitants' reliance on it. The assumption that everybody will own their own car and lead a highly mobile existence is reflected in the low-density layout of modern cities. Such cities were also planned with freeway systems, enabling people to drive great distances every day. However, this attitude takes no account of the elderly, the young, the poor and non-drivers.

a Read the paragraph on the right. What topic is discussed?

b Underline the topic statement. What supporting points are made?

2 A paragraph may also contain a qualifying statement which introduces a different perspective, and this may also be followed by supporting points. Qualifying statements are often introduced by concession links such as *but*, *despite* or *however*. Which is the qualifying statement in the paragraph above?

3 Read the following sentences and complete the table on the left.

Topic statement	....
Supporting point(s)	....
Qualifying statement	....
Supporting point(s)	....

1 Much rubbish was simply dumped in a convenient place.
2 There is a shortage of space for depositing waste.
3 In the past, waste disposal was cheap and easy.
4 Increased transport costs make waste disposal expensive.
5 Today there are numerous problems with waste disposal.

4 Write the sentences above as a paragraph, with appropriate links.

PRESENTING SOLUTIONS TO PROBLEMS
Task 2

5 Individually, write three paragraphs on the following topic.

> **What are the key problems facing the world's cities in the 21st century, and what can be done about them?**

Look back at the mindplan on page 30 to help you plan your ideas.
Follow this plan:

Paragraph 1 Introduce topic; outline two key problems
Paragraph 2 Propose possible solutions to first problem
Paragraph 3 Propose possible solutions to second problem

WRITING PRACTICE
Problem/solution (example answer)
▶ p. 236, ex. 2

Begin:
Almost half the world's population now live in urban areas and, as cities grow even larger, conditions for city dwellers are likely to get worse. Two of the most critical problems, it can be argued, are …

▶ EXAM BRIEFING Academic Writing: Task 2

In Task 2 you have to write a discursive essay. You may have to present and justify an opinion, present the solution to a problem, or compare and contrast evidence. You need to write about 250 words and you are advised to spend about 40 minutes on the task. This task carries more weight in marking than Task 1.

Focus on listening 2 *Case study: São Paulo?*

Section 4: Note completion

Notice that this task has two parts and that Questions 5–10 are in diagram form. Before you begin, read the *Task Approach* and study the diagram so you understand how the information is organised.

TASK APPROACH

- Look carefully at the headings and layout. Highlight key words.
- The sequence of question numbers tells you which way to follow the diagram.
- Remember: thinking about possible answers will help you listen more effectively.

Questions 1–10
Complete the notes below.
*Write **NO MORE THAN THREE WORDS AND/OR A NUMBER** for each answer.*

FACT SHEET: SÃO PAULO

Founded in **1** ....

Current population **2** ....

Important for manufacture of **3** ....

Also national centre for **4** ....

BRAZIL

São Paulo

Pacific Ocean

Atlantic Ocean

PUSH FACTORS
(reasons for leaving countryside)
- Poor harvest
- **5** .... to improve old farms
- Little chance of education in the countryside
- **6** .... damage land and houses

PULL FACTORS
(reasons for moving to the city)
- Greater **7** ....
- Higher wages
- More **8** .... opportunities
- Better **9** .... facilities
- Relations may already live in town

COUNTRYSIDE ⟶ SÃO PAULO

MIGRATION OBSTACLES
Little money for **10** ....
Relations do not want you to leave the village

ERROR HIT LIST

number/amount

A number of questions was raised.	A number of questions <u>were</u> raised
The number of burglaries have risen.	The number of burglaries <u>has</u> risen
There is a big amount of discussion.	There is a <u>considerable</u> amount of …

- The phrase **a number of** is followed by a **plural** verb.
- The phrase **the number of** is followed by a **singular** verb.
- Don't say **a big number** or **a big amount**. Use *large/considerable/substantial*.

percentage/proportion

A small percentage of students drops out of the course.	A small percentage of students <u>drops</u> out …
There is a big proportion of people over 60.	There is a <u>large</u> proportion …
London is large with proportion to Oxford.	London is large <u>in</u> proportion <u>to</u> Oxford.

- If the noun after **percentage** is plural, the verb is usually plural.
- Don't say **a big percentage** or **a big proportion**. Use *high/large* and *small/low*.
- Something is small/large, etc. **in proportion to** something else.

level/standard

There is a big level of air pollution.	There is a <u>high</u> level of air pollution.
The level of living in the inner city …	The <u>standard</u> of living in the inner city …

- Don't say **a big/large level** or **a small level**. Use *high/low*.
- When you are talking about the quality of something, the usual word is **standard**.

compared with / compared to / in comparison

✗	✔
Comparing with other countries, the UK …	<u>Compared</u> with other countries, the UK …
By comparison to the USA, Canada has …	By comparison <u>with</u> the USA, Canada has …

- Use **compared with** or **compared to** when comparing two or more things. **In comparison (with)** or **by comparison (with)** can also be used to compare things but these are fairly formal and are most often used in written English.

Critical Thinking 1 *What is critical thinking?*

What is critical thinking?

Critical thinking is a way of careful, analytical thinking which is essential for effective communication. It is the key to success in IELTS and also to your future academic studies. Using critical thinking skills will help you become a more active learner by reasoning, questioning and making connections.

The basis of critical thinking is comparing and grouping ideas and information. To do this we need to ask basic questions such as: *Are these things the same or different? True or false? Relevant or irrelevant?* Like so much else, critical thinking improves with practice.

1 Write a general category for each of the following groups of words.

Example: ice hockey   skiing   sky-diving   snowboarding   golf

Answer: sport(s)
1   letter   voicemail   email   text message   note
2   cotton   wool   silk   nylon   leather
3   comma   full stop   colon   plus sign   question mark
4   documentary   soap opera   news bulletin
    current affairs programme
5   wood   coal   natural gas   oil
6   square   circular   triangular   rectangular   cubic
7   however   but   although   and   nevertheless
8   contents   title page   index   introduction   preface

Identifying differences

2 One word in each group in exercise 1 is different from the rest in some way. Underline the odd one out and give reasons. You may find more than one answer.

e.g. ice hockey – played in team, or ski-diving – done from above the earth

Making connections

3 Think about the process of learning a language. Which of the following activities is most similar? Which is most different? Give reasons for your answers.

1   Learning to drive a car
2   Learning to use a computer
3   Learning to swim
4   Learning mathematics
5   Learning to cook
6   Bungee jumping

Critical thinking in the classroom

4 Which of the following classroom and exam activities require critical thinking skills?

1   analysing an examination writing topic
2   identifying the main argument in a reading text
3   writing down a dictation
4   studying a grammar rule
5   deciding how to record new vocabulary
6   making a mindplan of ideas for a speaking or writing task
7   repeating a phrase after the teacher or tape
8   discussing a topic in pairs or groups

Critical Thinking for IELTS

Critical thinking skills are needed in all parts of the IELTS test. They will help you:

- evaluate an argument in a reading text
- distinguish between correct and incorrect options in a reading or listening task
- analyse a writing topic and develop a logical argument
- understand an interview discussion point and respond appropriately

5 ▶ Hurry sickness

"There is more to life than increasing its speed"
(Mahatma Gandhi)

In this unit you will practise	Key Language	Exam Focus
• Talking about the pace of life and work patterns • Reading and forming a general picture; fact v opinion • Reading and matching headings; multiple choice; summary completion; dealing with unknown vocabulary	Prepositions Tense review Word building: affixes	**Speaking:** Parts 1,3 **Reading skills**

Lead-in

1 Work in pairs to answer these questions. (Key on page 253).

Slow down?

1 Do people tell you that you talk too quickly?
2 Do you seem to glance at your watch more than others?
3 When someone takes too long to get to the point do you want to hurry them along?

4 Are you often first to finish at mealtimes?
5 When walking along a street, do you feel frustrated when you are stuck behind others?
6 Would you become irritable if you sat for an hour with nothing to do?
7 Do you walk out of restaurants or shops if there is even a short queue?

2 Which of the following cities would you expect to have the fastest pace of life, and which the slowest? Discuss your ideas. (Answers on page 253)

Cairo (Egypt)	*Guangzhou (China)*	*Madrid (Spain)*
New York (USA)	*Singapore*	*Wellington (New Zealand)*

3 Read the following article.

AN EXPERIMENT conducted in 32 cities has revealed that average walking speeds have increased by about 10 per cent since 1994. The steepest acceleration was found in Asian 'tiger' countries such as China and Singapore, which have experienced particularly marked social and economic change. Pedestrians in these nations walk between 20 and 30 per cent faster than they did in the early 1990s.

Richard Wiseman, a professor of psychology at the university of Hertfordshire, who led the study, said the results were significant because walking speed was a good indicator of the pace of people's lives.

Previous research carried out in 1994 showed that walking speeds are linked to other indicators of behaviours and even health. As people move faster they become less likely to help others, and also tend to have higher rates of coronary heart disease.

Professor Wiseman said: "While the effect of stress itself is actually quite small, what happens is that as people get more stressed and hurried they spend less and less time with their friends, they don't have time to exercise, they smoke more. It's these factors that build up to cause the risk."

4 **Answer the following questions in your own words.**

1 How have people's walking speeds changed in recent years?
2 Why are researchers interested in people's walking speeds?
3 What problems are associated with higher walking speeds?

5 **Find words in the text on page 48 which mean the same as the following. All the answers are from the *Academic Word List*.**

1 carried out   2 shown   3 important   4 sign   5 earlier   6 connected

Focus on speaking 1 *Stereotypes*

Part 1: Interview

1 **When you mention a stereotype, a popular view about something, it's a good idea to say if you agree with this or not. Study the *Useful language* below.**

Useful language: Talking about stereotypes

Tokyo **is supposed to be** a very safe city.

Australians **are supposed to have** a relaxed and laid-back attitude to life.

… **but I'm not sure if that's true or not.**

… **but** (actually/in my experience) **I don't think that's true** (of all Australians)

---

2 **Which country/city/people do you associate with the following? Make sentences using *supposed to be/have*.**

> the best food   very modern architecture   the most skilful footballers
> the most beautiful scenery   very friendly people   the highest crime rate

▶ *Focus on Academic Skills for IELTS page 16*

3 Make sentences using *supposed to be/have* to describe some of the different people/parts of your country.

Focus on reading 1 *Hurry sickness*

FORMING A GENERAL PICTURE

1 **a** Look at the title of the article on page 51. What do you think 'hurry sickness' could be?

b Read through the article quickly and decide which of the following, A, B, C or D best describes its overall topic.

A Ways to improve your efficiency at work.
B Illnesses caused by working too hard.
C Problems arising from the increased pace of life.
D The importance of relaxation.

SCANNING FOR SPECIFIC INFORMATION

2 Complete these sentences with words or phrases from the text.
1 Barton Sparagon is a doctor who researches …
2 The term 'hurry sickness' has been in use for …
3 Jill Stein works as …

INTRODUCING EXAM
TASKS

Headings

▶ *Focus on Academic Skills for IELTS* pages 34–35

3 Study the *Exam Briefing* and *Task Approach* below and answer questions 1–6.

▶ **EXAM BRIEFING** **Academic reading: headings**

In this task you have to identify the main topic of each paragraph or section by choosing the correct heading from a list. There are always more headings than you need so you need to choose carefully.

TASK APPROACH

- Study the headings and underline or circle new words.
- Study examples to help guide your approach.
- Read the first section carefully and try to summarise the main idea in your mind.
- Choose the heading which best sums up the section as a whole.

Questions 1–6
*The reading passage has eight sections, **A–H**.*
Choose the correct heading for each section from the list of headings below.

List of headings

i	The effects of social change
ii	How do we begin to tackle the problem?
iii	What are the effects on our health and why are we so susceptible?
iv	Who is responsible for the problem?
v	Danger signs
vi	A disease with no age limits
vii	What is the main reason for 'hurry sickness'?
viii	A treatment for heart disease
ix	What is the cause?
x	Is there a cure?

Example	Section A	*Answer* **v**
1	Section B	.vii
2	Section C	ix.

Example	Section D	*Answer* **i**
3	Section E	iii
4	Section F	vi.
5	Section G	x.
6	Section H	ii.

hurry sickness

by Alyson Geller, MPH

A According to statistics, it is becoming increasingly rare in many Western countries for families to eat together. It seems that people no longer have time to enjoy a meal, much less buy and prepare the ingredients. Meanwhile, fast food outlets are proliferating. Further evidence of the effects of the increasing pace of life can be seen on all sides. Motorists drum their fingers impatiently at stop lights. Tempers flare in supermarket queues. Saddest of all is the success of an American series of books called *One Minute Bedtime Stories*. What, one has to ask, do parents do with the time thus saved?

B According to Barton Sparagon, M.D., medical director of the Meyer Friedman Institute in San Francisco, and an expert on stress-related illness, the above are all symptoms of a modern epidemic called hurry sickness. The term was invented nearly 40 years ago by a prominent cardiologist, who noticed that all of his heart disease patients had common behavioural characteristics, the most obvious being that they were in a chronic rush. Hurry sickness has been an issue in our culture ever since, but the problem is escalating in degree and intensity, leading to rudeness, short-tempered behaviour and even violence, alongside a range of physical ills.

C The primary cause, according to Sparagon, is the increasing prevalence of technology – like email, cell phones, pagers and laptop computers. We can bring work home, into our bedrooms and on our vacations. Time has sped up for so many people, and there is increased pressure to do more in the same number of hours, says Sparagon.

Jill Stein, a sociologist at the University of California at Los Angeles, agrees that time is being more compressed than ever. "In the past, an overnight letter used to be a big deal. Now if you can't send an e-mail attachment, there's something wrong. Because the technology is available to us, there is an irresistible urge to use it."

D What about those annoying people who shout into their cell phones, unaware of those around them? Stein says that self-centred behaviour is related to larger social trends as well as technology. "There is a breakdown of the nuclear family, of community, of belonging; and an increased alienation and sense that we're all disconnected from one another. This breakdown came before the technology, but the technology has exacerbated it." Now we connect through this technology, says Stein, and we don't have face-to-face interaction.

Ironically, as people pull their cell phones out in the most unlikely venues, our personal lives are available on a public level as never before. People are having work meetings and conversations about their spouses and their therapy sessions with complete impunity. Ordinarily we'd never be exposed to this information, says Stein.

E Sparagon claims that there is more a sense of entitlement now than ever ("Why should anyone slow me down?"). But he warns that there is more than civility at stake. "This chronic impatience is damaging not only to our social environment, but to our physical health. It builds, and then it doesn't take much to explode. And for those who repress it, it's equally damaging."

The high-tech revolution and the lifestyle it has produced have brought with them a wide range of serious health problems, including heart attacks, palpitations, depression, anxiety, immune disorders, digestive problems, insomnia and migraines. Sparagon says that human beings are not designed for prolonged, high-speed activity. "When you look at our heart rates, brain-wave patterns – our basic physiology has not evolved to keep pace with the technology – we are hard-wired to be able to handle a 'fight-flight' response where the stress ends within five to ten minutes. In our current culture, though, we struggle for hours on end."

F Even children are not spared the negative effects of modern-day overload. There's a hidden epidemic of symptoms like hypertension, migraines and digestive problems among children as young as ten – disorders never before seen in children, says Sparagon. Whether these problems result from being swept into the maelstrom of their parents' lives, or from full loads of extracurricular activities and unprecedented homework requirements – up to five hours a night for some – children are facing the same sense of overload, time pressure and demands that their parents experience, says Sparagon, "and they don't have coping mechanisms to deal with it."

G Recovery is possible, but Sparagon emphasises that there is no quick fix. Many of these stress-related behaviours have become deeply ingrained to the point where people are hardly aware of them. The greatest paradox, he says, is that even when people are ready to change their behaviour, they are in a hurry to do so.

H Sparagon works with people to become aware of their stress and the impact it's having on their lives. They examine their belief systems (What is really important? What can they let go of?) and they learn to challenge their behaviours. One popular exercise is to assign a chronically impatient person to stand in the longest line in the grocery store.

The only answer is to take it one day at a time. The irony is that all the techniques and technology designed to streamline our lives may ultimately be counterproductive. As Sparagon says, "People are finding that all of this multi-tasking, rushing and worrying is not only making life intolerable, but actually making them less efficient than they could otherwise be."

Multiple choice

> **► EXAM BRIEFING**   **Academic reading: multiple choice**
>
> There are two main kinds of multiple-choice task. In the first you choose one correct answer from a list of four options. This type may focus on a specific section of text (like Question 7 opposite) or on the overall topic of the passage. In the second type you pick more than one answer from a longer list of options (like Questions 8–10 on page 53).

---

4 The approach to both types of multiple-choice task is the same. Study the *Task Approach* below.

TASK APPROACH

- Look at the sentence opening or question.
- Find the relevant section of text and read it very carefully.
- For each option, ask yourself these key questions:

1 **Is it mentioned in the text?** The idea may look true or logical but be sure it's actually in the text.

2 **Is it true?** The text may contain similar words to those in the question, but check that the meaning is exactly the same.

3 **Is it relevant?** It may be mentioned in the text, and true, but not answer the question.

► *Focus on Academic Skills for IELTS pages 36–37, 51*

Question 7

Choose the correct letter, **A**, **B**, **C** or **D**.

7   One result of technology and the increased pace of life is that people

    A   frequently meet work colleagues in public places.

    B   have personal telephone conversations in public.

    C   need to visit therapists on a regular basis.

    D   no longer have offices to work from.

Questions 8–10

Choose **THREE** letters, **A–G**. Which **THREE** factors contribute to 'hurry sickness'?

    A   Jobs are less secure and people must work harder to keep them.

    B   Our bodies are not designed to cope with stress for long periods.

    C   People are becoming more short-tempered and violent.

    D   People are expected to try and achieve more in the time available.

    E   Too much stress can lead to physical disease.

    F   Globalisation has led to 24-hour trading.

    G   People want to use the new technology which is available.

EXTRA PRACTICE

Summary completion

5   **In addition to the four correct answers, find:**

- two which are **results** rather than causes of 'hurry sickness'.
- two possible factors which are **not mentioned** in the passage.

> **EXAM BRIEFING**   **Academic reading: notes / summary completion**
>
> In this task you have to complete notes or a short summary using information from the passage. There are two versions. In one you have to write up to three words and/or a number from the passage (as in the task below). In the other you choose answers from a box of options. Answers may not be in passage order.

▶ *Focus on Academic Skills for IELTS* pages 10, 37

6   **Study the following advice.**

TASK APPROACH

- First, read through the whole summary for general understanding.
- Read it again carefully, studying the words before and after each gap and thinking about the general meaning.
- Find the relevant section of text and re-read carefully to find the answer.
- Make sure your answers fit logically **and** grammatically.

Questions 11–14
Complete the summary below.
Choose **NO MORE THAN THREE WORDS** *from the passage for each answer.*

Hurry sickness is not a new condition but it has increased both in
11 ~~degree and intensity~~ .... in recent years, mainly as a result of the rapid development
of 12 ~~physical ills (technology)~~ .... Typical symptoms include chronic impatience, which
experts believe can have potentially serious effects not only on those around us but
also on our 13 .... The fact that children are also beginning to
suffer from a variety of health problems suggests that they are as vulnerable to the
pressures of modern life as their parents. Curing the condition is a slow process,
which requires the sufferer to 14 .... the stress in their lives, and
try to change their behaviour patterns.

VOCABULARY

KEY LANGUAGE
Parts of speech
▶ p. 210, ex. 1

7 The following words occur in the text on pages 51–52. Study the context and choose the correct meaning from the list below. This will be easier if you first identify what part of speech each one is.

1 … fast food outlets are *proliferating* (Section A)
2 … a modern *epidemic* called 'hurry sickness' (B)
3 The primary cause … is the increasing *prevalence* of technology … (C)
4 This breakdown came before the technology, but the technology has *exacerbated* it. (D)
5 … conversations about their *spouses* … (D)
6 … full loads of *extracurricular* activities … (F)
7 The greatest *paradox* … is that even when people are ready to change their behaviour, they are in a hurry to do so. (G)
8 … all the techniques and technology … may … be *counterproductive* (H)

KEY LANGUAGE
Word building: affixes
▶ p. 216–217, ex. 9
e.g. *extracurricular,
counterproductive*

a) *n*   widespread existence
b) *n*   statement which seems to be impossible because it says two opposite things
c) *v*   made worse
d) *adj* having the opposite effect to that intended
e) *n*   something which develops and spreads quickly (e.g. an infectious disease)
f) *n*   husbands or wives
g) *adj* outside the regular course of work in a school or college
h) *v*   rapidly increasing in numbers

Focus on reading 2 *Distinguishing fact from opinion*

1 When you read a detailed argument, it's important to distinguish between facts (statements which are known to be true or based on generally accepted evidence) and opinions (personal beliefs which may or may not be true).

Which of the statements (or parts of the statements) should be read as Fact (F) and which should be read as Opinion (O)?

On my way to work once, I saw a man walking down the street while shaving with an electric razor, which seemed to me extraordinary.

James Gleick is a science writer and the author of several fascinating books including *Faster: The Acceleration of Just About Everything.*

We are subject to certain biological constraints. For example, diseases can't be cured more quickly because we're in a hurry.

Despite the undoubted speed of the internet, there's a sense in which it has made us even more impatient.

2 Which of the following phrases are more likely to be associated with facts (F) and which with opinions (O)?

1 Professor Brown argues that …
2 According to the latest statistics, …
3 Several experts claim that …
4 Scientists have discovered …
5 Some people say …
6 Research findings confirm that …
7 It is a commonly held belief that …
8 In his view, …
9 Many scientists suspect that …
10 As has been frequently demonstrated, …

For more information on reporting verbs see *Critical Thinking 5*, page107 and *Key Language* page 219, ex. 12, page 233, ex. 33.

Focus on speaking 2 *Priorities*

Part 3: Discussion

Prioritise the following, according to how important they are in your life. Then discuss your decisions in pairs.

| *Health* | *Wealth* | *Family* | *Career growth* | *Intellectual growth* |

Academic Style 3 *Nouns and Noun Phrases 1*

Introduction

There is a high proportion of nouns in academic writing, and this reflects the vital role that nouns play in communicating information. This section looks at two important uses of nouns and noun phrases in academic writing.

A **noun** refers to a person, place, thing, or abstract quality or idea, e.g. *secretary, school, water, justice*.

A **noun phrase** is a group of words containing a main noun (or headword) together with additional information, e.g. *a dangerous situation, an electricity supply, a point of information*.

General nouns

General nouns are a way of briefly summarising information. They are an important feature of academic writing because they help to avoid repetition and link a text together.
NB General nouns may refer backwards (as in example 1) or forwards (as in example 2). Look at the examples in bold in the following sentences.

1 Tests have shown that fish become disorientated in water with a high level of CO_2. This **effect** is potentially devastating for a wide range of fish populations.
2 One of the most common **reasons** people gave for taking time off work was stress.

1 Choose suitable general nouns from the list below to complete the sentences, using singular or plural forms as appropriate.

activity	device	problem	purpose
benefit	effect	reason	trend
change	issue	result	type

1 The country is facing a range of .... including inflation and high unemployment.
2 Cinema attendance has fallen steadily in recent months and this .... looks set to continue.
3 The subject of discrimination will be among several other .... to be discussed.
4 The new mayor promised to crack down on drug dealing and other illegal ....
5 Nouns can be countable or uncountable and each .... has its own grammatical rules.
6 Members get free entry to exhibitions as well as other .... such as a regular newsletter.
7 Unfortunately an E grade wasn't the .... he had been hoping for.
8 Washing machines and other labour-saving .... have transformed our lives.

Noun + noun combinations

Noun + noun combinations are a very common kind of noun phrase in academic prose. In these, the first noun defines the second (or headword) in some way. For example, it may describe:
a material, e.g. glass bottle (bottle made of glass)
a purpose, e.g. safety regulations (regulations designed to improve safety)
an area of specialisation, e.g. finance director (director with responsibility for finance)

2 Explain the meaning of the following noun + noun combinations.

1 fossil fuel
2 sports centre
3 business correspondent
4 bottle bank
5 laser surgery
6 sign language

3 The following are common parts of noun + noun combinations in academic English. Choose nouns from the list to combine with words 1–6 below. Check the meanings of any combination you're not sure of.

information	research	laboratory
computer	language	university

1 .... superhighway, technology
2 .... education, lecturer
3 .... printout, software
4 .... barrier, teacher
5 .... grant, scientist
6 .... experiments, equipment'

4 Which noun + noun combinations match the following definitions?

1 the time of day when traffic is at its heaviest
2 the time of year when there are most tourists in a place
3 the enjoyment you get from doing your work
4 the buying and selling of military weapons
5 the cheapest type of seats in a plane
6 angry or violent behaviour by drivers towards other drivers

> **Language Fact**
> There are typically three to four times as many nouns as verbs in academic writing. By contrast, nouns and verbs are equally frequent in conversation.

Academic Vocabulary 3

Grammar/Meaning

1 The following words appeared in the text on pages 51–52. Decide what part of speech each word is, noun (N), verb (Vb), adjective (Adj) or Adverb (Adv), then match to the correct definition from the list a)–h). If necessary, go back to the text to see how the word is used.

1	issue	*Hurry sickness has been an **issue** in our culture* (B)	*N, d)*
2	nuclear	*a breakdown of the **nuclear** family* (D)	......
3	unprecedented	***unprecedented** homework requirements* (F)	......
4	mechanism	*children don't have the coping **mechanisms*** (F)	......
5	impact	*the **impact** that stress is having on their lives* (H)	......
6	challenge	*People learn to **challenge** their behaviours* (H)	......
7	assign	*One exercise is to **assign** an impatient person to stand in the longest line in the store* (H)	......
8	ultimately	*these techniques may **ultimately** be counterproductive* (H)	......

Definitions

> a) finally, after everything else has been done and considered (*Adv*)
> b) the effect that a situation has on people or things (*N*)
> c) to refuse to accept something (*Vb*)
> d) subject or problem that is often discussed or written about (*N*)
> e) a system or way of behaving (*N*)
> f) never having happened so much before (*Adj*)
> g) relating to a family which consists of just a husband, wife and children (*Adj*)
> h) to give someone a particular job (*Vb*)

Word building: Opposites

2 Choose the correct prefix to form the opposite of the following adjectives.

ab-	in-	un-

1	accurate	5	normal
2	available	6	reliable
3	aware	7	secure
4	capable	8	significant

3 Complete these sentences with words from exercise 2.

1 Tests revealed an .... level of cholesterol in his blood.
2 The problem only affected an .... number of people.
3 You will lose marks for .... spelling in the IELTS Listening test.
4 Two-thirds (62%) of parents are .... of their child's online contacts.
5 Unfortunately, funding for new computer equipment is .... at present.

Word building: *Nouns and adjectives*

4 Make nouns and adjectives from the following verbs:

Verb	Noun	Adjective
1 analyse		
2 attach		
3 connect		
4 emphasise		
5 interact		
6 require		
7 stress		
8 vary		

5 Complete the sentences with words from completed exercise 4 above.

1 After half-term, the .... of the course will change to exam preparation.
2 Moving home is supposed to be one of the most .... life events.
3 It's important to eat a .... diet rather than one particular group of foods.
4 Price is decided through the .... of supply and demand.
5 They made a detailed .... of the data before drawing any conclusions.
6 I sent the photograph by email as a(n) ....

6 Choose five academic words from this page to learn, and write personal examples to help you remember them.

1 ....
2 ....
3 ....
4 ....
5 ....

6 ▶ Time out

time out *n* **1** take time out (to do sth) *informal* to rest or do something different from your usual job or activities: *In between jobs, Liz always took time out to return to her first love – travelling.* (Longman Exams Dictionary)

In this unit you will practise	Key Language	Exam Focus
• Discussing leisure activities • Describing a leisure activity; discussing topic issues • Listening and completing notes • Structuring an argument: analysing the question; providing evidence; giving supporting reasons; evidence-led approach • Vocabulary: describing people; pronunciation: word stress	Cohesion: reference links **Writing practice** Task 1: Presenting data Task 2: Structuring an argument	**Speaking:** Parts 2, 3 **Listening:** Sections 1, 2 **Writing:** Task 2

Lead-in

Work with a partner.

1 a Think about how you spend your free time. Number the leisure activities below 1–10 according to how much time you spend on them (1 = most).

going to the cinema	1
internet/emailing	
listening to music	1
playing computer games	
reading	
shopping	1
spending time with friends/family	2
sport/exercise	1
visiting museums/galleries	0
watching TV	4

b Compare lists with your partner and discuss any differences. Find out more about their leisure habits. For example, ask which TV programmes they never miss, and which they turn off immediately!

2 Discuss these questions, giving reasons for your answers.

a Consider differences between the sexes. Which <u>two</u> leisure activities would you expect to be

• most popular with both sexes?
• more popular with women than men?
• more popular with men than women?

b Compare your answers with the results of a UK survey on page 237. Are there any surprises? What differences, if any, would you expect in a similar survey in your own country?

> **WRITING PRACTICE**
> Presenting and comparing data (guided practice, example answer)
> ▶ pages 237–238, ex. 3, 4

Focus on vocabulary *Describing people*

Work in pairs to do these exercises.

1 Sociological studies have shown that people commonly associate a number of distinct attributes with particular leisure activities. What adjectives would you use to describe the people below? Try to think of two or three for each.

> *Weight trainer   Guitarist   Kayaker   Volleyball player   Chess player*

2 Match each person with one of the following lists of attributes. Check any vocabulary you're not sure of.

A *Volleyball player*

Athletic *sport*
Competitive
Concerned with
  physical appearance
Energetic
Health conscious
Physically fit
Sports minded
Team player

B *Chess player*

Able to concentrate
Analytical
Cerebral
Competitive
Good problem-solver
Logical
Maths-minded
Quiet
Strategic

C *Weight*

Athletic
Competitive
Concerned with
  physical appearance
Health conscious
Physically fit
Sports-minded

D *Guitarist*

At peace with
  themselves
Creative
Determined *don't give up*
Introspective
Intelligent
Patient
Quiet

E *Kayaker*

Adventurous
Fun
Fun loving
Likes scenic beauty
Loves fresh air
Outdoor type
Sociable

3 Which adjectives would you use to describe a backpacker?

4 Work in pairs to describe someone you know or admire. Spend a few moments making notes before you begin.

PRONUNCIATION:
WORD STRESS

5 Words consist of one or more syllables, each containing a vowel sound. Study the examples and put the words into the correct group. There should be five words in each.

1-syllable words O e.g. *fun, team*	2-syllable words Oo e.g. *player, study*	3-syllable words Ooo e.g. *gallery, internet*

air	good	outdoor	problem	straight
concentrate	health	patient	scenic	volleyball
conscious	logical	physical	sociable	type

6   Words of three syllables or more are commonly stressed on the third syllable from the end, e.g. adjective Ooo (AD-jec-tive), comparison oOoo (com-PA-ri-son). For more information see the *Language Fact box* on page 118.

Practise saying the following 3- and 4-syllable words with this stress pattern.

activity	attribute	general
adventurous	competitive	intelligent
argument	energetic	particular
associate	exercise	similar

Focus on listening 1 *Student interviews*

Section 1: Note completion

▶ Focus on Academic Skills for IELTS pages 14–15

You are going to hear interviews between a Student Counsellor and two students. You have to complete the Counsellor's notes.

Before you listen, look through the headings and the example answers. Think about the kind of questions the Counsellor might ask, and the answers the students might give.

Questions 1–10
Complete the notes. Use **NO MORE THAN THREE WORDS** *for each answer.*

Interview One

Name:		Linda Richmond
Course:	1	....
Where living:	2	....
Membership of student societies/clubs:	3	....
Comments on facilities:		Quite good
Suggestions for improvements:	4	....
Other leisure activities:	5	....

Interview Two

Name:	6	....
Course:		Marine Biology
Where living:		5 kilometres away
Membership of student societies/clubs:	7	....
Comments on facilities:	8	....
Suggestions for improvements:	9	....
Other leisure activities:	10	....

Focus on speaking *Leisure activities*

Part 2: Long turn

EXAM TIP You can ask the examiner to explain any words in the topic you don't understand

1 Study this topic card for a Part 2 task. How many discussion points are there?

> **Describe a leisure activity that you enjoy.**
>
> > **You should say:**
> >
> > > **what the activity is**
> > > **where and when you take part in it**
> > > **what it involves**
> >
> > **and explain why you enjoy it so much.**

MINDPLANS

2 In pairs, think of a heading for each set of notes on this mindplan.

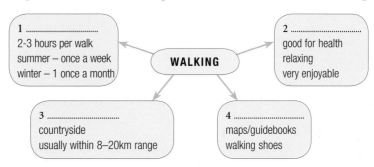

1 ....
2-3 hours per walk
summer – once a week
winter – 1 once a month

WALKING

2 ....
good for health
relaxing
very enjoyable

3 ....
countryside
usually within 8–20km range

4 ....
maps/guidebooks
walking shoes

3 Prepare to discuss your own leisure activity. Make notes using a mindplan.

4 Work in pairs. Take it in turns to describe your chosen leisure activity in as much detail as possible. Try to keep talking for one to two minutes. Afterwards, tell the class two things about your partner's activity.

Part 3: Discussion

5 Work in pairs to discuss the following questions.
● Why is it a good idea for a child to have a hobby?
● Do young people get enough physical exercise these days?
● Is watching television a good way of relaxing?
● What leisure activities would you recommend as a way of combating stress?

► *Focus on Academic Skills for IELTS* page 41, ex. 3

Focus on listening 2 *Ten ways to slow down your life*

Section 2: Sentence completion

1 You are going to hear advice on how to deal with stress in everyday life. While you listen, you have to complete a set of sentences containing key information on the topic.

Sentence completion is slightly more challenging than note completion because your answers must fit into the sentence grammatically as well as logically. Read the following advice.

TASK APPROACH

- Study the instructions to find out how many words you can write.
- Read the heading and questions, and think about possible answers. This process will help you listen more effectively.
- Look for grammatical clues to see what kind of word or phrase is needed in each space.

2 **Work with another student to discuss the following questions.**

KEY LANGUAGE
-ing forms vs infinitives
▶ p. 229–230, ex. 27

1 What part of speech is needed for answers 1–4 (e.g. noun/noun phrase, verb/verb phrase)? How do you know?
2 What verb form is needed for answers 7 and 8 (e.g. infinitive with/without 'to', *-ing* form?) How do you know?
3 Think of some possible answers to questions 2, 3, 7, 8 and 10.

3 **Now answer the following questions.**

EXAM PRACTICE

Questions 1–10
*Complete the sentences below. In this practice task, each answer is **TWO WORDS**.*

TEN WAYS TO SLOW DOWN YOUR LIFE

At work
1 Decide on a ......*finishing time*...... and stick to it.
2 Make sure that you take a ......*lunch break*...... of at least 30 minutes.
3 Prioritise your emails, faxes and ......*phone calls*......
4 Make good use of the ......*waste paper bin*......
5 Accept that there will still be things in ......*in-out tray*...... at the end of the day.
6 Talk to someone about something ......*outside work*......

At home
7 After work, concentrate on ......*listening to*...... other people.
8 Avoid ......*watching TV*......
9 Play a part in your ......*local community*......
10 Take up an activity like painting, learning a ......*musical instrument*...... or a new sport.

Focus on writing *Structuring an argument*

Task 2

TASK APPROACH

1   Read the following advice on structuring an argument.

- **Analyse** the question carefully. Underline or circle the **key points** and consider what you understand by them.
- Decide on your **overall response**, and think about the **evidence** you need to provide, including any personal experience you have.
- Make a **paragraph plan**. This will help you cover all the key points, organise your writing clearly, and **link ideas** logically.

ANALYSING THE QUESTION

2   Read the following Task 2 question. The key points in this task have been underlined for you. Consider carefully what you understand by them and discuss the questions below with a partner.

> Write about the following topic:
>
> ***Do young people today make <u>good use</u> of their leisure time? Or do they spend <u>too much time</u> watching television and playing video games, instead of taking part in <u>more productive activities</u>?***
>
> Give reasons for your answer and include any relevant examples from your own knowledge or experience.
>
> Write at least 250 words.

- *good use*   Is there a right and wrong way to use leisure time?

- *too much time*   How much is too much? Is there an acceptable level?

- *more productive activities*   What makes an activity 'productive'? What kind of activities are 'more productive' than watching TV?

PROVIDING EVIDENCE

3   Discuss these questions, mentioning any relevant personal experience you've had. Make notes of the main points using a mindplan (see page 51).

1   What **problems** (if any) do you see in children spending a lot of time watching TV or playing video games?

2   What **benefits** (if any) might children gain from these activities?

▶ *Focus on Academic Skills for IELTS pages 42–43*

3   List a few **alternative activities** and suggest how these can be more 'productive'.

4   When providing evidence, you may need to discuss the reasons for something. Read the following *Useful language* box and answer questions 1 and 2.

Useful language: Expressing reasons	
Because	**Because** children spend so much time indoors, they … Children may have health problems **because** they ….
because of / as a result of	Their schoolwork can suffer **because of / as a result of** …
so / such	Some games are **so** realistic that children may … Some games have **such** realistic effects that …

1   What is the difference in usage between *because* and *because of*?
2   What is the difference between *so* and *such*?

PRESENTING
SUPPORTING POINTS

5   When presenting a written argument, it's important to make it clear whether you are stating a reliable fact or expressing an opinion – your own or someone else's.

Stress is arguably one of the most serious modern diseases. According to a survey carried out by the Institute of Management, approximately 270,000 UK workers take time off work every year because of work-related stress, at a cost to the nation in sick pay, lost production and medical bills of about £7 billion.

Experts have often suggested that stress is less of a problem for bosses than for their subordinates, and this view is confirmed by the survey, which found that only nine per cent of junior managers looked forward to going to work. Furthermore, only seven per cent felt they were in control of their jobs.

KEY LANGUAGE
Reference links
▶ p. 217–218, ex. 10
e.g. a survey / the survey
the UK / the nation

1   Circle words or phrases in the text used to introduce or indicate an opinion.
2   In order to present a convincing argument, opinions need to be supported by facts. Which facts are used to support the opinions you identified in the text above?
3   When you have more than one supporting reason, you can use linking expressions like the following.

Useful language: Linking expressions		
In the first place, …	One reason for this is …	Another (reason) is …
In addition, …	Furthermore, …	Moreover, …

Think of two facts to support the following opinions. Then make statements linking the points suitably.

- It's a bad idea to give children too much pocket money.
- Mobile phones are an extremely useful means of communication.

EVIDENCE-LED APPROACH

6 Here is a basic model for a Task 2 answer. In this approach, you consider all the evidence and work towards an overall conclusion. This is known as an *evidence-led* approach. An alternative approach will be discussed in Unit 12.

Study the paragraph plan below and then complete the sentences in the first two sections with your own ideas.

PARAGRAPH PLAN	SAMPLE LANGUAGE
Opening paragraph	
• Introduce topic	Since television became widely available in the 1950s, it has grown steadily
• Provide background information	in popularity. Nowadays, many families …
Middle paragraphs	
• Analyse evidence	Some experts believe that young people are becoming more and more …
• Start a new paragraph for each point	In evidence of this, they …
• Give reasons/examples to illustrate your views	On the other hand, it can be argued that watching TV can actually …
Closing paragraph	
• Summarise main points	We have seen that …
• State your overall conclusion	To sum up, …

EXAM PRACTICE

7 Now write your answer to the task.

> **WRITING PRACTICE**
> Structuring an argument
> (exam task)
> ▶ p. 239, ex. 5

8 When you have completed a writing task, it's important to look through it again in order to find and correct any mistakes. The following exercise practises this process, which is called 'proof reading'. See also *Reflective Learning 4*, page 147.

Most of these sentences contain common errors. Identify and correct the errors.

1 There never seems to be anything worth watching on the television.
2 Young people tend to hear the radio more than older age groups.
3 According to statistics, Americans spend 2.9 hours a day seeing television.
4 She finds playing piano the best way to relax.
5 Why don't you get rid of the television if you never watch it?
6 Ninety per cent of people in Britain listen the radio at some time during the day.
7 Do stop talking and concentrate in your driving.
8 You have to take a two-year training course in order to qualify as a teacher.

Check your answers by referring to the *Error Hit List* on page 66.

ERROR HIT LIST

television/TV/radio

✘	✔
Is there anything on the television tonight?	… anything <u>on television</u> tonight?
I'd rather stay at home and see television.	… <u>watch</u> television.
Did you hear the radio last night?	… <u>listen to</u> the radio …

- Use **television** and **TV** (without an article) to talk about the system of broadcasting programmes, e.g. *Television can be educational. What's on TV?* Only use **the television** and **the TV** to talk about the piece of furniture, e.g. *Put that chair in front of the television.*

- Say **watch television**, not 'see television'. When you are talking about a particular programme, you can say **see** or **watch**, e.g. *Did you see the weather forecast?*

- Say **listen to the radio**, not 'hear the radio'. When you are talking about a particular programme, you can say **hear** or **listen to**, e.g. *Did you hear the news yesterday?*

concentrate/listen/play

✘	✔
You must be concentrated in your work.	You must <u>concentrate on</u> …
Be quiet. I need to concentrate myself.	I need to <u>concentrate</u> ~~myself~~.
I enjoy listening jazz.	I enjoy listening <u>to</u> jazz.
I wanted to learn to play guitar.	… to play <u>the</u> guitar

- **concentrate** takes the preposition *on*. It is never used with reflexive pronouns.

- **listen** takes the preposition *to*.

- In British English, we say 'play **the** guitar/piano/flute', etc. In American English, the definite article is sometimes omitted.

game/match

✘	✔
We had a match of football.	… a <u>football match</u>/a <u>game of</u> football.

- Although **match** and **game** have the same meaning, they are used slightly differently. **Match** is only used after the name of the sport, while **game** is usually used in the phrase **a game of**.

plural expressions with numbers

✘	✔
We have a ten years old daughter.	… a <u>ten-year-old</u> daughter.

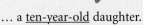

- When qualifying expressions with numbers are used before nouns, singular forms are used. Use a hyphen between the number and the noun it refers to, e.g. *a three-week holiday; a two-litre bottle, a four-hour journey.*

Reflective Learning 2 *Self-evaluation and setting learning goals*

Introduction

An important aspect of reflective learning is to establish learning goals. For this you need clear **aims** and a realistic idea of your **strengths and weaknesses**. A useful approach is to fill in a checklist like the one below and discuss it with your teacher.

Identifying aims

1 Write down your aims in studying English. Think about the IELTS test and the score you hope to achieve, as well as more general communication needs. Be as specific as possible. Mention exactly what you want to be able to do in English and the skills you need to improve.

Assessing language skills

2 Study the checklist. If you want to add extra skills, continue on another piece of paper.

Tick one of the first three columns to assess your ability in each skill. In the last column add up to three stars to show how important you think a particular skill is for you.

No star = not important   * not very important
** quite important   *** very important

Setting goals

3 Use the completed list to work out your **learning goals**. Any skills in the third column which also have three stars will be your **top priorities**. Choose no more than two or three to focus on. If possible, ask your teacher for advice. Repeat this process at regular intervals in order to monitor your progress and adjust your learning goals as necessary.

1 ……………………………..………………………..……......

2 ……………………………..………………………..……......

3 ……………………………..………………………..……......

Reviewing goals

4 Work with a partner. Check the three reflective learning goals you each listed on page 27. Discuss any success you've had or difficulties you've encountered in achieving these goals. Revise these goals if necessary and remember to review them regularly.

	How well do you perform?			How important?
	Well enough	Quite well	Not very well yet	No star * ** ***
1 Reading long texts and understanding the main ideas				
2 Reading for detail to answer exam questions				
3 Working out the meaning of difficult vocabulary				
4 Finding information in dictionaries and reference books				
5 Understanding everyday conversation				
6 Understanding recorded conversations and lectures				
7 Listening to answer exam questions				
8 Having enough ideas for essays				
9 Having enough vocabulary to express yourself in writing				
10 Structuring an argument and linking ideas in an essay				
11 Interpreting graphs and diagrams				
12 Speaking and writing reasonably accurately				
13 Taking part in everyday conversation				
14 Taking part in discussions in class				
15 Answering questions in the Interview				
16 Having enough vocabulary to express yourself in speaking				
17 Speaking reasonably fluently				
18 Speaking with reasonably clear pronunciation				

7 ▶ Retail therapy

retail therapy *n* [U] the act of buying things that you do not need when you are unhappy because you think it will make you feel better – often used humorously. (Longman Exams Dictionary)

In this unit you will practise	Key Language	Exam Focus
• Discussing likes and dislikes; consumer topics; describing objects • Sampling a text; dealing with unknown vocabulary • Short-answer questions; summary completion; matching; True/False/Not Given • Topic vocabulary and pronunciation • Pronunciation: sounds	Linking expressions Talking about research Noun + noun combinations	**Speaking:** Parts 1–3 **Reading skills** **Speaking / Writing**

Lead-in

1 Work in pairs. Read the following statements and decide whether the missing word in each space is 'men' or 'women'.

KEY LANGUAGE
Linking expressions
▶ p. 219, ex. 11

1 When they shop, 70 per cent of ...*men*...... become 'hunters', aiming for a defined product in a specific shop. 80 per cent of ...*women*... , on the other hand, act as leisurely 'gatherers', roaming round in a less purposeful manner.

2 ...*Men*... have normally exhausted their patience after 72 minutes of shopping. Meanwhile most ...*women*... prefer to carry on shopping for at least another 28 minutes.

3 Generally speaking, ...*women*... buy their own clothes, without seeking other people's advice. However, around a quarter of ...*men*... admit to relying on the input of other people to choose what they wear.

2 Check your answers on page 253 and discuss how true the statements are of you personally, and of other people you know.

3 Underline linking expressions within each pair of statements.

Focus on speaking 1 *Discussing likes and dislikes; consumer topics*

Part 1: Interview

▶ EXAM BRIEFING Speaking: Interview Part 1

Questions about likes and dislikes are very common in Part 1, so it's important to know a variety of expressions to describe your feelings. It may be useful to start with a brief introduction to help you give a more specific answer. If you need to give a negative opinion, it's a good idea to begin with a softening phrase.

1 Study the *Useful language.* Notice the introduction and softening phrases.

Useful language

Introduction

It depends what kind of … / what you mean by …

Softening phrases

To be honest, … I'm afraid, …, Actually …

Likes

I (quite/really) enjoy/I don't mind …

The *(kind of)* … I enjoy most is/are … because …

I find … *(very/extremely/really)* interesting/relaxing/enjoyable, etc.

Dislikes

I don't *(really)* like/enjoy … *(very much/at all)*

I'm not *(very/all that)* keen on … don't like it

I find … *(rather/really)* boring/frustrating/annoying, etc.

---

2 Practise answering the following Part 1 questions with a partner. Remember to use expressions from the *Useful language* above.

1 How do you feel about shopping in general?
2 What is your least favourite kind of shopping?
3 Do you prefer shopping alone or with someone else?
4 What kind of shopping do you do on the Internet?

Part 3: Discussion

3 Discuss the following questions. Try to present two sides of the argument using the expressions below. Use introductory sentences or softening phrases as appropriate.

1 Are large out-of-town hypermarkets and shopping malls a good thing?
2 Do you think people are too materialistic these days?
3 Is there too much advertising on TV?

EXAM TIP Answer questions as fully as possible by giving reasons for opinions and mentioning examples from your experience.

Useful language

On the whole … / Generally speaking … *(I think)* …

(But) **On the other hand …**

Focus on reading *Retail therapy*

▶ **EXAM BRIEFING**

One challenge of the Reading paper is dealing with a large amount of text in a short time. A single passage may be up to 900 words long, and the three passages together contain 2,250–2,700 words. At least one passage will put forward a detailed, logical argument, which needs careful analysis.

Academic reading: tackling long texts

● Begin by forming a general picture of the content and how it is organised.
● Study the questions to find out what information is needed.
● Scan the text to locate the relevant section, then read closely for detail.

SAMPLING A TEXT

1 Sampling is a way of forming a general picture of a text. The main topic is usually set out in the first paragraph, and sub-topics are often made clear in the first sentence of each paragraph, so these are good places to begin.

Read the first paragraph of the text on page 73, and the first sentence of each of the following paragraphs. Then decide which answer (A–D) best describes the overall topic.

A A history of the marketing industry
B Effective sales techniques for the retail industry
C Information on credit card debt and how to avoid it
D Research findings that can help us reduce our spending

EXAM PRACTICE
Short-answer questions

2 Read paragraphs 1–4 of the text on page 73 and answer questions 1–3 below.

TASK APPROACH

• Check the **instructions** to find how many words you can write.
• Underline **key words** in the questions.
• Use **skimming skills** to find the relevant section of text and **scanning skills** to locate the information you need. The answers are in text order.

Questions 1–3
Answer the questions below.
*Choose **NO MORE THAN THREE WORDS** from the passage for each answer.*

1 What aspect of shopping causes dopamine to be released?
2 What research method did Gregory Berns use in his work?
3 Which institution was responsible for a report on shoppers' attitudes to credit cards?

Summary completion

3 This task was introduced in Unit 5. In this second type, you have to choose answers from a box of options. Read the advice for this task below.

TASK APPROACH

KEY LANGUAGE
Grammatical terms
▶ p. 210, ex. 1

• Study each gap and think about the part of speech that is missing, eg. noun, verb, adjective, etc. This will help you narrow the choice.
• Search the list of options for words of that kind, and try them in the space.
• Locate the relevant part of the text and re-read carefully, looking for parallel expressions which help identify the correct answer.

PARTS OF SPEECH

4 Before you start the exam task, do this practice exercise.

a Decide what part of speech is missing in each space in the text on page 71. Choose from the list below and say what clues helped you decide.

Ns (noun singular)	**V** (plain verb)
Npl (noun plural)	**V+-ing** (-ing form, N or V)
Number	**V+-s** (3rd person singular)
	V+-ed (past participle)

b Identify suitable words from the box and choose the best answer in each case.

administered ⁶	living ⁸	scientists ₁	8.9 %
condition ⁵	recognize ⁹	seek ₁₀	
consumers ³	resisting ₄	shopaholic ²	

1 ………. have developed a new test which aims to tell if you are a 2 ……….. .
The test is designed to identify 3 ………. who regularly spend money on items,
regardless of need, and who have difficulty in 4 ………. the impulse to buy. This
5 ………. is known as compulsive buying. When the test was 6 ………. to a sample
of 550 university staff members, the results revealed that nearly 7 ………. would be
considered compulsive buyers. The authors concluded that we are 8 ………. in a
consumption-orientated society and people need to be educated to 9 ………. if
compulsive buying is a problem in their lives so that they can 10 ………. help.

5 Now do the exam task. If necessary, remind yourself about the general *Task Advice*
on page 53 and the specific advice on page 70 before you begin.

Questions 4–12
Complete the summary using the list of words, A–Q, below.

Many studies into the psychology of shopping have been carried out, not only by experts in 4 ….…I…… (n)
like Jennifer Argo, but also by 5 ……O…… like Gregory Berns, and the results can be found in various (n/adj)
6 ……A….. and professional journals. Among other things, researchers have looked at the difference
between shopping alone or with 7 ….K………. , and at the effect of shopping when you have 8 ….J………
problems. Much of this research into shopping is 9 ….G….T…… by the marketing industry, in order to
discover how to 10 ….E………. consumers to buy more and more products they don't need. 11 ……B……. ,
it is also possible to use the same research to help people to control their 12 ……P……. .

A *academic*	G *funded*	M *psychologists*
B *additionally*	H *make*	N *retailers*
C *aimed*	I *marketing*	O *scientists*
D *companion*	J *money*	P *spending*
E *encourage*	K *others*	Q *time*
F *fortunately*	L *popular*	

Matching

REMINDERS

6 This task was introduced in Unit 3. Study the following reminders.

• Scan the text and underline the points to match in the text (in this case journals).
• Underline key words in the questions.
• Study the relevant sections of the text, looking for parallel expressions.

Questions 13–17

Look at the following advice on how to avoid overspending when shopping (Questions 13–17), based on research published in a number of journals (A–D).
Match each piece of advice with the correct journal. NB You may use any letter more than once.

13 Use only cash as a method of payment for goods.

14 Avoid shopping in the company of other people.

15 Try to resist the attraction of designer brands.

16 Be particularly cautious if you have financial problems.

17 Take time to consider before making a purchase.

A	The Journal of Consumer Research
B	The Journal of Experimental Psychology: Applied
C	The Journal of Advertising Research
D	Behavioural Research Therapy

True/False/Not Given

TASK APPROACH

7 **Read the following advice on choosing between No/False and Not Given answers.**

- A No/False statement says the **opposite** to information in the passage. You can therefore make a No/False statement true by inserting *no* or *not*.
- There is **no information** in the passage to say whether a Not Given statement is true or false. Even if you know the information is true, you must choose Not Given if there is no evidence in the passage.

> **EXAM TIP** Answers to True/False/Not Given questions are in passage order.

8 **Read paragraph 8 again carefully, then say which of each pair of statements is False and which Not Given.**

1a 90 per cent of the world's population lives on less than $2 a day.
1b Purchasing power of $2 a day is defined as the international poverty line.
2a The term 'satisficing' comes from a combination of the words 'satisfy' and 'suffice'.
2b The term 'satisficing' was invented by the author of the article.

Questions 18–22

Do the following statements agree with information given in the passage?
Write:

TRUE	*if the statement agrees with the information*
FALSE	*if the statement contradicts with the information*
NOT GIVEN	*if there is no information on this*

18 Shoppers' first concern when buying something is whether it is good value or not.

19 Wendy Liu holds the position of Assistant Professor of Marketing.

20 After buying a product, the level of dopamine in the body increases rapidly.

21 The 'pain of paying' is likely to be experienced when using a credit card.

22 People with more than one credit card are more likely to get into debt.

Retail therapy

1 The marketing industry has spent billions of dollars scientifically perfecting ways to appeal to shoppers' primitive brain responses of instinct and emotion so that they buy products which their reasoning higher brain knows that they don't need or particularly want. The good news is that much of this research can be turned on its head, enabling us to control our instincts and spend less.

2 To take a simple example: pausing briefly between choosing something and taking it to the checkout can dramatically increase the chance of resisting the urge to buy, according to a study in the *Journal of Consumer Research*. Wendy Liu, of the University of California, Los Angeles, ran four tests where she interrupted people's purchasing. She found that a break in the buying process changed their priorities. Before the interruption, shoppers focused on whether the object they desired was a bargain, whereas after the interruption, they returned with a far more objective, higher-brained view, which questioned whether they really wanted the item at all.

3 The need to cool off our consumer brains is reinforced by Gregory Berns, a neuroscientist at Emory University, Atlanta, Georgia. His brain scan studies show how the feelgood chemical dopamine is released in waves as shoppers see a product and consider buying it. However, it is only the anticipation, rather than the buying, that releases the chemical. Once an item has been purchased, the chemical high dissipates rapidly, often leaving a sense of regret. In fact, with practice it is possible to stimulate the dopamine release merely by window-shopping, without making any purchase.

4 Another area of enquiry has been methods of payment. Four studies on 330 people in the *Journal of Experimental Psychology: Applied* confirm the suspicion that it's much easier to spend money in the form of a credit card. The New York University-led report concludes that we regard anything but hard cash as 'play money' and that real currency is the only thing that gives you the 'pain of paying'. Credit cards might not only anaesthetise retail pain, they may also create a physical craving to get the dopamine high from spending, according to Professor Drazen Prelec, a psychologist at the Massachusetts Institute of Technology. He cautions that when you see and touch the plastic it is just like smelling biscuits baking when you are hungry. You feel compelled to spend in order to satisfy the craving.

5 Researchers have also looked at the phenomenon of designer brands. These have proved highly effective at persuading people to spend more money on 'special' goods which are actually only of average quality. Such brands are painstakingly developed to encourage people to identify with them, to believe, in effect, that their favourite labels have exactly the same human values as they do. A study in the *Journal of Advertising Research*, which investigated this area, reveals how our primitive brains are built to relate to other people and animals – and this way of relating attaches to inanimate objects too.

6 One aspect of shopping psychology studied by Jennifer Argo, an associate professor of marketing at Alberta University, arose from personal experience. Argo realised that whenever she went shopping with a friend, she changed her habits, choosing costlier foods and clothes. She subsequently employed mystery shoppers to stand by a rack of batteries, and found that their mere presence made the battery buyers pick the most expensive brand. If no one was there, they chose cheaply. The result, published in the *Journal of Consumer Research*, was consistent in three separate studies. "We will spend more money in order to maintain our self image in front of other people," she says. One answer, according to a separate study, may be to shop with relatives: apparently we buy fewer things when accompanied by family members.

7 A final point of potential interest is that we are more liable to spend when in financial difficulty: under stress we can feel driven to hoard, according to a study of students in *Behavioural Research Therapy*. This residual instinct can help to explain how sales campaigns may work by collectively preying on our deepest insecurities – you're not good enough, no one likes you.

8 The fact is that we need to look wider, to the global neighbourhood, remembering that about half of humanity lives on less than $2 a day according to UN statistics. Meanwhile, a fifth of the Earth's people buy nearly 90 per cent of all the consumer goods. 'Satisficing', a term originally from the social sciences, is the sensible alternative to maximising. When you satisfice, you don't let an impossible search for the perfect option destroy your enjoyment of the merely satisfactory. We have an opportunity to decide that life in the developed world today, with its unprecedented levels of healthcare, comfort and personal safety, is probably as good as it will get, and there is no need to try buying any more contentment. We just need to convince our primitive brains of this.

**DEALING WITH
UNKNOWN VOCABULARY**

KEY LANGUAGE
Talking about research
▶ p. 219, ex.12
e.g. According to a study …

Remember these points:

- you are not expected to understand every word in a text.
- if a word is not important to understanding, ignore it!
- if a word is important to understanding, try to guess the general meaning.

9 Find and underline two examples of the word 'craving' in paragraph 4. This word is helpful to general understanding and it's possible to work out the meaning. What information about the word is given? What do you think it means?

10 Look at the way the expressions below are used in context and try to guess the general meaning.

1 to turn something on its head (paragraph 1)   4 inanimate (5)
2 to dissipate (3)   5 liable (7)
3 to compel (4)

Focus on vocabulary *Business and Economics*

TOPIC VOCABULARY

KEY LANGUAGE
Noun + noun
combinations,
▶ p. 220, ex. 13
e.g. designer brand, self image

1 Categorise the following words and phrases according to whether they relate mainly to:

A Types of business   **B** Success and failure in business   **C** Economics

Check any meanings you're not sure of.

bankruptcy *B*   currency *C*   debt *C*   gross national product *C*
inflation *C*   loss *B*   manufacturer *A*   multinational (corporation) *A*
profit *B*   recession *C*   retailer *A*   service industry *A*

2 Complete the following sentences with words from the list above, using singular or plural forms as necessary.

1 BMW is a leading car ...... *manufacturer* in Germany
2 It is often cheaper to buy goods on-line rather than from a high street ...... *retailer*
3 The production of food is now dominated by huge ...... *multinationals* like McDonalds.
4 The city has attracted a large number of ...... *service industry* such as insurance.
5 There was high ...... *inflation* during the 70s and prices increased rapidly.
6 The ...... *currency* of Japan is the yen.
7 One in ten people only pay off their credit card ...... *debt* by the minimum amount each month.
8 The poor economic situation has led to an increase in companies facing *bankruptcy*

PRONUNCIATION: SOUNDS

3 The letter 'o' can be pronounced in several ways. Put the following words under the correct heading according to the way the letter 'o' is pronounced.

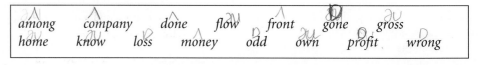

among   company   done   flow   front   gone   gross
home   know   loss   money   odd   own   profit   wrong

/ ɒ / e.g. *hot*	/ əʊ / e.g. *note*	/ ʌ / e.g. *son*

Focus on speaking 2 *Describing objects*

Part 2: Long turn

1 In some Part 2 tasks you need to describe an object. If so, think about the key aspects: size and shape, colour, what it's made of and how the object is used.

Complete the following descriptions and say what the objects are.

A These are long thin sticks about 25 centimetres long, and they come in pairs. They're made of wood, plastic or ivory and they sometimes have beautiful decorations on them. You hold them both in one hand and they're used for …

B This is an extremely thin piece of metal about four centimetres long. It's got a hole in one end and the other end is pointed and sharp. It's used for …

C This is a flattish object which is usually square or rectangular in shape and made of plastic. There are buttons with numbers and mathematical symbols on them on top, and also a small clear window. You use it for …

A
B
C
D
E

2 Practise describing objects A–E on the left. Before you begin, study the *Useful language* below.

> **Useful language**
>
> It's a thing/a gadget/a device you use for … *(+-ing)* (purpose)
>
> It looks *(a bit)* like … (appearance)
>
> It's *(roughly/sort of)* square/rectangular/circular, etc. (shape)
>
> It's made of … (material); It's soft/hard (texture); It's red, etc. (colour)

3 Work in pairs to describe objects and see if your partner can identify them.

Student A: Turn to page 253. **Student B:** Turn to page 255.

EXAM PRACTICE

4 Work in pairs.

1 Read the topic card below and think of a suitable possession to describe. Notice that describing appearance is only one part of the task, so you don't need to go into a lot of detail.

2 Spend a few moments making brief notes in the form of a mindplan.

3 Take it in turns to describe your chosen possession. You should try to keep talking for two minutes, without interruption. Keep an eye on the time while your partner is speaking and let them know when their time is up.

> **EXAM TIP:** You don't need to know the exact word for something as long as you can describe it clearly.

> **Describe a personal possession which means a lot to you.**
>
> **You should say:**
>
> **what the item is**
> **what it looks like**
> **where you keep it**
>
> **and explain why it's important to you.**

Academic Style 4 *Nouns and Noun Phrases 2*

Introduction

This section looks at the use of nouns and noun phrases in academic writing in more detail.

Compare:

- Most people would agree that regular exercise is important. (general English)
- There is widespread **agreement** about the **importance** of regular exercise. (academic English)

By using nouns (e.g. *agreement*) rather than verbs (**e.g.** *agree*) actions are turned into abstract concepts. Personal subjects (**e.g.** *Most people*) are often removed, making academic writing more impersonal and formal.

Noun phrases

In a noun phrase the additional information can come before the headword (main noun), e.g *the most recent* **development** or after it, e.g. a **development** *that was not expected*

Noun phrases can act as the subject, object or complement (following verbs like *be* or *seem*) of a sentence:

- *The latest report* will be published today. (Subject)
- Have you read *the latest report*? (Object)
- The figures are in *the latest report*. (Complement)

Noun phrases with 'of'

Noun phrases linked by *of* are one of the most common types of noun phrase, particularly in academic English, e.g. *the importance of regular exercise*. Other typical examples include:

a point **of** view
parts **of** the world
the rate **of** change
the cost **of** living

1 Underline all the noun phrases with *of* in the text. Then say which ones act as the subject of the sentence.

In coastal areas of Senegal, the gradual disappearance of the mangrove forest has caused great damage, particularly for fishing, while the quality of farmland has also deteriorated, owing to rising concentrations of salt. But last year, a process of regeneration began. During the rainy season, teams of volunteers planted 6.3m mangrove seed pods over an area of about 1,260 hectares. The scheme, which took months of preparation, far exceeded its goal, and plans for next year's campaign are already in hand.

2 Complete the following noun phrases in a suitable way and then use them in sentences.

1 one **of** the most important …   2 the main aim **of** …
3 a fear **of** …

Forming noun phrases

To convert a verbal expression into a noun phrase, the verb must be changed into its noun form and any adverb must be changed into an adjective.

e.g.
The journal reported *that prehistoric remains <u>had recently been discovered</u>* in Colombia.
The journal reported <u>*the recent discovery*</u> of prehistoric *remains* in Colombia.

3 Rewrite the following sentences replacing the words in italics with a suitable noun phrase. Most, but not all, are noun phrases with *of*.

The report had not recognised *how severe global warming would be* this century.

1 The report had underestimated
.... this century.

The only way *to diagnose the disease accurately* is to obtain a blood sample.

2 A(n) ....
.... depends on obtaining a blood sample.

Many countries *are dangerously dependent on oil* as a source of energy.

3 Many countries have
.... as a source of energy.

You can insure yourself against losing your income if you become *unemployed*.

4 There is ....
caused by ....

Piaget is known for his studies of *the way children developed intellectually*.

5 Piaget is known for his studies of
....

> **Language Fact**
> '*of*' is the second most common word in English after '*the*'.
> This reflects the importance of '*of*' in noun phrases.

Academic Vocabulary 4

Meaning

1 Study these extracts from the text on page 73 and then choose the answer which best matches the meaning of the academic words in bold. If necessary, go back to the text to see how the word is used.

1 The need to cool off our consumer brains is **reinforced** by Gregory Berns. (Section 3)

   A supported   B disputed   C researched

2 A university report **concludes** that we regard anything but hard cash as play money. (Section 4)

   A ends   B studies   C finds

3 The result … was **consistent** in three separate studies. (Section 6)

   A the same   B made up of   C obvious

4 … our deepest **insecurities**, you are not good enough, no one likes you. (Section 7)

   A lack of success   B lack of money
   C lack of confidence

5 Satisficing is the sensible **alternative to** maximising. (Section 8)

   A different word for   B different choice from
   C different explanation for

Word building: Verbs ending -ise/-ize

2 Study the following definitions and then complete each example with a verb ending in *-ize*. NB These words are sometimes spelled *-ise*, especially in British English.

Example Increase as much as possible: *The company's aim is to <u>maximize</u> profit.*

1 Give a short account including only the main points: *to ……………. the results in a table.*

2 Complete the last details of an arrangement: *to ……………. a conference programme.*

3 Be a sign or symbol of something: *The Olympic rings ……………. the five continents.*

4 Put into groups according to type: *to ……………. patients according to sex and age.*

5 Make as small as possible: *to ……………. any risk to the public.*

6 Put things in order of importance: *to ……………. your emails.*

Grammar

3 Rewrite the following sentences using the academic words in brackets, so that the meaning is the same. Do not change the form of the word in brackets.

Example The data is not correct (**error**)

   ..There is an error in the data.………………………

1 There should be at least five characters in your password. (**consist**)

2 Some drivers have no idea about the rules of the road. (**unaware**)

3 Scientists have analysed the latest data. (**analysis**)

4 Students are expected to play a full part in discussions. (**participate**)

5 The minister said a market economy was the only option. (**alternative**)

6 Pollution has significantly affected many coral reefs. (**impact**)

Word partners

4 Match each academic word below to a group of words that regularly combine with it.

consumer	environmental	global
credit	financial	

1 ………………. aid, assistance, institution, success,

2 ………………. demand, goods, society, spending

3 ………………. economy, market, scale, view

4 ………………. account, agreement, card, note

5 ………………. damage, issues, policies, problems

5 Complete the following examples using word combinations from exercise 4 above.

1 The website lists all the banks and other ………………. ………………. in the UK.

2 ………………. ………………. for cheaper foreign cars led to higher imports.

3 The lecture is about ………………. ………………. such as global warming.

4 The study compares spending on ………………. ………………., compared with cash.

5 We need to take a ………………. ………………. , rather than a narrow national one.

6 Choose five academic words from this page to learn, and write personal examples to help you remember them.

8 ▶ What's on

> If an event is **on**, it has been arranged and is happening or will happen OPP **off**: *The transport union has confirmed that the strike is definitely on.* (Longman Exams Dictionary)

In this unit you will practise

- Discussing cultural attractions; describing an event
- Topic vocabulary and word stress
- Listening and answering multiple choice questions; sentence and table completion; short answers; labelling a plan
- Describing tables and graphs
- Presenting and justifying an opinion: disagreeing; discussing implication
- Pronunciation: word stress

Key Language

Cohesion
Conditionals

Writing Practice

Task 1: Describing information from a table
Task 2: Presenting and justifying an opinion

Exam Focus

Speaking: Parts 1, 2
Listening: Sections 1, 2
Writing: Tasks 1, 2

Lead-in

1 Organise the words or phrases in the box into one of these categories:

a) Cinema   b) Theatre   c) Concert   d) Museum / Gallery

> act   backing group   cast   catalogue   collection   composer   conductor
> exhibit   playwright   portrait   programme   scenery   screen
> sculpture   soloist   soundtrack   special effects   stage   stunt   subtitles

PRONUNCIATION:
WORD STRESS

2 Examples A and B show two different word stress patterns. Each word has three syllables, represented by the number of circles. The large circle shows which syllable is stressed in each case. Find four more examples for each pattern from the categories and words above.

A museum oOo   *composer, conductor*

B gallery Ooo   *scenery, collection, cinema*

Focus on speaking 1 *Discussing cultural attractions*

Part 2: Long turn

Work in pairs to talk about the following topic. You can make a few notes before you begin. Try to speak for two minutes without interruption. Refer to the language in the *Useful language* box below.

Describe a visit you can remember to one of the following places and explain what you remember especially about it.

museum   cinema   historic building   art gallery   theatre   concert hall

> **Useful language**
>
> **The thing I remember most** (about it / the film, etc.) **was …**
> **What I liked** (most) (about it / the day, etc.) **was …**
> **The** (best / most interesting, etc.) **thing** (about it) **was …**
> **It was the** (best / worst / most beautiful, etc.) **…   I've ever …** (seen / been to / heard, etc.)

Focus on listening 1 *Music festival*

Section 1: Multiple choice; table completion; sentence completion

The following task contains various question-types. Remember to read through the different instructions and the questions in advance.

Question 1 below introduces a new type of multiple-choice question where you have to choose more than one answer from a list of options.

TASK APPROACH

- Look through the list and say each item silently. Thinking about the pronunciation will make it easier to identify the answers when you hear them.
- Listen carefully – the information may come quickly, and the words you need may be combined in longer phrases.

Question 1
Choose **TWO** letters, A–G.

1 Which **TWO** of the following types of music will be performed at the festival?

   A rap   C jazz   E folk music   **G** dance music

   B rock music   **D** opera   F country and western

Questions 2 and 3
Choose the correct letter, **A**, **B** or **C**.

2 When does the festival begin?

   A 9th May   **B** 12th May   **C** 16th May

3 How long does the festival last?

   A a weekend   **B** a week   C two weeks

Questions 4–8
Complete the table below.
Write **NO MORE THAN TWO WORDS AND/OR A NUMBER** for each answer.

Event	Time	Ticket price
Cuban music: talk	4 10:30 a.m	£6
'The sounds of Scotland'	2 p.m.	5 £8
6 'African alive	7 p.m.	£15
Canal boat cruise (with 7 lunch and talk)	2–5 p.m.	8 £14.50

Questions 9–10
Complete the sentences below.
Write **NO MORE THAN THREE WORDS** for your answer.

9 The friends intend to visit an art exhibition at the ...bus stop... gallery

10 Maria should take her ...student... with her.
card

79

Focus on listening 2 *The Museum of Anthropology*

Section 2: Short answers; labelling a plan; sentence completion; table completion

You will hear information about a museum. For questions 4–6 you have to label a plan. Read the following advice before you begin.

► EXAM BRIEFING

In this task you have to complete the labels on a visual such as a diagram, plan or map. You either choose answers from a list of options A, B, C, etc. or write in words you hear on the recording. The instructions will tell you how many words you can write. Correct spelling is essential.

Study the visual including any labels already marked and ask yourself some basic questions. like those opposite.

Listening: labelling a diagram, plan or map

- **a plan** (e.g. a building): Is it a floor plan or a cross-section? Which is the way in?

- **a map** (e.g. a region): Which way is north? What are the main features (rivers, towns, etc.)?

- **an object** (e.g. a machine): Which is the top/bottom, back/front, etc.? What are the key features?

- **a process:** Where does the process start and end? What are the stages?

Questions 1–3
*Write **NO MORE THAN THREE WORDS AND/OR A NUMBER** for each answer.*

1   When was the museum originally founded?   ....

2   How many floors does the museum have?   ....

3   The museum is famous for its collection of cultural items from the people of which region?   ....

Questions 4–6
Label the plan.
*Write **NO MORE THAN THREE WORDS** for each answer.*

5   ....

6   ....

Rotunda

Gallery   Gallery

Ramp

Visible storage

4   ....

Entrance

Questions 7–10
Complete the sentences below.
*Write **NO MORE THAN THREE WORDS AND/OR A NUMBER** for each answer.*

7   The sculpture in the Rotunda took .... more than three years to create.

8   The best way of getting to the museum is ....

9   The museum is closed on .... in winter.

10   The museum is open late on Tuesdays ....

Focus on writing 1 *Describing tables and graphs*

Task 1
INTERPRETING STATISTICS

1 Read the following findings from a museum survey into visitor satisfaction, then answer questions 1–3.

Visitors surveyed:	10,000
'Very satisfied':	2,000
'Satisfied':	5,080
'Quite satisfied':	2,320
'Not satisfied':	500
'Don't know':	100

- **Twenty per cent / a fifth** of the people surveyed said they were 'Very satisfied'.
- **Approximately / just over 50 per cent of / half** the visitors said they were 'Satisfied'.
- Only **one per cent of / one in a hundred** visitors had no opinion.

1 What proportion of visitors were 'Very satisfied' or 'Satisfied'? *20%*
2 What percentage of visitors to the museum had no opinion? *5%*
3 What percentage of visitors expressed dissatisfaction? *1%*

2 Statistics can be expressed in a number of ways, as fractions (half, a quarter, etc.), percentages (20%) or in expressions like 'one in ten'. Match each of the percentages 1–6 with expressions from the box below.

1 10 per cent   4 33 per cent
2 20 per cent   5 75 per cent
3 25 per cent   6 90 per cent

a third	*three out of four*	*one in three*	*three-quarters*
one in ten	*a half*	*a quarter*	*nine out of ten*	*a fifth*
a tenth	*one in five*	*one in four*	*two-thirds*

QUALIFIERS

3 It's often helpful to describe statistics in terms of the nearest 'round figure', e.g. 47% = approximately/almost 50%; 25.5% = just over a quarter / one in four.

Useful language: Qualifiers			
exactly	about	more than	less / fewer than
	approximately	(just) over	(just) under
	almost / nearly		

Rewrite the following statistics. Use expressions from the box in exercise 2 and a suitable qualifier.

1 48.5% *just under 50%* 4 65% *exactly 65%*
2 30 people out of a total of 90   *a third*   5 seven in 100 *just under 10%*
3 43 out of 80 *just over half*   6 74 out of 100 *almost*

GRAPH

4 Study the graph and answer the questions.

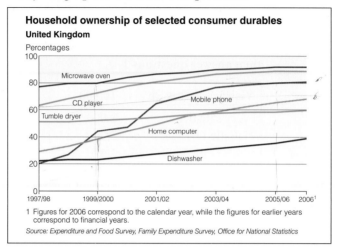

Household ownership of selected consumer durables
United Kingdom

1 Figures for 2006 correspond to the calendar year, while the figures for earlier years correspond to financial years.

Source: Expenditure and Food Survey, Family Expenditure Survey, Office for National Statistics

1 What percentage of the British public owned
   a) a microwave oven in 1999/2000? *80%*
   b) a CD player in 1997/98? *just over 60%*
   c) a home computer in 1999/2000? *just under 40%*
   d) a mobile phone in 2005/06? *80% microwave oven in 2006/90%*
2 Which product increased in popularity most over the whole period? By how much? *mobile phone in 1997/8 20%*
3 Which product increased in popularity least over the whole period? By how much?
4 Compare the ownership of mobile phones and home computers in 1997/98, and again in 2006. *home computer were slightly higher than mb with 30% against 20% but in 2006 home computer is significant lower than with just over 60% compared to 80%.*

ORGANISING AND PRESENTING DATA

5 Use information from the table to complete the text. Before you begin, read the following advice.

TASK APPROACH

- Begin with an **introductory statement**, e.g. *The table/graph shows …*
- Don't try to describe every detail. Look for **significant features**, e.g. the biggest change, the overall trend, etc.
- Don't speculate about reasons for trends. **Stick to the facts**.
- End with a **comment on general trends**, e.g. *The figures for the period suggest that …; From this evidence we can conclude that …*

Selected arts events attended in a 12-month period, by age, in the UK (percentages)				
Age	16 – 24	25 – 44	45 – 64	All aged 16 and over
Theatre performance	29	37	42	36
Carnival and street art	28	31	27	26
Live music event	34	29	25	24
Exhibition of art, photography or sculpture	16	23	26	22
Craft exhibition	5	14	21	15
Classical music performance	3	5	12	8

Source: Social Trends 38

> **WRITING PRACTICE**
> Describing information from a table (guided practice)
> ▶ p. 240, ex. 6

The table shows details of attendance at various arts events over a year, according to the age of the participants. Overall, the most popular type of arts events during the period were theatre performances, which were attended by **1** _36 %_ of all adults aged 16 and over. By contrast, the least popular events were classical music performances, attended by just **2** _36–74 8%_ of adults. People aged **3** _45–64_ were more likely than other age groups to attend a theatre performance (42 per cent), while **4** _live music event_ were more likely to be attended by those aged 16 to 24 (**5** _34 %_). The differences **6** _between_ age groups were particularly marked in the case of craft exhibitions and classical music, where attendance rates were around **7** _4 times_ higher for older people **8** _than_ for the younger ones. It is clear from the evidence that age plays a significant role in the popularity of the arts events listed. (*151 words*)

Focus on writing 2 *Presenting and justifying an opinion*

Task 2

In exam topics which require you to present and justify an opinion, you may need to express disagreement or discuss the implications of an assertion.

EXPRESSING DISAGREEMENT

1 As part of your answer to a Task 2 question, you may wish to challenge a fact or claim or point out a false conclusion. Study the *Useful language*.

> **Useful language: Challenge a fact or claim**
> e.g. *Insurance fraud is a crime without a victim.*
> It's not (*completely*) true to say that …
> Many people would disagree with the assertion/idea that …
> It's hard to believe that …

> **Useful language: Pointing out a false conclusion**
> e.g. *A lot of people exceed the speed limit so it must be acceptable.*
> The fact that … doesn't mean …
> (*Just*) Because … it doesn't necessarily follow that …
> It may be true that … but …

2 Read the following statements. Decide which three you disagree with most and write sentences giving reasons and/or pointing out false conclusions.

1 Teaching children is easier than teaching adults.
2 Everyone would benefit from taking more exercise.
3 The prison population has increased, so more crimes must have been committed.
4 Motor cycles should be banned – they're the most dangerous form of road transport.
5 Only a fifth of hospital consultants are female. Women doctors can't be very ambitious.
6 It's not worth trying to give up smoking, because a lot of people try and fail.

DISCUSSING IMPLICATIONS

KEY LANGUAGE
Conditionals
▶ p. 221–222, ex. 15

3 It's often important to consider the implications of an assertion. One way to do this is to use a conditional tense. Another is to ask a rhetorical question.

Argument: Increasing the price of petrol would encourage people to use public transport.
But **if** *petrol costs* **rose**, *the cost of many goods* **would** *also* **be affected**. (conditional).
And what about *people who live in the countryside, who have no regular bus service?* (rhetorical question).

With a partner, take it in turns to suggest some of the implications of the following arguments.

1 The sale of cigarettes should be banned.
2 Cars should not be allowed to enter city centres.
3 Income tax is too high. We should vote for the party which would lower taxes.
4 Tertiary education should be free for all students.

EXAM PRACTICE

4 Refer to the *Task approach* on page 63 before you begin.

You should spend about 40 minutes on this task.

Write about the following topic.

> *The government spends about £220 million a year supporting museums and galleries in the UK, and a similar amount subsidising the visual and performing arts.*
>
> *This is a huge sum to spend on minority interests, and the money would be better spent on more important things. It should be up to the people who enjoy cultural attractions to pay for them.*
>
> *What are your views?*

Give reasons for your answer and include any relevant examples from your own knowledge or experience.

Write at least 250 words.

WRITING PRACTICE
Presenting and justifying an opinion (example answer)
▶ p. 241, ex. 7

SPOT THE ERROR

5 After completing the task, remember to proof read your work. Identify and correct the errors in the following sentences.

1 One of the most important things in life is a good health.
2 Four out of five tourists who visit the country arrive by air.
3 It is worth to point out that this is not the only possible cause of the problem.
4 There has been an increase of interest in classical music in recent years.
5 Only half the people who responded to the survey were satisfied.
6 In the end of the period in question, imports had increased by ten per cent.
7 It can be true that people are living longer, but what about their quality of life?
8 The new airport will be only two and quarter kilometres away from the school.
9 Although you can encourage people to stop smoking, you can't force them to.
10 The training scheme was unpopular, and at the end the government had to abandon it.

Check your answers by referring to the *Error Hit List* on page 86.

Focus on speaking 2 *Describing an event*

Part 2: Long turn

One of the things you may be asked to do in Part 2 of the interview is to describe an event, either public or private. Look at the example task in the box on the right before doing the exercises.

> **Describe a big public event that you have attended.**
>
> **You should say:**
>
> > **what it was**
> > **when it was held, and why**
> > **what happened**
>
> **and describe how you felt about being there.**

1 Work in pairs and discuss the following questions.

1 Make a list of as many public events as you can you think of, big or small.
2 What kind of public events do you enjoy attending? Why?
3 Is there anything you dislike about such events?

GUIDED EXAM PRACTICE

2 Think of a public event you have attended. Before you tell your partner about it, spend a moment or two preparing.

- Choose a particular event you remember well.
- Use a mindplan to note down the key points. Main headings could include *When*, *Why*, *What* and *How*, and subheadings could include *music, fireworks,* etc.
- Study the *Useful language* below and also that on page 78.

> **Useful language: Introducing a topic**
>
> **I'd like to talk/tell you about …. which …**
>
> **The …. I want to talk about is/was …**
>
> **It was a really exciting/enjoyable/special occasion because …**
>
> *I'd like to talk about a family celebration which was held a few years ago for my brother's graduation. It was a really special occasion because so many members of the family came … .*

▶ *Focus on Academic Skills for IELTS* page **78**

EXAM PRACTICE

3 With a partner, take it in turns to do this exam task.

> **Describe a family celebration you particularly remember.**
>
> **You should say:**
>
> > **why the celebration was held**
> > **who attended**
> > **what happened**
>
> **and explain what made it memorable.**

ERROR HIT LIST

at the end/in the end

✗	✔
They fought the case for years, but at the end they lost.	… <u>in the end</u> they lost.
In the end of the course there is a test.	<u>At</u> the end of the course …

- **At the end** refers to the point where something finishes, and it is usually followed by the preposition *of*.
- **In the end** means 'after a long period of time' or 'eventually'. It is never followed by *of*.

half/a quarter

✗	✔
I've written the half of my essay.	I've written ~~the~~ <u>half</u> (of) my essay.
We've only got half of a kilometre to go.	We've only got <u>half</u> ~~of~~ a kilometre to go.
I've been living here for two and half/quarter years.	… for two and <u>a</u> half/quarter years.

- Don't use *the* before **half** except when talking about a particular half of something, e.g. *The second half of the match was pretty boring*.
- You can say **half** or **half of**, but **half** is more common.
- Use **half** (not **half of**) in front of measurement words like *kilometre, litre* or *hour*.
- After numbers, **half** and **quarter** take an indefinite article, e.g. *two and <u>a</u> half metres; four and <u>a</u> quarter years*.

one in ten/nine out of ten

✗	✔
It was a one out of a million chance.	It was a one <u>in a</u> million chance.
Three in four cats prefer 'Moggie' cat food.	Three <u>out of</u> four cats prefer …

- Use the preposition *in* to talk about very small proportions, e.g. *one or two in ten*.
- Use the prepositions *out of* to talk large proportions, e.g. *99 out of 100*.

worth/value

✗	✔
The museum is certainly worth to see.	… is worth <u>seeing</u>.
The current worth of the property is £100,000.	The current <u>value</u> of the property …

- **it's worth doing something; something is worth doing.** These phrases take an *-ing* form, not an infinitive.
- **worth** is usually used as a preposition, e.g. *The car is **worth** £100*. The noun related to **worth** is value, e.g. *The **value** of the car is £100*.

Critical Thinking 2 *What is an argument?*

Introduction

When you put forward an argument, you express an opinion and give reasons in order to persuade other people to agree with you. The ability to produce a sound argument in a piece of writing or to evaluate an argument in a reading text is important for success in the IELTS test and is also a key element of academic study.

Structure of an argument

In academic writing, an **argument** consists of a point of view on a subject, usually called a '*thesis statement*', together with *supporting evidence*. The following diagram shows the basic structure of an argument:

thesis statement		Evidence
X happens/ should happen, etc.	because of	**y**

An argument which begins with a thesis statement like this is described as **thesis-led** (See page 65). Sometimes it is more appropriate to discuss the evidence first before reaching a conclusion. This kind of argument is described as **evidence-led** (See page 122).

Evidence		thesis statement
y	so/therefore/ thus	**X** happens/should happen, etc.

Notice the expressions *because of*, *therefore*, etc., which may signal an argument but be aware that not all arguments have clear signalling like this.

Identifying arguments.

1 An argument requires a clear thesis statement. Which of the following are arguments, and which are just sets of statements describing evidence?

1 Most scientists agree that the burning of fossil fuels is causing the climate to change dramatically. Global warming will expose millions of people to the risks of hunger, drought and flooding. The development of clean, renewable forms of energy are therefore essential.

2 Wind power does not produce dangerous waste or contribute to global warming. It is abundant, reliable and affordable. The wind industry could also create thousands of new jobs, especially in the field of offshore engineering.

3 Fruit and vegetables are good sources of many vitamins and minerals. There is mounting evidence that people who eat plenty of fruit and vegetables are less likely to develop chronic diseases such as coronary heart disease and some cancers. Yet many people have diets low in these foods.

4 We need to protect the world's forests. Forests provide many benefits. They help stabilise the world's climate by storing large amounts of carbon, they protect against soil erosion and they keep rivers and reservoirs free from silt. Forests are also home to two-thirds of the world's land-based plants and animals.

5 Governments should discourage people from owning private cars and make alternative forms of transport more attractive. Public transport needs to be made cheaper and more reliable, and there should be an advertising campaign to promote cycling as an enjoyable and economical way to travel about.

Providing evidence

2 Decide whether you agree or disagree with the following thesis statements and provide two or three pieces of evidence for your view.

1 Children should study at least one foreign language.
2 The first priority for government spending should be education.
3 Modern technology will never replace the book.
4 Learning about the past has no value for us today.
5 Not every important lesson in life can be learned from books.

Critical Thinking for IELTS

- When developing an argument in a writing task, make sure your thesis statement is clear and well-supported with evidence.

- When reading a text, look for the thesis statement and consider what evidence is provided. Is it sufficient? Is it convincing?

9 ▶ Water, water everywhere

Only a fool tests the depth of the water with both feet. (African proverb)

In this unit you will practise	Key Language:	Exam Focus
• Discussing water resources and water use • Skimming, scanning a text • Reading and completing a table; classification; sentence completion; multiple choice	Introducing sentences Word building: nouns	**Speaking:** Part 3 **Reading skills**

Lead-in

1 Work with another student to discuss which activity in each of the following pairs uses the most water.

1 taking a bath
  taking a shower

3 one day's cooking
  one day's drinking

2 washing dishes by hand
  using a dishwasher

4 washing the car
  watering the garden

Check your answers on page 254 and write in the number of litres for each activity.

2 The bar chart below shows how much water (in litres) is needed to produce various foods. Use the information in the following sentences to complete the bar graph.

- It takes nearly **50% more** water to produce a glass of **milk** than it does to produce a serving of pasta.
- It takes over **six times as much** water to produce a serving of chicken **as** it does to produce a glass of milk.
- Producing a serving of tomatoes takes **less than a quarter** of the water needed to produce a serving of pasta.
- Producing a serving of oranges takes **nearly twice as much** water as producing a serving of tomatoes.

How much water does it take to produce one serving of:

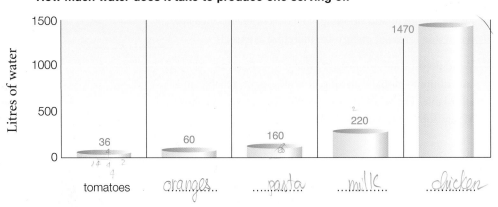

(single servings)

KEY LANGUAGE
Numerical and other
comparative expressions
▶ p. 214 ex. 7

3 Write four sentences comparing the amount of water needed in each pair of activities in Exercise 1.

Begin: *Taking a shower uses …*

or   *It takes … to take a shower …*

Refer to the language of comparisons on pages 214–215 and the qualifiers on page 81 if necessary.

Focus on speaking *Water issues*

Part 3: Discussion

▶ *Focus on Academic Skills for IELTS page 71*

1 Discuss these points with another student.

1 Do you generally use water carefully or do you use it without thinking?

2 Are there ever any restrictions on water use in your country?

3 What are some of the ways of saving water in the home?

2 Work with a partner to answer as many of these questions as possible. Follow the instructions on page 90 to find the answers to the Water Quiz.

Water Quiz

1 Which of the following accounts for most of the world's water use?
a) agriculture
b) industry
c) domestic uses

2 How many litres of water does one person require each day (for all domestic purposes) in order to enjoy a reasonable quality of life?

3 Which **two** of the following countries have the highest consumption of water per person per day, and which country has the lowest?

Austria   Italy
Switzerland   Germany
Japan   UK
India   Spain
USA

4 What percentage of the Earth's surface is covered with water?

5 Name **three** other water resources in addition to the sea.

6 What percentage of the Earth's total water resources can be transformed into usable water?
a) 1%   b) 10%   c) 25%

7 What percentage of disease could be prevented in developing countries if safe, clean water was available?
a) 20%   b) 50%   c) 80%

8 Which of these countries has the most available drinking water, and which has the least?
a) Brazil   b) Ethiopia
c) Egypt   d) India

Focus on reading 1 *Water: Earth's most precious resource*

SKIMMING/SCANNING

Find the answers to the quiz questions on page 89 as quickly as possible by skimming and scanning the following text and tables.

1 Skim the text so that you have a general idea of what it's about. Read the *title*, the *headings* for Figures 1–4, and look quickly at each *table*.
2 Read the first question from the quiz.
3 Scan the text to find the section which contains relevant information, and locate the answer. NB Don't expect to find the exact words in the question. Look for topic words and parallel expressions.

WATER: Earth's most precious resource

Over the last 300 years, world population has increased sevenfold, but water use has increased by 35 times. Since 1950, the amount of annually renewable fresh water available per human being has fallen by more than half.

Figure 1: Contribution to Earth's total water resources in %

Sea	97.3
Glaciers	2.1
Underground aquifers	0.6
Lakes and rivers	0.01
Atmosphere	0.001
Biosphere	0.0006

Although 70% of the Earth is covered by seawater and a further 3% by ice, neither of these is easily transformed into usable water. Less than 1% of the Earth's total water resources is usable for drinking, farming or industry.

Figure 2: Water consumption by sector

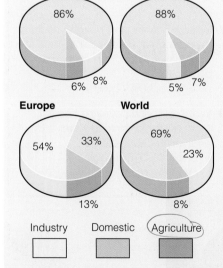

Asia 86% 6% 8%
Africa 88% 5% 7%
Europe 54% 33% 13%
World 69% 23% 8%

Industry Domestic Agriculture

While domestic users in rich countries tend to be wasteful in their use of water, regarding it as essentially free and plentiful, they play only a small part in total water use. On the other hand, the quality of water needed for domestic use is much higher than that needed for industry or farming.

Figure 3: Domestic daily water consumption per inhabitant in litres

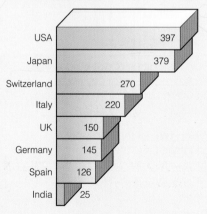

USA	397
Japan	379
Switzerland	270
Italy	220
UK	150
Germany	145
Spain	126
India	25

As a general rule, 80 litres of water per person per day are enough for a reasonable quality of life, but the regional differences are considerable. An American uses 400 litres, while an inhabitant of Burundi may have to survive on 10 litres or less. Consumption is much higher where pipelines are laid than in regions where water has to be carried from a well. Thus the provision of piped water services – while highly

desirable from a health point of view – greatly increases water use, putting a further strain on scarce resources.

Figure 4: Percentage of the population with access to drinking water

It is difficult to establish precise figures

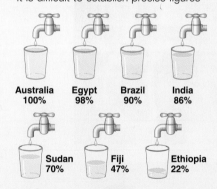

Australia 100%	Egypt 98%	Brazil 90%	India 86%
	Sudan 70%	Fiji 47%	Ethiopia 22%

for access to safe drinking water, but it is thought that 1.3 billion people worldwide, around a fifth of the world's population, do not have this basic service. Not surprisingly, the problem is much worse in rural areas than in towns. In a recent estimate, 94% of urban areas had access to safe water, compared with only 71% in rural areas. Dirty water is the world's biggest health risk, accounting for as much as 80% of disease in the Third World. According to WHO* statistics, 1.8 million people die annually from polluted drinking water, 90% of whom are children under 5.

*World Health Organisation

Focus on reading 2 *The Ecology of Hollywood*

1 The tasks below are based on the text *The Ecology of Hollywood* on pages 92–93. Before you start, look through the reading passage quickly in order to form a general picture.

▶ **EXAM BRIEFING** | **Academic Reading: table/flow chart completion**

In this task you have to fill gaps in a table or flowchart which summarises specific information in the passage.

There are two versions: in one you select words from the passage; in the other you choose from a list of options. The answers may not be in text order.

- Read the instructions carefully so you know exactly what to do.
- Make sure you understand how the information is organised.
- Look through the questions so you know what topics to search for in the text.

Table completion

2 Before you begin this practice task, read the advice below.

TASK APPROACH

- Study the table carefully. Notice what kind of information is needed in each gap.
- Go through the text and underline references to the four aqueducts.
- Read those sections carefully to answer the questions.

The Los Angeles Aqueduct

KEY LANGUAGE
Relative clauses
▶ p. 222, ex. 16
e.g. *The Los Angeles Aqueduct, which was completed in …*

Questions 1–3
Complete the table below. Choose **NO MORE THAN TWO WORDS AND/OR A NUMBER** *from the passage for each answer.*

Project	Los Angeles Aqueduct	Extension to Los Angeles Aqueduct	Colorado River Aqueduct	Californian Aqueduct
Year completed	1913	1940	1 .... *1964* *1941*	
Length	2	168km		720km
Source	Owens Valley	3	Colorado River	

The Ecology of HOLLYWOOD

1 Los Angeles is an unlikely city. Built over a major seismic fault, on the edge of one of the world's most inhospitable deserts, the city has developed like the extension of a Hollywood movie set, a sprawling urban fantasy which many people feel should not really exist. Scientists have estimated that the land and water in the area could naturally support 200,000 people, not the 15 million that live there.

2 Since the 1880s, Los Angeles has been transformed from a sleepy cattle town with a population of 4,000, to a seething metropolis that now accounts for nearly one per cent of global greenhouse emissions. It is the car culture par excellence, with nine million cars contributing to the ubiquitous smog and air pollution and 40 per cent of the population suffering from respiratory problems due to vehicle emissions. Surprisingly, LA is now becoming the forum for some of the most progressive environmental thought in the US.

3 The city is full of contradictions. Often regarded as the apotheosis of consumerism and material extravagance, it is seen as the essence of anti-nature. Paradoxically, people often move to Los Angeles because of nature; attracted by its climate, the snow-capped mountains, the ocean and the beaches. The movie industry came here because of the clarity of the light, the 270 days of sunshine per year and the diversity of location close by.

4 The fantasy has always depended on one fundamental resource – water. No metropolis on the planet has looked farther afield for its supply than LA has, and the fact that there are "no more rivers to bring to the desert" is a cause of much concern. The natural water table was exhausted after four decades in the 1890s. In 1913, when the controversial Los Angeles Aqueduct was first opened, diverting water over 350 kilometres from Owens Valley, chief engineer William Mulholland proclaimed that it would supply Hollywood's lawns and swimming pools for ever.

5 Within ten years, the city needed more. In 1940, the aqueduct was extended 168 kilometres north to Mono Lake, while the following year southern California was able to tap into Arizona via the Colorado River Aqueduct. However, neither supply has been without problems. In 1964, the US Supreme Court settled in favour of Arizona's claim to supply from the Colorado River, and LA's entitlement was reduced by about 50 per cent. And in the 90s, with the water level in Mono Lake falling to dangerously low levels, LA was ordered to reduce its water intake from this source as well. The city is also dependent on the State Water Project, which brings more than a trillion gallons of water per year along the 720-kilometre Californian Aqueduct, supplying irrigation systems for the vast agricultural base of the San Joaquin Valley. This effectively removes half the water that would otherwise flow into the San Francisco Bay area, altering the flow of fresh and saltwater in the Sacramento Delta, with inevitably harmful consequences for fish and wildlife.

6 Almost a third of the water feeding Los Angeles is now obtained by extraction from underground aquifers*. However, a combination of illegal dumping, run-off from commercial fertilisers and leakage from garbage landfills, has left some 40 per cent of the wells in southern California contaminated above federal limits. To compound the problem, half of the considerable winter rainfall, which would permeate the soil and recharge the aquifers, is swallowed by concrete drainage systems and diverted into the Pacific. Since intensive farming methods require around 200,000 litres of water to produce what an average Californian eats in a day, the issue of water supply is never far away. Desperation has led to some ambitious proposals, ranging from a plastic pipeline from Alaska to towing icebergs from Antarctica.

7 What few Angelinos are aware of today is that the city is actually built on a river. The so-called LA river, which stretches 92 kilometres from The Valley down Long Beach, passing through Hollywood studios and Chinatown, is the central natural feature of the city. At one time, it was shaded by sycamores, oaks and willows. However, as the city was paved over, the winter floods created a threat to economic expansion and, in the 1930s, work began to erase the river altogether. "The Army Corps of Engineers built a concrete trough, put the river inside it and fenced it off with barbed wire," explains Jennifer Price, an environmental writer. "The river became the ultimate symbol of LA's destruction of nature."

8 Inevitably, the concrete flood-control system had disastrous ecological consequences, destroying wetland areas which provided an important staging area for migratory birds on the Great Pacific Flyway. The empty concrete channel is now used as an area for training municipal bus drivers to turn around, and it has been suggested that it be used as a freeway during the dry season. Fittingly, it is best known today as the location for Hollywood car chases.

9 However, plans are now underway to restore the river, recreate wetland areas to attract birds, and establish nature walks, cycle paths and equestrian trails. Led by the Friends of the LA River, a pressure group formed by poet and filmmaker Lewis McAdams, the project has pulled people together from government agencies, environmental groups and neighbourhood associations, all working together in what is being seen as a symbolic attempt to heal the split between the population and the landscape of the city.

10 Being a prime example of nature's confluence with human culture, Los Angeles clearly provides the perfect platform to examine this interaction and make progress towards a sustainable urban environment. "If we actually rethought how to retain the water that falls from the sky, we wouldn't be so dependent on water sources hundreds of miles away," says Price. Various initiatives have now been implemented in this vein: a huge waste-water recycling plant has been built in Santa Monica while environmental groups like The Tree People are redesigning drainage systems to collect run-off rainwater from buildings, and redirect it into underground aquifers.

11 There is a feeling of optimism about the future of nature in a city which has always been regarded as being in fundamental opposition to it, leading to a more integrated vision of environmentalism in the 21st century. Those involved with the restoration of LA rivers see it as not only important for ecological sustainability and a way of linking disparate communities but also as being of tremendous significance symbolically. "There is a feeling that if you can fix the LA river, you can fix the city," believes Price. "And if you can fix this city, it seems possible that you can fix any city."

*aquifer: a layer of rock or soil that can absorb and hold water

Matching

3 This task was introduced in Unit 3. Read these reminders before you begin.

REMINDERS

- Study the list of problems and underline key words.
- Locate and highlight each water source in the text and read the information.
- Check to see which problem applies. Look for *parallel expressions* in the text.

Questions 4–7
Look at the following methods of obtaining water (4–7). Match each method with the correct problem (A–D).

Method of obtaining water

4 Los Angeles Aqueduct ␣ B

5 Colorado River Aqueduct ␣ D

6 Californian Aqueduct ␣ A ␣

7 Extraction ␣ C ␣ A

Problems

A Taking water from this source has had adverse effects on the environment.

B The supply from this source proved inadequate.

C Much of the water from this source is impure.

D The amount of water which can be drawn from this source is now restricted.

Sentence completion

4 This task was introduced in Unit 3. Read these reminders before you begin.

REMINDERS

- The sentences appear in the same order as information in the text.
- Underline key words or phrases in the questions.
- Check the text, remembering to look for parallel expressions. Think about grammar too: not every phrase can complete each statement.

Questions 8–11

*Complete each sentence with the correct ending, **A–J** from the box below.*

8 Many LA citizens have health problems caused by ⟶ J

9 LA is unique in the distances from which it brings its ⟶ A

10 The water shortage could be relieved by utilising more ⟶ I

11 The LA river was destroyed in the interests of the city's ⟶ B

A	water supply.	**F**	drainage systems.
B	trade and industry.	**G**	winter rainfall.
C	global warming.	**H**	unpromising location.
D	the good weather.	**I**	irrigation systems.
E	saltwater.	**J**	exhaust fumes.

Multiple choice

▶ *Focus on Academic Skills*
for IELTS page 51, ex. 3

5 This task was introduced in Unit 5. In this version you choose several correct answers from a list of options. See *Task Approach* on page 52.

Questions 12–14

*Choose **THREE** letters, **A–G**. Which **THREE** of the following recent or planned developments in Los Angeles are mentioned by the writer?*

A recycling solid waste

B creating paths for walkers and horse riders

C collecting and storing rainwater

D converting the river bed into a freeway

E forming government agencies

F allowing the LA river to flow again

G planting a variety of trees

Focus on vocabulary

VOCABULARY MATCHING

KEY LANGUAGE
Introducing sentences
▶ p. 223, ex. 17
e.g. *Inevitably, By and large*

1 Use the paragraph numbers in brackets to find expressions 1–5 in the text and study the context. Then match the expressions to their meaning a)–e).

d 1 support *v* (1)   a) to make the situation worse
e 2 inevitably *adv* (5)   b) completely different in kind
a 3 to compound the problem *phrase* (6)   c) now happening
c 4 underway *adj* (9)   d) provide the necessities of life
b 5 disparate *adj* (11)   e) as you would expect

DERIVED ADJECTIVES

KEY LANGUAGE
Word building: nouns
▶ p. 223, ex. 18

2 Many adjectives are formed with a suffix (e.g. *-al, -ic*). Study the phrases from the text and say what topic the adjectives in italics refer to. Paragraph numbers are given in brackets. There is a list of topics to choose from below.

e.g. *global* greenhouse emissions – **global** refers to: the whole world

F 1 a major *seismic* fault (1)
H 2 *respiratory* problems (2)
G 3 contaminated above *federal* limits (6)
A 4 *economic* expansion (7)
C 5 disastrous *ecological* consequences (8)
D 6 *municipal* bus drivers (8)
E 7 *equestrian* trails (9)
B 8 a sustainable *urban* environment (10)

A trade, industry and the management of money
B town or city (as opposed to country)
C plants, animals, people and their environment
D the government of a town or city or the public services it provides
E horse riding
F earthquakes
G central government (US)
H breathing

3 Use vocabulary from exercises 1 and 2 to complete the sentences below.

1 There is a shortage of accommodation once the tourist season gets .... *underway*
2 More and more people are moving out of the countryside into .... *urban* areas.
3 The destruction of the rainforests is a(n) .... *ecological* disaster for the world.
4 Switzerland is a(n) .... *federal* republic.
5 No single solution can satisfy so many .... *disparate* groups of people.
6 Rising unemployment will .... *inevitably* lead to an increase in crime.
7 The lake is now too polluted to .... *support* fish.
8 In the current .... *economic* climate, we must try to keep costs down.

Academic Style 5 *Hedging*

Introduction

When academic writers discuss ideas, opinions and theories, they need to express themselves as carefully and accurately as possible. They must avoid suggesting that something is more likely, or that a rule applies more generally, than is really the case. Basically, they need ways of showing how sure they are about something.

This cautious approach is called 'hedging' in linguistics. This section looks at some of the key language that can be used in hedging to indicate various degrees of possibility.

1 Compare sentences a) and b) below. Underline the two additional words which qualify the statement in sentence b). Which statement are you more likely to believe? Why?

   a) Cancer drugs serve as an unexpected new weapon against deadly antibiotic-resistant bacteria.

   b) Cancer drugs may serve as an unexpected new weapon against some deadly antibiotic-resistant bacteria.

2 Underline the words which are used to qualify the following statements.

   1 The decline in sea ice cover in the Amundsen Sea appears to be linked to the warming of West Antarctica.

   2 Logging companies are sometimes asked to protect certain areas of undamaged habitat to compensate for the damage their operations do.

   3 Extra doses of a molecule that helps to protect lung cells from the damage caused by smoking might one day reduce some of the dangers associated with the habit.

Key hedging language

This table shows some key language used in hedging.

3 Use hedging language from the table below to qualify the following statements where appropriate.

Example

New evidence shows that early dinosaurs crawled on all fours before learning to stand upright.

New evidence ~~shows~~ suggests that some early dinosaurs may have crawled on all fours before learning to stand upright.

   1 Olive oil has a similar anti-inflammatory effect to the drug ibuprofen, which explains why the Mediterranean diet protects against cancer and other diseases.

   2 The earth beneath our feet contains 100 times as many species of bacteria as we thought. According to recent research, one gram of soil harbours up to a million microbial species.

   3 Skeletons recently discovered in Scotland indicate that ancient Britons practised the art of mummification at the same time as the Egyptians.

   4 The floods caused by Hurricane Theo will create the perfect breeding ground for mosquitoes, which transmit West Nile virus, and it will be at least a month before we know the scale of the risk to public health. Conversely, the hurricane will also have the opposite effect and get rid of the disease altogether.

4 Answer the following questions, using expressions from the table below.

   1 What is the cause of global warming?

   2 What is the current evidence for global warming?

   3 What will be the effects of global warming?

> **Language Fact**
> The most common use of modal verbs in academic writing is to express possibility.

Effect	Language	Example
Saying things are more or less certain or probable	Modal auxiliary	e.g. *will, may, might, can, could*
	Adverb or noun	e.g. *certainly, possibly, perhaps, There is a possibility that …*
	Verb	e.g. *It shows/indicates that …* *It seems/appears that …* *This suggests that …* *It tends to …*
	Adjective	e.g. *It is certain, likely, probable that …*
	Time expression	(very) *soon, at some point, one day*
Saying things are more or less common or general	Frequency adverb	e.g. *always, sometimes, often, rarely*
	Quantifier	e.g. *all, most, many, some, certain*

Academic Vocabulary 5

Meaning/word partners

1 Choose the correct word from each pair to complete the phrases below. Try to explain the difference in meaning and use in each case. Check in a dictionary of necessary.

1 **source(s)/resource(s)**: a renewable …; natural …; financial …

2 **source(s)/resource(s)**: the main … of income; a vital … of energy; data from various …

3 **economic/economical**: policy; an … crisis; … development

4 **economic/economical**: at … prices; the most … option;

5 **initial/prime**: the … cause; of … importance; a … factor

6 **initial/prime**: the … stages; the … response; my … reaction

2 Use words or phrases from exercise 1 to complete the sentences.

1 Smoking is the …………… …………… of lung cancer.

2 Small cars are more …………… to run than large ones.

3 …………… results from clinical trials have been encouraging.

4 Trees are an extremely valuable …………… …………… .

5 The country has serious …………… problems.

6 Beans are a good …………… of protein.

Word building: Noun formation

3 Complete the table by writing the nouns formed from the verbs 1–8.

Verb	Noun
1 achieve	
2 consume	
3 contribute	
4 estimate	
5 expand	
6 locate	
7 regulate	
8 survive	

Pronunciation

4 Examples A–C show three different word stress patterns. The circles represent the number of syllables, and the large circle shows which syllable is stressed.

Match each **word** from the table in exercise 3 to a stress pattern A–C. Once you've checked your answers, practise saying the words with the correct stress patterns.

A **oO** e.g. *locate*

……………………………………………………………

B **Ooo** e.g. *locally*

……………………………………………………………

C **oOo** e.g. *location*

……………………………………………………………

Revision

5 There is one mistake related to vocabulary use in each sentence. Underline the mistakes and correct them. Page numbers are given in brackets for you to check your answers if necessary.

1 There has been a decline of the sales of DVDs recently. (17)

2 Volunteers are needed to participate with clinical trials. (17)

3 Parents make an important role in their child's learning. (37)

4 There was a meeting to discuss environment issues. (37)

5 A bank loan enabled that the business could expand. (37)

6 The government seems uncapable to deal with the problem. (57)

7 I was only able to go to university with finance assistance from my parents. (77)

8 For non-drivers, there was no alternative from go by public transport. (77)

6 Choose five academic words from this page to learn, and write personal examples to help you remember them.

1 ……………………………………………………………

2 ……………………………………………………………

3 ……………………………………………………………

4 ……………………………………………………………

5 ……………………………………………………………

10 ▶ Hazard warning

hazard /ˈhæzəd/ *n* [C] something that may be dangerous or cause accidents or problems. [+**to/for**] *Polluted water sources are a hazard to wildlife.* (Longman Exams Dictionary)

In this unit you will practise	Key Language	Exam Focus
• Discussing personal risk-taking and natural hazards • Describing a sequence of events; discussing risk • Listening and labelling a diagram; completing notes; multiple choice • Describing a process: introductory sentences, marking stages	Cause and result **Writing Practice** Task 1: Describing a process Task 2: Presenting and justifying an opinion	**Speaking:** Parts 1–3 **Listening:** Sections 3, 4 **Writing:** Task 1

Lead-in

1 Look at the picture and answer the questions.

tight rope

1 Describe what is happening.
2 How does the picture make you feel?
3 Would you enjoy watching such an event? Why/ Why not?

2 Work in pairs to answer the quiz below. Score one point for each 'yes' answer.

QUIZ

Are you a risk-taker?

1 Were you a child who enjoyed climbing to the top of the tallest tree?
2 Would you go to a party where you didn't know anyone?
3 Would you resign from a job you didn't like without having another one to go to?
4 Have you dramatically changed your appearance in the past two years?
5 Have you ever gone white-water rafting, bungee jumping or scuba diving?
6 Have you spoken or performed in front of an audience in the past two years?
7 In a restaurant, would you order the most unusual thing on the menu?
8 Would you be willing to climb an active volcano and look into the crater?

Check your score on page 254.

3 Discuss the following questions.

1 What are the times in life when it may be important to take a risk?
2 In what situations would you advise someone not to take a risk?
3 Can you think of a risk you have taken in your life? What happened?

Focus on speaking 1 *Natural hazards*

Part 1: Interview

1 Work with another student to discuss this question.

Have you experienced any of the natural hazards below?
If so, tell your partner what happened.
If not, say which you'd least like to experience, and why.

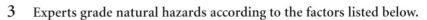
bụi cây cháy hạn hán

Earthquake	Volcano	Bush fire	Drought	Tsunami
Tornado	Flood	Landslide		

PRONUNCIATION: SOUNDS

2 In English the same vowel sound can often be spelt in different ways. For example, the sound /iː/ can be spelt *ee* as in *sheep* /ʃiːp/, *ie* as in *chief* /tʃiːf/, or *ea* as in *read* /riːd/.

    a The word *drought* /draʊt/ rhymes with *out*. The vowel sound /aʊ/ can also be spelt *ow* as in *brown*. Find five other words from List A with the same vowel sound.

    b The word *flood* /flʌd/ rhymes with *mud*. The vowel sound /ʌ/ can also be spelt *u* as in *mud*, *o* as in *son* or *ou* as in *tough*. Find five other words from List B with the same vowel sound.

    LIST A:

brown	grown	shown
cousin	now	thought
doubt	round	vowel

    LIST B

blood	food	good
cough	front	rough
done	gone	won

3 Experts grade natural hazards according to the factors listed below.

length of event	economic loss
area affected	social effect
loss of life	long-term impact

Discuss which *two* natural hazards from exercise 1 have the most severe impact, and which *one* has the least severe impact. Before you begin, study the *Useful language*. You can check your answers against the official ranking on page 254.

KEY LANGUAGE
Expressing cause and
result
▶ p. 224, ex. 19

Useful language: Expressing cause and effect

cause (something) or **cause** (something to happen)
A flood may cause economic loss / … may cause people to suffer economic loss.

result in/lead to (+ object) or **result in/lead to** (+ object + *-ing*)
*A flood may **result in** economic loss.*

*A flood may **lead to** people suffering economic loss.*
as a result of (+ noun or noun phrase)
*There can be serious economic loss **as a result of** a drought.*

Focus on listening 1 *Predicting a volcanic eruption*

Section 3: Labelling a diagram

You will hear a conversation between two students about an assignment on volcanoes. Before you begin, study the diagram and questions carefully.

Questions 1–10
Label the diagram below. Write **NO MORE THAN THREE WORDS** *for each answer.*

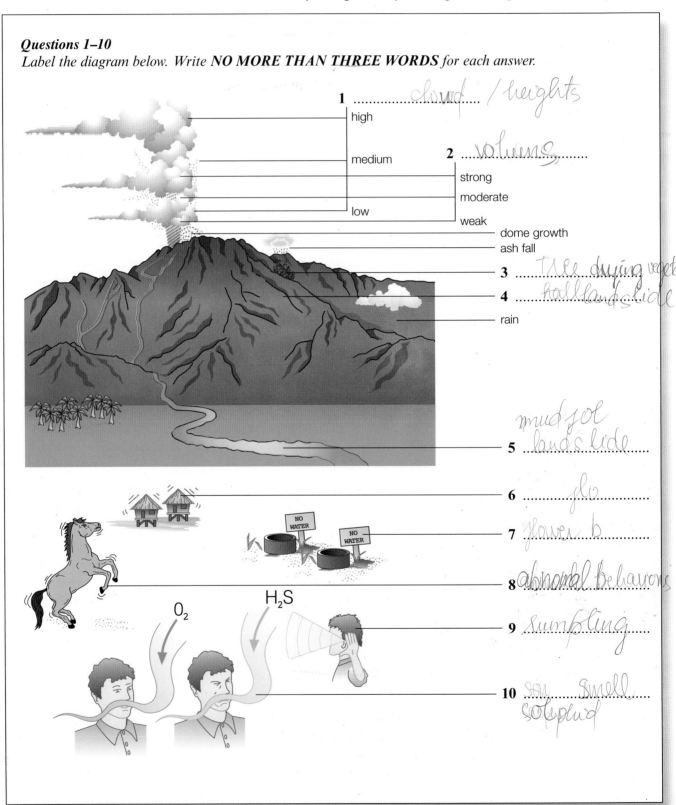

1 .... cloud .... / heights

high

medium

2 .... volcaens ....

strong

moderate

low

weak

dome growth

ash fall

3 .... Tree drying vegetation

4 .... fall landslide

rain

5 mud flo landslide

6 .... flo

7 flower b

8 abnormal Behaviors

9 sumpling

10 sou Smell sulphed

Focus on listening 2 *Tsunami*

Section 4: Labelling a diagram; note completion; multiple choice

Before you listen, look through the questions and remember the approach for each task type.

Questions 1–3
*Label the diagram below. Choose **THREE** answers from the box and write the letters A–F next to Questions 1–3.*

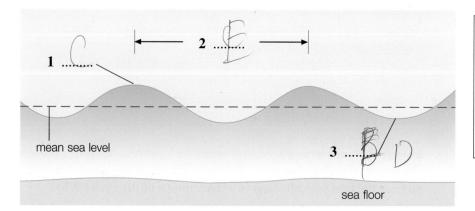

1 C
2 .... E
3 .... B D

mean sea level

sea floor

A   Wave height
B   Depth
C   Crest
D   Trough
E   Wave length
F   Wave period

Questions 4–9
Complete the notes below.
Use NO MORE THAN THREE WORDS AND/OR A NUMBER *for each answer.*

Tsunamis

Main cause:	4	earthquake
Percentage occuring in Pacific Ocean:	5	19 80 – 90
Maximum wave height in open ocean:	6	quiet small 760 & half metter
Country where largest tsunami ever was recorded:	7	Japan Kawisawa
Average wave length in Pacific:	8	500 millians 480 killomot
Travel at speeds up to:	9	700 kph

Question 10
Choose the correct letter, A, B or C.

10   What was the result of the Crescent City tsunami?
   A   Many people were killed or injured.
   B   Many buildings were flooded.
   C   Many high-rise buildings were destroyed.

Focus on writing *Describing a process*

Task 1: Describing a process

> **EXAM BRIEFING**   **Academic writing: describing a process**
>
> In this task you have to summarise the information in a diagram of a process. Variations include explaining how a machine or other device works. As with all Task 1 tasks, you will be assessed on your ability to select the most significant points to write about, on how clearly you organise the information, and on the accuracy of your language.

TASK APPROACH

1   Read the following advice on describing processes.
  - Study the diagram and make sure you understand the process. Is there a beginning and end or is it a cycle?
  - Begin with an introductory sentence, summarising the whole process and end with a suitable concluding sentence.
  - Describe each main stage in your own words, as far as possible. You don't need to include every minor detail.

INTRODUCTORY SENTENCES

2   **a**   Introductory sentences need to summarise a process or cycle. Look at the diagram of the global water cycle below. Which of the sentences A–C would serve as the best introduction to a description of the cycle? Why?

     A   There is water in the clouds and in the sea.
     B   Water moves in a continuous cycle.
     C   Snow falls from the clouds to the mountain tops.

The water cycle

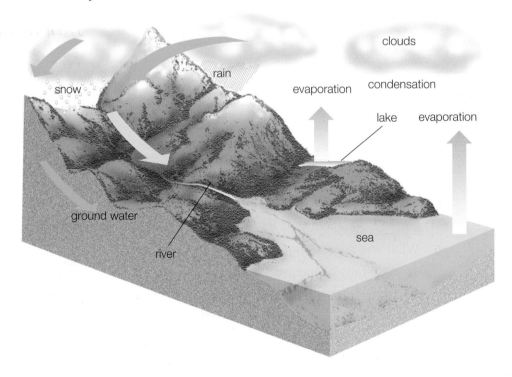

▶ *Focus on Academic Skills for IELTS pages 68–70*

b   Write the correct introductory sentence from exercise 2 on the dotted line in the description of the water cycle below.

MARKING THE STAGES IN A PROCESS

3   Study the diagram of the global water cycle in exercise 2 and complete the gapped description below. Use the verbs below in active or passive forms, as appropriate.

reach	*fall*	*absorb*	*rise*	*run*	*cause*	*release*	*blow*

The water cycle

....

The heat of the sun **1** .... water to evaporate from seas, rivers and lakes. In addition, water vapour **2** .... from the soil and from plants. As the water vapour then **3** .... into the atmosphere, it cools and condenses into clouds. The clouds **4** .... by winds until they **5** .... high ground. At this stage, the water droplets **6** .... back to earth as rain, hail or snow. After rain has fallen on land, it either evaporates into the air or it **7** .... by soils and plants. Some of it also **8** .... into rivers and lakes and eventually reaches the sea.

4   What tenses are used in the description of the water cycle? Why?

5   True or False? When describing a process, all verbs should be in the passive form.

6   Underline the words and phrases in the description which indicate the sequence of events.

7   The following expressions mark stages in a process. Answer the questions.

First,	*Next,*	*Then,*	*Meanwhile,*	*Later,*	*During this process,*
Afterwards,	*At this stage,*	*Subsequently,*	*Eventually,*	*Finally,*	

1   Which expressions mark stages which happen at the same time?
2   Which one marks a stage which happens after a long time?
3   Which two would **not** be used in describing a cycle like the water cycle? Why?

GUIDED WRITING TASK

8 Write a short description of the carbon cycle using the diagram and notes below. Try to include several of the sequence expressions on page 84.

WRITING PRACTICE
Describing a process
(example answer)
▶ p.242, ex 8

Begin: *Carbon is used repeatedly in a process called the carbon cycle.*

The carbon cycle

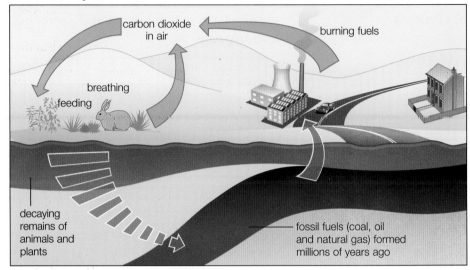

Plants take in …
Animals then …
When plants and animals die …

Over millions of years…
Eventually, …

EXAM PRACTICE

9 Now complete the following exam task.

WRITING PRACTICE
Describing a process (guided
practice and exam task)
▶ p.243–244, ex. 9, 10

You should spend about 20 minutes on this task.

The following diagram shows how pencils are manufactured.

Summarise the information by selecting and reporting the main features, and make comparisons where relevant.

Write at least 150 words.

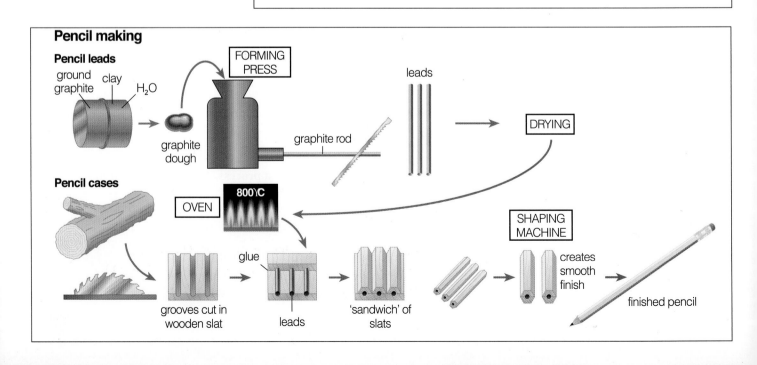

Focus on speaking 2 *Describing stages, discussing risk*

SPOT THE ERROR

1 Before you begin the speaking task, revise some grammar key points. Identify and correct any errors in the following sentences.

1 The country is experiencing serious economic problems. (HL10)
2 At first, the machine must be switched on. (HL10)
3 It's more economic to travel by bus than by train. (HL10)
4 News of the event didn't reach the city until several hours after. (HL10)
5 The report has taken a year to complete, but it's available at last. (HL10)
6 Firstly I enjoyed the course, but gradually I began to lose interest. (HL10)
7 There has been an increase of spending on childcare. (HL2)
8 The landslide caused a big amount of damage. (HL4)
9 There was a report about the earthquake on the television. (HL6)
10 It rained every day, and in the end we decided to go home. (HL8)

Check your answers by referring to the section in brackets at the end of each sentence. HL = *Error Hit List*

Part 2: Long turn
DESCRIBING A SEQUENCE
OF EVENTS

2 Work in pairs. Choose one of the topics below and make brief notes of the stages you need to describe. Then tell your partner about it, remembering to use a range of sequence expressions.

▶ *Focus on Academic Skills for IELTS page 85, ex. 3*

A Your education up to now.
B Your work experience up to now.
C How you have learnt English.
D How you qualify to drive in your country.
E How you arrange a holiday abroad.
F How you plan a party.

Part 3: Discussion
EXPRESSING OPINIONS
AND GIVING REASONS

3 a In pairs, discuss which of the following risks are most likely to kill you. Put the risks in order by writing 1–10 in the spaces provided (1 = most probable). Be prepared to give reasons for your choices.

Probability of dying in any one year from various causes			
Accident at work	....	Hit by lightning	....
Accident at home	....	Influenza	....
Accident on road (driving in Europe)	....	Smoking ten cigarettes a day	....
Earthquake (living in California)	....	Playing field sports	....
Floods (living in Bangladesh)	....	Wind storm (living in northern Europe)	....

SOURCE: Coburn and Spence, 1992

WRITING PRACTICE
Presenting and justifying an opinion (exam task)
▶ p. 254, ex 11

b Compare your answers with the table on page 254. How accurate was your perception of risk? What can you say about the risks posed by natural hazards?

ERROR HIT LIST

economic/economical/financial

✗	✓
Travelling by public transport is easy and economic.	… easy and <u>economical</u>.
Underdeveloped countries need economical support.	… <u>economic</u> support.
He's got serious economics problems.	… serious <u>financial</u> problems.

- **economical** describes something which is cheaper to buy or use than something similar, e.g. *Coach travel is an **economical** alternative to rail travel.*
- Use **economic** to talk about the way a country's money is produced, spent and controlled, e.g. *The Labour party is proposing a number of **economic** reforms.*
- **financial** means 'connected with money'. Use it to talk about the way people and organisations use and control their money, e.g. *The company got into **financial** difficulties; I had to draw up a **financial** plan.*

at first/firstly/first

✗	✓
There are two problems. At first, we have no money.	<u>First of all/Firstly/First</u> …

- **First**, **firstly** and **first of all** introduce the first item in a list or sequence. The next item in a sequence is normally introduced by **then** or **next**, and in a list by **second/secondly**, etc.
- **At first** means at the beginning of an event or period, especially when the situation changes, e.g. *We liked living abroad at first, but we got homesick later.*

at last/lastly

✗	✓
At last, I'd like to thank everyone for coming tonight.	<u>Lastly</u>, I'd like to …

- Use **lastly** like **finally** to introduce the last in a sequence or list.
- Use **at last** when something good happens after a long period of waiting, e.g. ***At last** the government is doing something about unemployment.*

after/afterwards

✗	✓
I left school and went abroad a month after.	… a month <u>later</u>.
There was thunder and after it began to rain.	… and <u>then/afterwards</u> it began to rain.

- When you mention a time in the past that is measured from an earlier time in the past, don't use **after**. Use **later** instead, e.g. *They met in July and married two years later.*
- Don't use **after** on its own as an adverb. Use **afterwards, later,** etc. instead. **After** can be used in informal styles in phrases like *immediately after* and *not long after.*

Reflective Learning 3 *Learning and recording vocabulary*

How do you learn vocabulary?

1 Discuss these questions in pairs. Which is the closest to what you do? Which is the most helpful approach?

1 How do you decide what vocabulary to learn?
  A I rely on the teacher to tell me.
  B I write down every new word I meet.
  C I try to focus on the most useful words in English.

2 Which of the following do you mainly use? What are the advantages and disadvantages of each?
  A electronic dictionary
  B English-English learner's dictionary
  C bilingual dictionary

3 What do you do when you meet an interesting new English expression outside class?
  A I mean to remember it (but usually don't).
  B I write it on any piece of paper that's handy.
  C I write it in a special notebook and check it later.

4 When do you review new vocabulary you have learnt?
  A soon afterwards   B once a week
  C the night before a test   D rarely

What dictionaries can tell us

2 Good dictionaries can tell us which words are useful to learn by indicating how common they are. Study the following entry from the *Longman Exams Dictionary*.

> **learn·ing** [S3] [W2] /ˈlɜːn ɪŋ/ *n* [u]
> knowledge gained through reading and study: *a man of great learning / Motivation is one of the factors that affects the **learning process.***

The word appears in a blue lozenge, which tells us it is very common and therefore worth learning. The codes [S3] and [W2] tell us it is one of the 3,000 most common words in spoken English and one of the 2,000 most common words in written English.

1 Apart from indicating how common the word is, what other information is given in the top line?
2 What example of a **noun + noun combination** with 'learning' is given? (See page 56)

Recording vocabulary

3 Discuss these ways of recording new vocabulary. Do you do anything like this? What is useful about each method?
A Mindplan

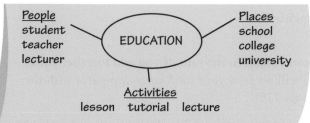

People
student
teacher
lecturer

EDUCATION

Places
school
college
university

Activities
lesson   tutorial   lecture

B Word card

card 1	card 2
'education'	/edʊkeːʃən/ (pronunciation) εκπαίδευση = the process of teaching and learning e.g. *He gave his children a good education;* have/get/receive an education; (collocations) *the education system, the local education authority, higher education* (related expressions)

Ideas for vocabulary learning

Learning a word takes **time**. Try to use different **sources of information** such as your teacher, other English speakers, a good dictionary and the internet.

- Look the word up.
- Ask your teacher to explain the word and give examples.
- Find different examples of the word in use.
- Revisit the word often and explore different aspects.
- Record the word carefully with all the relevant information.
- Experiment with using the word.

Setting goals

4 How do you rate your vocabulary learning? Give yourself a mark out of 10. Aim to continue doing what you already do well. Make a note of **one** new strategy you intend to try.

Reviewing goals

5 Work with a partner. Check the three learning goals you each listed on page 67. Discuss any success you've had or difficulties you've encountered. Revise these goals if necessary and remember to review them regularly.

Language Facts
- Learning the 2,000 most common words in English, will enable you to understand 75 per cent of all written and spoken English.
- In order to remember a word, you need to revisit it 5–7 times over a short period of time.

11 ▶ Use it or lose it

brainpower *n* U **1** intelligence, or the ability to think: *A lot of brainpower went into solving the problem.* **2** educated intelligent people who have special skills, especially considered as a group: *the country's shortage of scientific brainpower* (Longman Exams Dictionary)

In this unit you will practise	**Key Language**	**Exam Focus**
• Talking about learning and memory	The verb suffix *-en*	**Speaking:** Parts 2, 3
• Prediction; skimming; scanning; reading for detail	Articles	**Reading skills**
• Reading and answering multiple-choice questions, sentence completion; matching; True/False/Not Given		
• Vocabulary: word families; dependent prepositions		

Lead-in

1 Study the words on page 254 for exactly two minutes. Then turn back to this page and write as many words as you can remember in the spaces below.

MEMORY TEST: PART 1

1	6	11	16 ....
2	7	12	17 ....
3	8	13	18 ....
4	9	14	19 ....
5	10	15	20 ....

2 Now answer the following questions.

1 How did you get on? Which words were easiest to remember? Why?
2 Does writing things down help you to remember them?
3 What other techniques (if any) did you use to remember the words?
4 If you had to learn another set of words, would you do it differently?

3 Work with another student. Discuss how you normally remember the following:

- things you need to buy
- someone's birthday
- an important telephone number
- what you need to say in a telephone conversation
- things you have to pack for a holiday
- someone's name after you've been introduced
- directions for getting somewhere
- new English vocabulary

Part 2 of the Memory Test comes later in the unit. If you add together your scores for the two parts, you will see how your total score compares with the average for these tests (see page 115).

Focus on reading 1 *Sleep*

PREDICTION

1 Making guesses about the content of a text by looking at the heading, subheading and any visuals will help you read more efficiently.

Look at the newspaper headline below and say what you think the article is going to be about.

Sleep better than midnight oil on eve of exams

NB Headlines often rely on fixed phrases and colloquialisms. If you are unsure about the meaning of this headline, look up the idiom *to burn the midnight oil*.

SKIMMING

2 Skim the article quickly to check or correct your prediction. Note that the text below is shorter than an exam passage.

By Mark Henderson
Science Correspondent

STUDENTS who stay up all night to cram for an exam are doing themselves more harm than good, according to research into the link between sleep and memory published yesterday.

Scientists at Harvard Medical School discovered that people who deprive themselves of sleep so that they can study until the last minute are unlikely to remember anything that would improve their performance, while suffering the crippling effects of fatigue.

The scientists found that the brain needs good-quality sleep immediately after practising a task if it is to learn to improve at it. Those who substitute study for sleep, particularly those who miss deep or 'slow-wave' sleep, will get little benefit from their extra effort.

Instead, they may perform worse than expected because tiredness is a major cause of poor decision-making.

The findings, published in *Nature Neuroscience*, add to a growing body of evidence that sleep is vital to the learning process.

In the study, a team led by Robert Stickgold, assistant professor of psychiatry at Harvard Medical School, asked 24 volunteers to practise a 'visual discrimination task' that involved identifying the orientation of diagonal lines on a computer screen.

Half the volunteers were then kept awake all night, while the other half had a normal night's sleep. To eliminate the effects of fatigue on the sleep-deprived group, both groups then slept normally for two further nights. They were then tested again on the same exercise.

Among the group who slept normally, the volunteers showed a marked improvement. Those who had not slept showed none, despite the two nights of sleep to catch up.

The results, Professor Stickgold said, suggest that a good night's sleep immediately after learning is "absolutely required" to embed new skills in the memory. "We think that the first night's sleep starts the process of memory consolidation," he said. "It seems that memories normally wash out of the brain unless some process nails them down. My suspicion is that sleep is one of those things that nails them down."

From *The Times*

SCANNING

3 Scan the article to find the answers to these questions as quickly as possible.

1 What was the subject of the scientists' research?
2 Where did the research take place?
3 Where can the results of the study be found?
4 How many people volunteered to help with the study?
5 What kind of task were they asked to do?

READING FOR DETAIL

4 Exam reading passages often discuss causes and effects, and you may need to identify and match these in order to answer a question.

Find the relevant sections of the article on page 109 and read them carefully in order to match the causes and effects.

Causes

1 Students stay up all night studying.
2 Scientists have carried out research.
3 Some volunteers stayed awake all night.
4 The volunteers who had stayed awake slept normally for the next two nights.
5 Some volunteers slept normally.
6 Learning is followed by a good night's sleep.

Effects

A They showed an improvement in the task.
B The effects of fatigue were eliminated.
C New skills are retained in the memory.
D They showed no improvement in the task.
E They do not improve their performance in the exam.
F More is known about the effects of sleep on learning.

1 ..E.... 2 ..A.... 3 ..B.... 4 ..B.... 5 ..A.... 6 ..C....

Focus on reading 2 *Use it or lose it*

Multiple choice, sentence completion, matching, True/False/Not Given

1 Questions 1–14 on pages 111–113 are based on the following reading passage. Glance through the text first before you look at them.

Use it or lose it: keeping the brain young

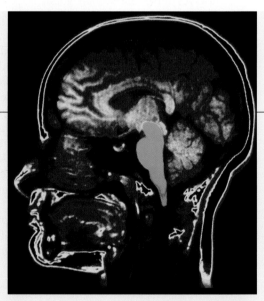

1 You hear the same complaint all the time as people get older: "My memory is terrible." Is it all in the mind, or do real changes take place in the brain with age to justify such grumbling? The depressing answer is that the brain's cells, the neurons, die and decline in efficiency with age.

2 Professor Arthur Shimamura, of the University of California at Berkeley, says there are three main ways in which mental function changes. The first is mental speed, for example how quickly you can react to fast-moving incidents on the road. Drivers in their late teens react quickly but tend to drive too fast, while the over sixties are more cautious but react more slowly. The near-inevitable slowing with age also partly explains why soccer players are seen as old in their thirties, while golf professionals are still in their prime at that age. This type of mental slowing results from a reduction in the efficiency with which the brain's neurons work.

3 The fact that adults find it harder to learn musical instruments than children points to a second type of mental loss with age – a reduction in learning capacity. The parts of the brain known as the temporal lobes control new learning, and are particularly vulnerable to the effects of ageing. This means that, as we get older, we take longer to learn a new language, are slower to master new routines and technologies at work, and we have to rely more on diaries and other mental aids.

4 "Working memory" is the third brain system which is vulnerable to the effects of ageing. Working memory is the brain's "blackboard", where we juggle from moment to moment the things we have to keep in mind when solving problems, planning tasks and generally organising our day-to-day life. Absent-mindedness occurs at all ages because of imperfections in the working memory system – so, for instance, you may continually lose your glasses, or find yourself walking into a room of your house only to find that you cannot remember what you came for.

5 Such absent-mindedness tends to creep up on us as we age and occurs because our plans and intentions, which are chalked up on the mental blackboard, are easily wiped out by stray thoughts and other distractions. Stress and preoccupation can also cause such absent-mindedness, in addition to age-related changes in the brain. The frontal lobes of the brain – located behind the forehead and above the eyes – are where the working memory system is located. Like the temporal lobes, which handle new learning, the frontal lobes are more vulnerable to the ageing process than other parts of the brain.

6 The news, however, is not all bleak. Although neurons reduce in number with age, the remaining neurons send out new and longer connecting fibres (dendrites) to maintain connections and allow us to function reasonably well with only relatively small drops in ability.

7 This and other evidence suggests that the principle "use it or lose it" might apply to the ageing brain. Professor Shimamura studied a group of university professors who were still intellectually active, and compared their performance on neuropsychological tests with that of others of their age group, as well as with younger people. He found that on several tests of memory, the mentally active professors in their sixties and early seventies were superior to their contemporaries, and as good as the younger people.

8 Research on animals provides even stronger evidence of the effects of stimulation on the brain structure. Professor Bryan Kolb, of the University of Lethbridge in Canada, has shown that animals kept in stimulating environments show sprouting and lengthening of the connecting nerve fibres in their brains, in comparison with animals kept in unstimulating environments.

9 The beneficial effects of continued mental activity are shown by the fact that older contestants in quiz shows are just as fast and accurate in responding to general knowledge questions as younger competitors, suggesting that at least part of their intellectual apparatus is spared the effects of ageing because of practice and skill.

10 Such findings lead to the intriguing possibility of "mental fitness training" to accompany jogging and workouts for the health conscious. Research in Stockholm by Professor Lars Backman and his colleagues has shown that older people can be trained to use their memory better, with the effects of this training lasting several years.

11 Just as people go bald or grey at different rates, so the same is true for their mental faculties. Why this should be the case for memory and other mental functions is not yet clear, but physical factors play a part. If Professor Shimamura is right, then the degree to which people use and stretch their mental faculties may also have a role to play.

By Ian Robertson in *The Times*

EXAM PRACTICE
Multiple choice

2 **This question tests your understanding of the topic and text structure.**

> ▶ **EXAM BRIEFING** | **Academic Reading: multiple-choice tasks**
>
> In multiple choice tasks with more than one answer, the answers may not be in the same order as information in the passage. In some tasks each correct answer scores a mark. In others, you may need to get all the answers correct to score a mark.

Question 1
Choose **THREE** *letters, A–E.*
Which **THREE** *of the following are given in the reading passage?*

A   a detailed description of the structure of the brain
B   an account of the effects on ageing on the brain
C   a report about the results of several research projects
D   a description of several methods of testing mental ability
E   an explanation of how mental decline can be limited

Sentence completion

3 **In this task, you need to match the causes and effects described in paragraphs 1–8 of the text on pages 110–111. The task was introduced in Unit 3.**

REMINDERS

- Underline **key words and phrases** in the questions.
- Scan the text and look for **parallel expressions**.
- The questions are in **text order**.

Questions 2–5
Complete each statement with the correct ending (A–H) from the box on the right.

2 As the neurons in the brain become less efficient,

3 As the temporal lobes of the brain are affected by ageing,

4 If a person is under stress,

5 When the frontal lobes of the brain are affected by ageing,

A absent-mindedness may become more frequent.
B people go bald or grey at different rates.
C reactions become slower.
D new connecting nerve fibres develop.
E the performance of some university professors was studied.
F it becomes harder to pick up new skills.
G older quiz competitors do better than younger ones.
H there is a gradual deterioration in the working memory.

Matching

4 **These questions focus on information in paragraphs 7–11 of the text. This task was introduced on page 32.**

REMINDERS

- In the text, underline or highlight each person listed (A–C).
- Read each section quickly and notice where the information begins and ends.
- Choose a section – e.g. one of the shorter ones – and read it carefully. Then look for matching information in the list of achievements.

Questions 6–10
Look at the following achievements and the list of people on the right (A–C). Match each achievement with the appropriate person.

A Professor Shimamura
B Professor Bryan Kolb
C Professor Lars Backman

6 investigated the memories of different groups of people.
7 established the effectiveness of memory training.
8 identified a number of areas in which mental function may change.
9 investigated the development of nerve fibres in the brain.
10 did a study including observation of the long-term effects on his subjects.

True/False/Not Given

5   **Study the** *Task Approach* **on page 13 if necessary before you start.**

REMINDER

- You can make a No/False statement true by adding a negative (*no/not*). This is not necessarily so with a NG statement.

Questions 11–14
Do the following statements agree with the information given in the passage?
Write

TRUE	*if the statement agrees with the information*
FALSE	*if the statement contradicts the information*
NOT GIVEN	*if there is no information on this*

Example	*Answer*
As people get older, their brain cells become less efficient.	**TRUE**

11   Absent-mindedness is not necessarily a sign of ageing.   ....

12   Research indicates that physical training can help to improve memory.   ....

13   Taking part in quizzes is the best way to stimulate the brain.   ....

14   Scientists now understand why people's mental faculties decline at different rates.
     ....

Focus on vocabulary *Word families*

KEY LANGUAGE
The verb suffix *-en*
▶ p. 225 ex. 20
e.g. *short* (adj) ➔ *shorten* (verb)

1   Complete the following table with the correct parts of speech. Most of the answers appear in the texts in this unit.

Verb	Noun	Adjective
suspect	1	2
decide	3	4
compare	5	6
7	8	long
9	ageing	10
11	memory	12

▶ *Focus on Academic Skills for IELTS* pages 82–83, ex. 2

2 Choose words from the table on page 113 to complete the sentences.

1 There is no ………. between learning on-line and learning with a tutor.
2 The Fisheries Commission has called for ………. action to save the blue fin tuna and other marine species.
3 The book gives tips on ways to ………. key facts for an examination.
4 The fastest population increase has been in those ………. 85 and over, the 'oldest old'.
5 We hope as many people as possible will attend Graduation Day to make this a really ………. occasion.
6 The body's ………. process depends on a combination of genetic and environmental factors.
7 Reducing risk factors like smoking and obesity can ………. a person's expected lifetime.
8 Contact the bank immediately if you ………. that your credit card has been stolen.

3 Fill in the missing prepositions in the sentences.

1 People who are deprived ………. sleep may suffer a decrease in cognitive functioning.
2 This research will add ………. our understanding of the disease.
3 We are still dealing with problems resulting ………. mistakes made in the past.
4 The company has had to make substantial reductions ………. staff numbers.
5 According to the reviewer, the new model is superior ………. the old model in a number of ways.
6 There are several things to keep ………. mind if you want to give up smoking.
7 The website gives ideas on things to do instead ………. watching TV.
8 The same principle applies ………. many industrial processes.

Focus on speaking *Memories*

SPOT THE ERROR

1 Before you begin the speaking task, test your knowledge of articles by identifying and correcting any errors in the sentences below.

1 I was born in United States but we moved to France when I was a baby.
2 People used to think that marriage was for the life.
3 He wanted to go to Oxford University but he failed entry test.
4 The school I went to when I was child was very strict.
5 Nowadays many crimes are related to the drugs.
6 I think best holiday I ever had was skiing in the Italian Alps.
7 One of the most important things in life is a good health.
8 Meetings take place on first Monday of the month.

> **KEY LANGUAGE**
> Articles
> ▶ p. 225, ex. 21
> *e.g. in Greece, in the UAE, at school, at the school*

Part 2: Long turn

▶ *Focus on Academic Skills for IELTS* page 78

2 Work in pairs to do this practice task. Choose one of the following topics and talk about it to your partner for two minutes. Your partner should ask you one or two questions at the end.

Before you begin, look back at the *Useful language* for introducing topics on pages 78 and 85.

1 A sporting event
2 Getting into trouble at school
3 A prize you won
4 A special present you gave
5 Your best childhood friend
6 A difficult journey

3 Choose one of the following topics and tell your partner about changes which have taken place since you were a child. Look at the *Useful language* and try to talk for about two minutes.

1 Your country   3 School   5 Crime
2 Your home town   4 Holidays   6 Marriage

> **Useful language: Comparing past and present**
> Years ago …   people used to …   But/whereas/now(adays) …
> In the past …   everybody had to …
> When I was a child …   I remember … *-ing*

4 Follow the instructions for the second part of the Memory Test and then check your results.

MEMORY TEST: PART 2

Instructions: Turn to page 255 and study the diagrams for exactly two minutes. Then turn back to this page and see how many you can reproduce in the space. You can reproduce them in any order.

Scoring: Give yourself a mark for every word you remembered in Part 1, and every diagram correctly drawn in Part 2. Add the marks together for your total score.

Your score .... (Average score: 17)

SUPERIOR (upper 10 per cent)	23–32
GOOD (next 20 per cent)	19–22
FAIR (next 30 per cent)	16–18
POOR (lowest 40 per cent)	0–15

Part 3: Discussion

5 Work in pairs to discuss the following questions.

1 Was there a difference between your scores for the two parts? If so, what might this suggest?
2 How important is memory in the IELTS test?
3 Is it a good idea to 'cram' for an exam, i.e. to try and learn a lot in short time just before the Big Day? Why/Why not?

Academic Style 6 *Signposting*

Introduction

Linking expressions like *and* or *but* act as signposts, helping to make the organisation of ideas clear to the reader. They are very frequent in academic writing and this reflects one of its main functions, to present and support arguments.

Ideas can be linked **within a sentence** using expressions like *and*, *but* or *in spite of*, or **between sentences** using expressions like *In addition*, or *as a result*.

Linking expressions

1 Underline the main linking expressions in the text below.

> There are two fundamental problems of knowledge at the centre of the book. First, we have the problem of induction, that is the fact that although we are only able to observe a limited number of events, science nevertheless advances unrestricted universal statements. Second is the problem of demarcation, which demands a separating line between empirical science and non-science. This book makes a major contribution to the philosophy of science and is therefore essential reading for anyone interested in the field.

2 Academic English uses all the main types of linking expressions to show the connections between ideas or facts. Match the following linking expressions to the correct sections of the table opposite.

although	in addition	overall
as a result	including	similarly
by/in comparison	in other words	such as
	in spite of (that)	then
consequently	in the first place	to sum up
due to	meanwhile	whereas
eventually	moreover*	while
finally	on the other hand	yet
furthermore*		

* Be careful when using the expressions *furthermore, moreover, nevertheless*. They are very formal and are used particularly to add force to an argument. Do not use them in a neutral description.

✔ *New equipment would be expensive. Moreover/ Furthermore, it is completely unnecessary.*

✘ *The school has ten classrooms. Moreover, there is a private study room. (Use In addition)*

Type of link	Example language
Addition	*and, also*
Reason / Result	*so, because, therefore*
Giving examples / restating	*For example, that is (to say)*
Contrast	*but, however, nevertheless**
Sequence/Listing	*First(ly),*
Summary	*to summarise, in conclusion*

3 Choose the most suitable expression to complete the sentences below.

1 At 500 metres, Earth's tallest sand dunes are already huge, *in other words / yet* they are set to grow even bigger as the world warms.

2 Water will be scarce, and *therefore / similarly* food production will need to be far more efficient.

3 Large parts of the earth's biodiversity will vanish *including / because* species won't be able to adapt quickly enough to higher temperatures.

4 Marks left by a criminal's tools can reveal important evidence. The use of a screwdriver to prise open a window, *for example / in addition* leaves scratches unique to the tool.

5 Music has been created by every known society *although / and* it is consistently rated as the most popular art form in surveys. *However / Consequently* the origins of music mystify scientists.

4 Choose suitable expressions from the box to complete the text below.

but	However	such as	for example
Furthermore		that is to say	

An exchange of smiles, in a shop or between a parent and child, **1** ……………, seems to be a simple act. **2** ……………, within those individuals, a smile can have powerful physical and emotional effects **3** …………… a reduction in stress-related cardiovascular response. **4** ……………, smiling creates a sense of trust and social wellbeing which spreads outward to others. Smiling may not solve the world's problems, **5** …………… it is the foundation of something that will outlast them, **6** ……………, the co-operative basis of human society.

Academic Vocabulary 6

Meaning

1 Study the examples and match each academic word in bold to the correct meaning. Check your answers in a dictionary if necessary.

principle/principal

1 … the **principle** of 'use it or lose it' might apply to the ageing brain.
2 … the country's **principal** export.
   A main or most important (*adj*)
   B the basic idea behind a plan or system (*n*)

factor/function

3 … physical **factors** like exercise can play a part in mental fitness.
4 … memory and other mental **functions**
   A something which causes or influences a situation (*n*)
   B the purpose of something (*n*)

construction/structure

5 … the effects of stimulation on the brain **structure**.
6 The **construction** of the new hospital has begun.
7 The house was a simple **structure** made of stone.
   A the process of building things like houses, bridges and roads. (*n*)
   B the way in which parts are connected with each other to form a whole. (*n*)
   C something which has been built (*n*)

Word partners: *Prepositions*

2 Fill in the missing prepositions in these sentences.

1 Customers will **benefit** ………. an improved service.
2 Chilli extract has been **identified** ………. a possible cure for diabetes.
3 The **link** ………. smoking and cancer is well-established.
4 Several schools are **involved** ………. the project.
5 Language can be **defined** ………. a system of vocal symbols.
6 Qualifications are useful but they are no **substitute** ………. experience.

Grammar

3 Rewrite the following sentences using the academic words in brackets, so that the meaning is the same. Do not change the form of the word in brackets.

1 If you run your own business you often have to work long hours. (**involves**)

2 The company made a profit even though the economic climate was poor. (**Despite**)
3 Many students receive financial support from their parents. (**rely**)
4 People typically work 40 hours a week. (**normal**)
5 Many fossils have been found here. (**location**)
6 There are some mistakes in the translation. (**accurate**)

Pronunciation

4 Examples A–C show three different word stress patterns. Cross out <u>one</u> word from each group which has a different word stress pattern from the rest. When you've checked your answers, practise saying the other words with the correct stress.

   A **Oo** factor, function, process, require, structure
   B **oO** define, despite, involve, normal, rely
   C **Ooo** accurate, construction, evidence, principal,

Revision

5 Replace the underlined expressions with more formal academic words from previous sections. Page numbers are given in brackets so you can check your answers.

Example It is not easy to <u>get</u> reliable advice.
Answer **obtain**

1 There is a Key which can be <u>bought</u> separately. (17)
2 The breakthrough <u>happened</u> as a result of computer technology. (17)
3 So far management has given no <u>answer</u> to the union's demands. (17)
4 Computers have had an important <u>effect</u> on the way students study. (57)
5 Many of the patients <u>need</u> specialised care. (57)
6 The website offers useful advice for <u>people who buy and use things</u>. (77)

6 Choose five academic words from this page to learn or revise and write personal examples to help you remember them.

1 ....
2 ....
3 ....
4 ....
5 ....

12 ▶ You live and learn

You live and learn *spoken* used to say that you have just learned something that you did not know before. (Longman Exams Dictionary)

In this unit you will practise	Key Language	Exam Focus
• Talking about school, studies and education	Collocations	**Speaking:** Parts 1–3
• Multiple choice; note completion; sentence completion	*The … the …* comparisons	**Listening:** Sections 2, 4
• Interpreting data: identifying key information; avoiding repetition	**Writing Practice**	**Writing:** Tasks 1, 2
• Presenting and justifying an opinion: thesis-led approach	Task 1: Describing data	
• Topic vocabulary and word stress	Task 2: Structuring an argument	
• Pronunciation: word stress		

Lead-in

▶ *Focus on Academic Skills for IELTS page 82, ex. 1*

1 Categorise the following words according to whether they relate mainly to *school* (S) or *college/university* (U). Check any meanings you're not sure of.

headmaster	lecturer	seminar
professor	undergraduate	fresher
degree	research	doctorate
class	lesson	secondary
pupil	tutorial	teacher
uniform	homework	campus

2 What's the difference between the following pairs of words?

1 a) term
   b) semester

2 a) department
   b) faculty

3 a) essay
   b) thesis

PRONUNCIATION: WORD STRESS

WE'RE TREATING HER FOR WORD STRESS.

3 Examples A–C show three different word stress patterns. The circles represent the number of syllables, and the large circle shows which syllable is stressed.

A **Oo**   e.g. German, science   ....

B o**O**o   e.g. Norwegian, computing   ....

C **O**oo   e.g. Arabic, algebra   ....

Find four examples of each stress pattern from the words in exercises 1 and 2.

> ▶ **LANGUAGE FACT**   Stress in long words
>
> There is a useful rule for words of three syllables or more with the following endings:
> *-ity -iety -logy -graphy -sophy -onomy -etry -ian -ate*
> Most of these words are stressed on the third syllable **from the end**.
> e.g. *poetry* **O**oo *society* o**O**oo *university* oo**O**oo

Focus on speaking 1 *Schooldays*

Part 1: Interview

TASK APPROACH

▶ *Focus on Academic Skills for IELTS page 48*

1 Read the following advice about answering questions in Part 1 of the Interview.

- Make sure you answer the question that is asked, not another, similar question!
- Don't give one-word answers. Give full answers with reasons, if possible, e.g.
  Q: Which subject did you find hardest at school?
  A: Well, I suppose the most difficult subject for me was maths. That's because I'm hopeless at figures. I even make mistakes when I'm using a calculator! So I always did very badly in maths tests at school.

2 Work in pairs to ask and answer questions about the following points.

Student A
1 What / enjoy about schooldays?

2 Favourite subject(s)?
3 How much homework / each night?
4 Worst exam?

Student B
1 What subject / studying / hoping to study?
2 How long / course?
3 Why / choose that course?
4 What job?

> **Useful language**
>
> The (*main*) **reason** I enjoyed … was that …
>
> The (*main*) **thing** I liked / enjoyed about … was …   That's because …
>
> **The best / worst thing** about … was … because …
>
> **One of the problems** about / with … was …

Part 2: Long turn

3 Work in pairs, each taking one of the topics below, and prepare to speak for about two minutes. Listen carefully while your partner is speaking, but don't interrupt. When your partner has finished, ask one or two simple questions.

Student A

> Describe a teacher who has had an important influence on your education.
>
> You should say:
>
> > where they taught you
> > what subject they taught
> > what you liked about their teaching
>
> and explain in what way this teacher influenced you.

Student B

> Describe a skill you learnt successfully.
>
> You should say:
>
> > what skill you learnt
> > when and where you learnt it
> > how you learnt it
>
> and explain what helped you to learn successfully.

119

Focus on listening 1 *The golden rules of listening*

1   Discuss the following statements. Say if you think they are True or False, and why.

THE REASON WHY WE HAVE TWO EARS AND ONLY ONE MOUTH IS SO THAT WE MAY LISTEN MORE AND TALK LESS.

DIOGENES

1   People may resist listening to others who blame or get angry with them.

2   People who have something they can't wait to say are good at listening.

3   Some people listen too much because they're afraid of revealing themselves.

4   Talking is more important than listening.

5   People who feel very emotional about issues make good listeners.

6   People are less likely to hear messages which agree with their view of themselves than messages which challenge those views.

You can check your answers on page 254.

EXAM PRACTICE
Section 2: Multiple choice, note completion

REMINDER

2   Listen to a short radio talk on the skill of listening and answer the questions below.

•   When you have to choose answers from a list of options, it's important to study each item in the list carefully in advance.

KEY LANGUAGE
Collocations
▶ p. 227, ex. 22
e.g. *take notes, do research*

Questions 1 and 2
*Choose **TWO** letters, A–F.*
*Which **TWO** topics will be covered in the programmes?*

A   taking notes in a lecture
B   taking part in a discussion
C   writing a letter of enquiry

D   preparing a job application
E   understanding body language
F   complaining on the telephone

Questions 3–10
*Complete the notes below. Use **NO MORE THAN THREE WORDS** for each answer.*

THE GOLDEN RULES OF LISTENING
• *Stop talking.*
• *Make a special effort to listen carefully when situation is* **3** ....
• *Relax – listening less effective when you're* **4** ....
• *Make it clear speaker has your* **5** ....
• *If you need* **6** .... , *explain what you are doing and why.*
• *Try not to let personal prejudices influence* **7** ....
• *Listen with reason and with* **8** ....
• *Your aim is to understand, not to* **9** ....
• *Be aware of what speaker* **10** ....

Focus on listening 2 *Making the most of your memory*

EXAM PRACTICE
Section 4: Note and sentence completion, multiple choice

KEY LANGUAGE
The … the **comparatives**
▶ p. 227, ex. 23
e.g. **The older** you are, **the more likely** this is to happen.

1 Always read the instructions and questions before you listen. Study the exam task below and answer these questions.
  1 How many words do you need to write for questions 1–4?
  2 What clue do you have about the answers to questions 3 and 4?
  3 Which parts of speech (e.g. verb, noun, etc.) must start each answer 5–9?
  4 What is the maximum number of words you can use in your answers?
  5 In question 10 what does the colour red represent?

2 Listen to the lecture and complete questions 1–10 below.

Questions 1–4
Complete the notes below. Write **ONE WORD ONLY** *for each answer.*

The five main memory systems:
Encoding
1 ....
Retrieval
2 ....
Visual

PQRST stands for:
3 ....
Question
Read
4 ....
Test

Questions 5–9
Complete the sentences below. Write **NO MORE THAN THREE WORDS** *for each answer.*

Before reading an article in detail, you should look **5** ....

When you have read an article carefully, you should **6** ....

'Implicit memory' allows us to learn information without **7** .... to it.

For this system to work efficiently, it is essential not to **8** ....

It is better to test yourself on things you **9** ....

Question 10
Choose the correct letter, **A, B** *or* **C.**

Which chart shows the percentage increase in brain cells of the mice who lived in luxury?

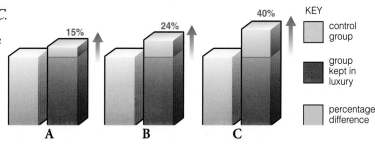

KEY
□ control group
■ group kept in luxury
□ percentage difference

TASK ANALYSIS

3 How helpful were the questions in exercise 1 in preparing you for the task? Did you find some questions more difficult than others? Which ones?

Focus on writing 1 *Presenting an opinion*

Task 2

REMINDERS

▶ *Focus on Academic Skills for IELTS* pages 80–81

1 **Read the following advice.**

- Analyse the **key points** of the question.
- Think of ways of **disagreeing** and **discussing implications**. (See page 69.)
- Make a **paragraph plan** so your argument is well structured.
- Use linking expressions to link sentences and paragraphs in a logical manner.

2 a **Read the task below. What are your views on the subject?**

b **Identify the key points you will need to address. Make some notes of the key evidence you will discuss. You will need this later when you attempt the task.**

You should spend about 40 minutes on this task.

Write about the following topic.

> *Too much emphasis is placed on testing these days. The need to prepare for tests and examinations is a restriction on teachers and also exerts unnecessary pressure on young learners.*

> *To what extent do you agree or disagree?*

Give reasons for your answer and include any relevant examples from your own knowledge or experience.

Write at least 250 words.

THESIS-LED APPROACH

3 We looked at an *evidence-led* approach in Unit 6 (page 65). Study this alternative model for a *thesis-led* approach.

4 **Answer the following questions.**

1 What is the main difference between the two approaches?

2 Which approach is more suitable when you agree/disagree strongly with a stated opinion (and can justify your view in some detail)?

3 Which approach is more suitable when your argument needs to be more balanced?

PARAGRAPH PLAN

Opening paragraph
- Introduce the topic.
- State your thesis (point of view).

Middle sections
- Justify your opinion.
- Start a new paragraph for each point.

Closing paragraph
- Restate your point of view.

PLAN

5 **Prepare a paragraph plan for the exam task above, based on this approach.**

JUSTIFYING YOUR OPINION

6 In Task 2, you may be asked to agree or disagree with a statement. When justifying your opinion, you may need to link ideas using expressions of concession or contrast. Study the expressions in the box and answer the questions below.

Useful language: Expressions of concession and contrast

although / even though
Although she did well in the exam, she didn't get a distinction.
He was arrested **even though** he had an alibi.

despite / in spite of
Despite its poor record, the government was re-elected.
The company's profits have increased **in spite of** the recession.

however
He claimed to be a doctor. **However**, he had no medical qualifications at all.

nevertheless
It was only a minor accident. **Nevertheless**, there could be serious repercussions.

while / whereas
While things are improving, there's still a long way to go.
Some people favour devolution, **whereas** others are bitterly opposed to it.

on the other hand
The new factory will provide employment. **On the other hand**, it may damage the environment.

▶ *Focus on Academic Skills for IELTS* page 83, ex. 4

1 What is the difference in usage between *despite/in spite* of and *although*?
2 Which three expressions are usually followed by a comma?
3 Which expression can be used to balance two facts or ideas?

7 Complete the following sentences and link the ideas using suitable expressions from the *Useful language* box above.

1 Football hooligans receive a lot of publicity. There are millions of spectators who cause no trouble at all.
2 Many people feel that censorship is unacceptable in a free society. It's undeniable that children need some form of protection from …
3 Medical advances are extending the human lifespan. Not everyone wants …
4 Smoking is known to cause … People have the right to …
5 City life undoubtedly has many advantages such as … city dwellers face many problems, including …

8 Read the following sentences and make the necessary corrections.
1 Nevertheless the economy is improving, recovery is still some months away.
2 Despite I agree with the idea in principle, I can foresee some problems.
3 He failed the exam in spite the fact he had studied very hard.
4 Although vaccines help fight disease, but they can have harmful side-effects.

WRITING PRACTICE
▶ Structuring an argument (example answer)
p. 246, ex. 12

EXAM PRACTICE

9 Now write your answer to the task.

Focus on speaking 2 *Teachers and students*

Part 3: Discussion

1 Read the following discussion question and look at answers A–D. Which is the best answer, and why?

> Do you think teaching is a rewarding job?

A | *Yes.*

C | *I think it depends on the situation. If the students are willing to learn, I'm sure it can be a very rewarding job. But in schools where the students are not motivated, I think it would be difficult and frustrating.*

B | *My teacher had a rewarding job because we were very good students who studied hard and got good exam results.*

D | *I think it is a satisfying job. A teacher helps people to learn. People can make a difference in their lives by studying. You see good results from your work.*

2 When giving reasons for an opinion it is often useful to refer to your own experience or to something you have heard or read.

Useful Language: Giving reasons for an opinion

Your own experience	Other people's opinions
I know from my own experience that …	Some people/experts/scientists **say/think** (that) … (but)
I remember … (e.g. a particular person/event)	**I read an article/watched a programme** … **which** …

---

3 Answer the question below in different ways, using the prompts a)–c). Before you begin, study the best answer in exercise 1 again. Refer to the *Useful language* on pages 69 and 115.

> Do you think your schooldays are the happiest days of your life?

a) It depends …   b) In the past/I remember when …   c) Some people think … but …

4 Work in pairs to discuss these questions. Give reasons for your opinions.
1 What's the most important quality in a good teacher?
2 Do well-behaved children deserve more of a teacher's attention than badly-behaved children?
3 Should a teacher encourage children to treat him/her like a friend?
4 Which is more important for children: freedom of expression or formal correctness?

Focus on writing 2 *Interpreting data*

Task I

REMINDERS

1 Read the following advice.

- Before you begin, analyse the graph carefully and **identify** key information.
- When writing your answer, **avoid repetition** by varying your language.
- Begin with an **introductory statement** and end by **drawing a conclusion** about any overall trends.

IDENTIFYING KEY INFORMATION

2 Study the chart in the exam task below and answer the following questions. In which subject(s) did:

1 pupils of both sexes have most success?
2 boys and girls have very similar results?
3 girls have most success? (Percentage?)
4 girls have a much better pass rate than boys?
5 boys have a better pass rate than girls?

AVOIDING REPETITION

3 Match each of the following to an expression in the box.

1 do badly (in an exam)   5 percentage
2 nearly twice as many   6 significantly (more, etc.)
3 achieve a good grade   7 comparable
4 exam pass rate   8 approximately

> WRITING PRACTICE
> Describing data (guided practice)
> ▶ p. 247, ex. 13

figure	*percentage of successful candidates*	*roughly*	*much*
get poor results	*almost double*	*equal*	*do well*

EXAM PRACTICE

You should spend about 20 minutes on this task.

The bar chart below shows the percentages of pupils who passed their school leaving exams, by subject and sex, during the period 2003–04.

Summarise the information by selecting and reporting the main features, and make comparisons where relevant.

Write at least 150 words.

Pupils passing school-leaving exams, by subject and sex, 2003–04

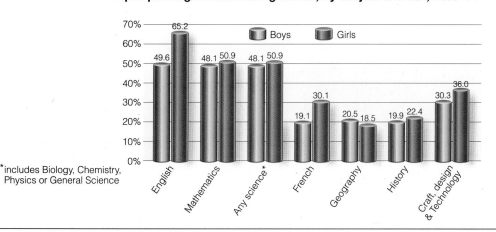

*includes Biology, Chemistry, Physics or General Science

ERROR HIT LIST

distinction/difference

✘	✔
You must make a difference between visual and verbal memory.	… make a <u>distinction</u> between …
I've noticed a difference about his attitude recently.	… a difference <u>in</u> …

- Use the phrase **to make** or **draw a distinction between** when you want to say that two things must be seen as separate and different.

- The noun **difference** takes the prepositions *in* or *between*.

differ/vary

✘	✔
British English varies from American English in several ways.	British English <u>differs</u> from …
Courses differ about length and cost.	Courses differ <u>in</u> …

- The verb **to differ** is used to say that two or more things have different qualities or features. It can be used without an object, e.g. *Opinions differ*. It can also take the prepositions *in* and *from*, e.g. *A differs from B. They differ in height.*

- The verb **to vary** is always used to refer to the way several things of the same type are different. It takes the preposition *in*, e.g. *Courses vary in length and cost.*

university

✘	✔
My brother went to the university.	… went to ~~the~~ university.
I hope to study in the university.	… <u>at</u> university.
My sister is in university, studying medicine.	… <u>at</u> university …
I am a student at a university.	I am a <u>university student</u>.
I am studying physics at University of London.	… at <u>the</u> University of London.

- Notice the prepositions in the phrases **be/study at university** and **go to university**. Notice, too, that these phrases do not include the definite article.

- You can use **university** before a noun, e.g. *a university campus, university studies.*

- Notice the use of the definite article in the two phrases: **London University** and **the University of London.**

make/do

✘	✔
Try not to do too many mistakes.	<u>make</u> a mistake/an error
I made this exercise for homework.	<u>do</u> an exercise/a test/homework
We had very little progress at first.	<u>make</u> progress
Please take an effort to be on time.	<u>make</u> an effort/an attempt
If you make your best, we'll be satisfied.	<u>do</u> your best
We must make the most out of our time.	make the most ~~out~~ of something

Critical Thinking 3 Questioning

Introduction

When applied to a reading or listening, critical thinking involves understanding, evaluating and responding to a point of view. For this you need to read or listen *actively* in order to engage with the information mentally and at a *personal level*.

The process begins with questions like:

- *What is this about?*
- *What do I already know about this subject?*
- *What does this writer think?*
- *What is the evidence?*
- *What is right or wrong in this argument?*

1 The following article is from a popular science journal. Read the title and the first two or three lines, then answer these questions.

1 What seems to be the main topic of the article?
2 What aspects of the topic do you think the article is likely to discuss?
3 Is this the kind of article that you would read for interest? Why/Why not?
4 Do you have any personal experience of this topic? (e.g. Do you use the internet for study purposes?) If so, say something about this.

2 Now read the whole article and then discuss these questions in pairs.

1 Did the article develop as you predicted? Was it more or less interesting than you expected?
2 What is the writer's main argument?
3 Do you agree with the writer's argument? Why/Why not?
4 What evidence is presented? Is this convincing? Is it enough to support the argument?
5 Can you suggest further evidence from your own experience to support the argument?
6 Are there any flaws in the argument that you can think of?

> **Critical Thinking for IELTS**
>
> Remember to try and engage with any reading or listening text as actively as possible.
>
> - Try to relate the topic to your own experience.
> - Ask yourself the kind of questions above, both before and during the task.

Lessons from the world's wide web

One of the greatest promises of the Internet relates to education. In times of teacher shortages, the benefits are obvious: one teacher online can instruct millions of pupils. There are obvious disadvantages, such as the lack of one-to-one teacher-pupil engagement, but mixing online with traditional education can reduce that problem. The Internet will also be one major way of delivering 'digital immersion learning'. This is learning that uses virtual technology to give students a sense of being realistically inside an environment so that they can learn more directly by participation. They can 'experience' historical events and fly like a bird over continents, through planetary systems or into cells and molecules.

Before the internet can confidently be used as an educational tool, however, some of its more serious problems must be addressed, chief of which is the unreliability of so much of the information it contains.

Here is a telling example. Suppose you wish to trace the author and context of a quotation you have encountered, as I did recently. On my search, the first web page cited by Google attributed it to the wrong poet, though this mistake was corrected in all of the following references. There were also frequent transcription errors on other web pages: 'no' for 'not', 'senses' for 'sense' and so on. These may be minor matters here, but would be far from minor if we were dealing with a mathematical or a chemical formula.

The lesson is that to make the best use of the Internet as an educational resource, its content has to be checked for reliability and a system of classification introduced. Given that the Internet is already the main resource for students, the need is urgent. I suggest that an international consortium of universities should set up panels of experts to assess the worth of websites, endorsing those that are reliable. They should not censor, nor comment on matters of opinion. But they should authoritatively identify worthwhile sites, and warn of factual error when it occurs. Without such expert monitoring, the Internet will increasingly be a problem rather than a boon, and limited in educational value.

From 'Lessons from the world's wide web' by A. C. Grayling in *New Scientist*

13 ▶ Bones to phones

inside information information that is available only to people who are part of a particular group or organisation: *Police believe the robbers may have had inside information.*
(Longman Exams Dictionary)

In this unit you will practise	Key Language	Exam Focus
• Discussing communication systems • Recognising participle phrases • Reading and matching; multiple choice • Comparing and contrasting • Vocabulary: introducing examples	Common verbs in *-ed* and *-ing* clauses The verb *doubt*	**Speaking:** Parts 2, 3 **Reading skills**

Lead-in

1 Work with another student. Can you identify each form of communication below?

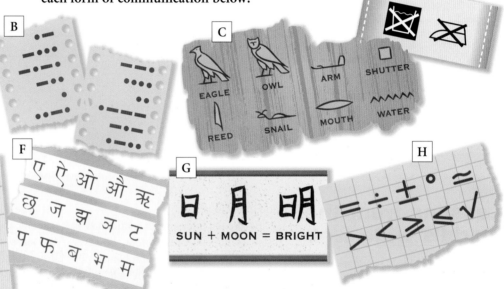

1 Which is the odd one out? Why?
2 What do the most ancient (**C**) and the most modern (**D**) have in common?
3 What other everyday examples like **D** can you think of?

2 a With your partner, put the following inventions in chronological order.

television	1 45 BC, Rome
mechanical clock	2 1092, China
printing press	3 1454, Germany
X-rays	4 1876, America
satellite	5 1895, Germany
calendar	6 1925, UK
telephone	7 1957, Soviet Union

b Which two of the above inventions have been the most significant, and which the least significant, in your opinion?

Focus on reading 1 *Communication devices*

1   Each of the following short texts is concerned with storing or communicating information. Read each text and guess which invention it refers to.

A

This device, first introduced in 1947 in America, did not come into general use until the 1980s. Since then, models have become progressively smaller and lighter, making them far more convenient to use. The original analogue operating system was replaced by digital networks in the 1990s, providing greater security for users. More than 24 million Britons, nearly half the population, now own one, and the device has even become something of a fashion accessory for the young.

B

Invented in Germany in 1500, this useful gadget became smaller and thinner as technology improved. At first regarded purely as 'ladies' fashion', it began to be worn by men after its successful use by soldiers in the First World War. In the 20th century, Switzerland took over from England and America as the dominant manufacturing country.

C

This important medium of communication, first became available in Greece in the second century BC, replacing papyrus rolls, which could be up to 35 metres in length. The new invention was far more convenient to use, being both portable and easy to access at any point. Having remained dominant for more than two millennia, it may now be under threat from item E.

D

This familiar item of business equipment dates back to 1910, when it was regularly used by newspapers to send and receive pictures. It was expected to become a common household appliance, and millions of dollars were spent on its development in the 1920s. However, it was another 40 years before it came into general office use.

E

This has been called the most liberating invention of the late 20th century. Having originated in technology developed in the early 1960s, it evolved through a miracle of international co-operation into the system we know today. Initially used only by scientists, it was released to the public in 1991, and by 1996 the number of users was doubling every 18 months.

Check your answers on page 254.

RECOGNISING
PARTICIPLE CLAUSES

▶ *Focus on Academic Skills for IELTS* page 69

2   Participle clauses are short versions of longer clauses, conveying the same meaning more economically. They have the effect of making a text denser, so that it requires more careful reading. This is relevant to the IELTS Reading paper because participle clauses are a feature of academic writing (see *Language fact* on page 130).

The two main types of participle clause are:

1   *-ing* **clauses**, which have an active meaning.
- *This was replaced by digital networks, **providing** greater security.*
(***providing*** = which provided)
- ***Having examined** the arguments in favour, we can consider the opposing views.*
(***Having examined*** = Now that we have examined)

2   *-ed* **clauses**, which have a passive meaning.
- *This device, first **introduced** in 1947, did not come into general use until the 1980s.*
(*first **introduced*** = which was first introduced)

3   Underline four more *-ing* clauses and four more *-ed* clauses in the texts above, and say how they could be expressed more fully.

4 **Rewrite the following sentences using participle clauses.**

1 He produced an essay which was based on information which he had downloaded from the internet.
2 The paper, which contains the results of the survey, is about to be published.
3 The damage which was caused by the flood will take years to be repaired.
4 Once he had finished his speech, the President answered the reporters' questions.
5 When he realised that he had lost the confidence of his team, the manager resigned.

KEY LANGUAGE
Common verbs in *-ed* and *-ing* clauses
► p. 228, ex. 24
Participle clauses are also relevant to IELTS writing skills.

► **LANGUAGE FACT** Participle clauses in academic writing

- Participle clauses are more common in academic writing than in other written forms, with -ed clauses being the more common of the two.
- The verbs most commonly used in these constructions in academic writing are:
  -ing clauses: *being, containing, using, concerning, having, involving*
  -ed clauses: *based, given, used, caused, concerned, made, obtained, produced, taken*

From *The Longman Grammar of Spoken and Written English*

Focus on reading 2 *Bones to phones*

1 Questions 1–15 on pages 132–133 are based on the following reading passage. Glance through the text before you start.

Bones to phones

Radio survived, the pneumatic mail didn't. Books are still here, but the Inca quipu *aren't. Why do some media die while others live on, asks Margaret Wertheim.*

The *inuksuit* were used as travel guides by the Inuit.

A With no books, no TV, no Internet, just how did our forebears exercise their minds around the campfire back in Palaeolithic times? One pastime seems to have been bone-notching. Across Europe and the Middle East, early humans took to etching parallel lines and crosses into pieces of bone. Why they did this is still a mystery, though present thinking is that the bones served as tally sticks or even a form of lunar calendar. Whatever their purpose, the bones were clearly important, or they would not have been used for so long – about 90,000 years. "I doubt very much that any form of media we have today will survive that long," declares Bruce Sterling with heartfelt admiration.

B Sterling, a Texas-based science-fiction writer, is a man who should know about such matters. He has spent much of the past five years sifting through the dustbins of history in search of dead media. He and fellow writer Bruce Kadrey are assembling an archive of the dead and dying. Their only criteria are that a device must have been used to create, store or communicate information, and that it must be deceased – or at least down to its last gasp.

C Appropriately, for a project about the transience of media, the Dead Media Project is housed on the Internet. Sterling and Kadrey set the ball rolling, but ultimately it is a communal effort, relying on a cadre of selfless workers around the globe who scour historical sources for arcane, obscure, forgotten and abandoned media. Most of these are not academic historians, just self-professed obsessives.

At present, the official archive, known as the Dead Media Working Notes, contains more than 400 listings. Take, for example, the *inuksuit* – huge stone relics that dot the Arctic landscape of North America. Their builders, the Inuit, used them as travel guides. By learning the shapes of individual sculptures and the sequences in which they appeared, the Inuit could travel vast distances over unfamiliar ground without getting lost. Then there are the *lukasa*, used by the Luba people of Zaire. These hand-held wooden objects, which were studded with beads or pins or incised with ideograms, were used to teach traditional lore about cultural heroes, clan migrations and sacred matters. Yet the symbols they carried were not direct representations of information, but designed to jog the memory.

In the category called "Dead Physical Transfer Systems", one group stands out – the multifarious systems designed to deliver mail. Pigeon posts have been around for 4,000 years, starting with the Sumerians. More recently, at the end of the nineteenth century, many cities boasted pneumatic mail systems made up of underground pipes. Telegrams and letters shot through the tubes in canisters propelled by compressed air. But perhaps the most bizarre postal innovation was missile mail. On 8 June 1959, at the behest of the US Post Office Department, the submarine USS Barbero fired a missile containing 3,000 letters at the Naval Auxiliary Air Station in Mayport, Florida. The postal service's website quotes an official at the time saying: "Before man reaches the Moon, mail will be delivered within hours from New York to California, to Britain, to India or Australia by guided missile." Sadly, the trial did not lead to a postal revolution.

Many cities in the nineteenth century had pneumatic mail systems.

F With his knowledge of media fossils and what has lived on, has Sterling noticed any qualities that select for survival? "It really depends on the society that gave birth to it," he says. "It helps a lot if it is the nerve system of how government information is transmitted." At the very least, he argues, successful media need a close association with some form of power in society. The Inca *quipu* illustrates the point. The Inca did not write, but kept records on complex arrangements of coloured, knotted strings, some weighing up to twenty kilograms and carrying tens of thousands of knots. These knots were tied by an official class – the Inca equivalents of historians, scribes and accountants.

G Unfortunately, the *quipu* did not survive long, but were burnt by the Spanish invaders. This demonstrates, as Sterling puts it, that media can be murdered. He believes that but for the Spanish, *quipu* could have been taken a great deal further. They are his favourite dead media. "One of the things that really fascinates me is that they were networks," he says.

"They had directories and even sub-directories, and all this just with strings and knots."

H Kadrey has noted another feature of long-lasting media: they tend to be simple. There are systems for sending messages with light, which have been invented time and again, starting with the Babylonians, Romans and Imperial Chinese, who operated a network of fires along the Great Wall. Before the invention of electrical telegraphy, the Russians, Czechs, British and Australians all experimented with optical telegraphy. These attempts may vary in their levels of sophistication but they're all based on the same simple idea. "All a person needs is a shiny thing and the Sun," says Kadrey.

I Another shining example that draws the admiration of both Sterling and Kadrey is that old standby, the book. "I have this argument all the time," Kadrey says. "So many people today claim that the book is dead. I don't believe it for a minute," he says. "It's a very powerful technology. Books are so dumb, just ink on a page, but they've lasted so long!"

From 'Bones to phones', *New Scientist*

EXAM PRACTICE

Locating information

2 Look at the *Exam Briefing* and *Task Approach* before answering the questions.

▶ **EXAM BRIEFING**	**Academic reading: locating information**
In this task you have to locate information in paragraphs or sections of a text. You may need to find specific details, a description or a comparison, for example. The questions are not in text order. Some paragraphs may have more than one matching item.	

TASK APPROACH

- Look through the questions 1–8 and underline key words and phrases.
- Study the first paragraph, looking for information which matches any of the questions.
- When you find a possible answer, check that there is an exact match between question and information in the text.
- Continue working through the text in the same way, paragraph by paragraph.

Questions 1–8
The reading passage has nine paragraphs labelled **A–I**.
Which paragraph contains the following information?
*Write the correct letter, **A–I** next to each question, **1–8**.*

1	where the Dead Media Project can be found	*Example*	C
2	a medium that was destroyed		....
3	an experimental medium which was not developed		....
4	a long-lasting but mysterious dead medium		....
5	a visual aid for teaching		....
6	how dead media are defined		....
7	a design feature shared by several successful media		....
8	the importance of a medium's role in society		....

Matching   **3**   Refer to the *Task approach* on page 32 if necessary.

Questions 9–13
Look at the following descriptions (Questions 9–13) and the list of media below.
Match each description with the correct medium.

Example	*Answer*
its inventors were very optimistic about its future	**D**

9 a widely used system in the 19th century, operating below ground level   ....

10 their meaning depended on their form and the order in which they
were placed   ....

11 made only by a certain group in the society   ....

12 may have been used to record years, months and their divisions   ....

13 various experimental systems using the same basic principle   ....

List of Media

A	bone-notching	**E**	Inca *quipu*
B	Inuit *inuksuit*	**F**	optical telegraphy
C	pneumatic mail	**G**	electrical telegraphy
D	missile mail	**H**	the book

Multiple choice

▶ *Focus on Academic Skills*
for IELTS page 90

4   Remind yourself of the three key questions you should ask yourself in choosing the correct answer. Refer to the *Task Approach* on page 52 if necessary.

Questions 14–15
Choose the correct letter, A, B, C or D.

14   What is the main role of Sterling and Kadrey in the Dead Media Project?

    A They have collected the majority of the dead media in the archive.
    B They were responsible for initiating the research.
    C They are writing a book about the subject.
    D They travel round the world searching for dead or dying media.

15   What is Sterling's opinion about the Inca *quipu*?

    A They represent the most important records of the time.
    B They were unnecessarily complicated.
    C They will never be fully understood.
    D They had potential for further development.

Focus on vocabulary *Introducing examples*

INTRODUCING EXAMPLES

1   Giving examples is a useful way of supporting or clarifying statements in an argument. The most common phrases used are *for example* and *such as*, but there are several other ways of introducing examples.

Underline the expressions used to illustrate examples in the following sentences.

1   The archive contains many fascinating media. Take, for example, the Inuit *inuksuit* …
2   In the category called 'Dead Physical Transfer Systems', one group stands out – the various systems designed to deliver mail.
3   Successful media need a close association with some form of power in a society. The Inca *quipu* illustrate the point.
4   The article discusses a range of dead media: bone-notching, Inuit *inuksuit* and Luba *lukasa*, to name but a few.

2   **Add examples to support the following statements, using some of the expressions above.**

1   Technology is moving so fast that it's hard for the older generation to keep up with the latest innovations.
2   Mobile phones are undoubtedly useful, but they also have their disadvantages.
3   Not every so-called labour-saving device actually makes life easier.
4   There are a number of concerns about children who spend too long at their computers.
5   There have been many wonderful inventions in the last hundred years.

> **KEY LANGUAGE**
> The verb *doubt*
> ► p. 228, ex. 25
> e.g. *I doubt very much that any form of media we have today will survive that long.*

Focus on speaking *Comparing and contrasting*

1   When comparing the following methods of communication, what factors would you consider (e.g. *speed, convenience*)?

2   **Work in pairs to extend this mindplan.**

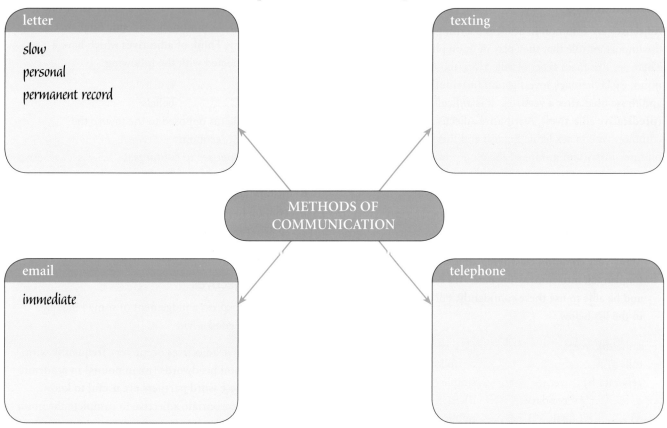

letter
slow
personal
permanent record

texting

METHODS OF
COMMUNICATION

email
immediate

telephone

EXAM PRACTICE
Part 3

3   Take it in turns to compare and contrast a pair below. Use your mindplan
notes and feel free to express your personal preferences.

A letter/telephone   C letter/email

B email/text   D email/telephone

Useful language

Expressing comparison

Both … and …	*Both* letters *and* texts provide a written record.
(just) *as … as*	It's just *as* easy to send a text *as* to make a phone call.
be equally …	Emails and phone calls can *be equally* effective as means of communication.

Expressing differences

comparatives	It's *cheaper* to send a text *than* make a phone call.
	Letters take a lot *longer than* emails to arrive.

Contrasting

but / while / whereas	Communication by email is almost instant, *whereas* letters can take days to arrive.

► *Focus on Academic Skills
for IELTS* page 86

Academic Style 7 *Attributive Adjectives*

Introduction

Adjectives are common in academic writing and this reflects the important role that they play in noun phrases. There are two main types of adjectives: those used **before a noun**, e.g. a *thorough* investigation (**attributive** adjectives), and those used **after a verb**, e.g. It is *difficult* to say (**predicative** adjectives). Attributive adjectives are the more common type in academic English and this section focuses on three important groups of these.

Classifying adjectives

These adjectives classify a noun according to type, e.g. *a **digital** camera, a **natural** material*

1   Many very common classifying adjectives in academic English fall into contrasting pairs. It's essential to know and be able to use these confidently. Fill in the opposites in the list below.

same/different	f) ……… (= earlier)/
full/ a) ……….	following
general / b) ……….	simple / g) ……….
c) ………. / secondary	h)………. / negative
d) ………. / final	public / i) ……….
major / e) ……….	

2   After checking your answers, choose from the list in exercise 1 to complete the sentences.

1   In ………. generations, elderly parents usually lived with their children's family.
2   An improved diet can have a very ……… effect on young children's behaviour.
3   The research is only in the early stages but the ……… results have been encouraging.
4   It was a very ……… operation which took several hours to perform.
5   The new law bans smoking in restaurants and other ……… places
6   The findings of the research are likely to be of ……… interest to psychiatrists.

3   Topical adjectives, which classify a noun according to subject area, are common in academic English, e.g *political* theory. **Think of adjectives which have a meaning connected with the following:**

1   science: …………… research
2   religion: ………….. beliefs
3   countryside (as opposed to the town): the …………… economy
4   town (as opposed to countryside) …………… areas
5   farming: …………… land
6   history: a place of …………… interest
7   relating to people (as opposed to animals or machines): ………….. nature
8   industry: ………….. countries

Evaluative adjectives

These adjectives express a judgement of some kind, e.g. *interesting* news, *good* advice.

4   Some evaluative adjectives occur very frequently with certain common headwords (main nouns) in academic English, so these word partners are useful to know. Choose the appropriate adjective to complete the noun phrases.

good   important   special   right

1   The survey is helpful because it provides a ………. indication of students' concerns.
2   Environmentalists say the increase in fuel tax is a step in the ………. direction.
3   It is now known that ice sheets play a(n) ………. role in climate change.
4   Business owners should maintain ………. communication with all staff.
5   Law Reviews are a(n) ………. case among research journals because they are edited by law students rather than qualified professionals.
6   45 per cent of people say that price is a(n) ………. factor in considering a purchase.

NB There is information about the use of other evaluative adjectives in *Critical Thinking 4*, page 167.

> **Language Fact**
> Attributive adjectives are more frequent in academic writing than in any other type of English.

Academic Vocabulary 7

Meaning

1 Study these examples of academic words used in texts in Unit 13. Think about the part of speech in each case, and match each one with a meaning from the box below.

1 Switzerland took over from England and America as the **dominant** manufacturing country.
2 Their only **criteria** are that a device must have been used to create ... information ...
3 **Appropriately** for a project about the transience of media, the Dead Media Project is housed on the internet.
4 By learning the shapes of sculptures and the **sequences** in which they appeared, the Inuit could travel vast distances without getting lost.
5 Perhaps the most bizarre postal **innovation** was missile mail.
6 The Inca kept records on **complex** arrangements of knotted strings.

> a) new idea or invention
> b) the order that something happens in
> c) consisting of many parts, complicated
> d) standards used for selection
> e) most important
> f) in a suitable way

Meaning: General nouns

2 General nouns were introduced on page 56. Choose from the list to complete the sentences.

device	issue	process
equipment	item	task
incident	medium	

1 Recovering after a serious illness can be a long, slow ....
2 The spacecraft performed various .... including collecting samples of lunar rock.
3 World leaders will be discussing child poverty among other important ....
4 The hospital lacks basic .... like blood glucose monitors and wheelchairs.
5 There have been several fights and other violent .... in the town recently.
6 Sales of luxury .... such as perfume and jewellery have fallen.
7 The book first became available as a(n) .... of communication in the 2nd Century AD.
8 A pedometer is a(n) .... which measures how far a person walks.

Word partners: *Pronunciation*

3 Choose an appropriate verb from the box to combine with each academic word

> | do | make | give |
> |----|------|------|

1	a contribution to	6	an alteration to
2	emphasis to	7	a commitment
3	a task	8	a demonstration of
4	an indication of	9	an adjustment to
5	research	10	priority to

4 Complete the sentences using word partners from exercise 2.

1 You will need to .... your calculations to take account of inflation.
2 The teacher .... us a practical .... how to operate the machine.
3 Students are expected to .... original .... for a thesis.
4 They .... me no .... when I might get the test results.
5 Einstein .... an outstanding .... Quantum Theory.
6 When lending money, the bank .... to people buying their first home.

Revision

5 Six of the words below, which all featured in previous Academic Vocabulary sections, are spelt wrongly. Underline the mistakes and correct them.

1	adequate	6	enviromental
2	aropriate	7	mecanism
3	assistence	8	previous
4	category	9	reinforce
5	consistant	10	speciffic

6 Choose five academic words from this page to learn or revise and write personal examples to help you remember them.

1 ....
2 ....
3 ....
4 ....
5 ....

14 ▶ The proper channels

channel *n* [C] **2** a system or method that you use to send or obtain information, goods, permission, etc: *All requests must be submitted through the proper channels.* (Longman Exams Dictionary)

In this unit you will practise

- Talking about information media
- Pronunciation: spelling and sounds; silent letters
- Listening and note completion; multiple choice; labelling a diagram
- Dealing with different data
- Presenting an opinion; opening and closing paragraphs

Key Language

Topic vocabulary: the media

Writing Practice

Task 2: Presenting and justifying an opinion

Exam Focus

Speaking: Parts 2, 3

Listening: Sections 1, 3

Writing: Tasks 1, 2

Lead-in

1 Can you understand what this quote says?

> GV A MN A FSH N U FD
> HM 4 A DY TCH A MN 2 FSH
> N U FD HM 4 A LFTM.
> Lao Tzu
> Chinese philosopher
> 6ᵗʰ Century BC

2 a Text-messaging relies on a simplified form of English spelling and the use of certain symbols. Can you guess the meaning of the following?

1 THRU
2 2MORO
3 4 EVA
4 R U THERE
5 CUL8R
6 BTW
7 THNQ
8 c%l

b Another way of expressing yourself electronically is through the use of 'emoticons'. Do you know, or can you guess, what the following emoticon symbols mean?

1 :-)   2 :-(3 ;-)   4 :-/   5 :-@

PRONUNCIATION:
SILENT LETTERS

3 a How is the word *thru* in exercise 2a above normally spelt? Which letters are silent, i.e. not pronounced?

b Most of the following words have silent letters. Circle them.

answer	combat	island	muscle
behind	doubt	ignorant	psychologist
calm	golfer	knife	receipt
climb	half	listen	wrist

Remember, you can check pronunciation in a good dictionary.

PRONUNCIATION: SOUNDS

4 Good dictionaries use phonemic symbols to show the pronunciation of a word. For example:

/ɑː/ is the sound in *hard*
/ɒ/ is the sound in *hot* or *wash*
/ɔː/ is the sound in *poor* or *all*

The letter 'a' can be pronounced in a number of ways. Put the following words in the correct column according to the way the letter 'a' is pronounced.

calm	half	raw	watch
class	law	swallow	water
command	past	walk	what
drama	quality	wander	
fall	quantity	warn	

1	**2**	**3**
/ɑː/ as in *far*	/ɒ/ as in *wash*	/ɔː/ as in *all*

Focus on speaking 1 *Communication problems*

1 Study extracts A–D for two minutes, then answer these questions.

1 Which forms of communication/technology do they discuss?
2 Which problems do they discuss?
3 Which problem do you think is the most serious?

A A survey of 600 British companies revealed that one in five had logged on to *Facebook* and other networking websites to vet potential employees. Jacqueline Thompson, from public relations firm *Brands2Life*, said that she had turned down one applicant after learning that he had used *Facebook* to criticise previous employers and discuss company information.

B Mobile phones are unlike previous fads because they undermine tradition and authority. There is no way to monitor the wide social circle within which a student might phone at school. Students sense this, hence the attraction of the mobile phone. Justine, 15, who goes to a school in central London, says: "When I have my phone, I can do what I want."

C Many managers are starting working an hour earlier to cope with the volume of emails. They don't know whether they are relevant or not until they have been opened. If they are away for a day, many managers feel threatened by the volume of emails, particularly because an instantaneous response is expected. That puts a lot of pressure on.

D The symbols have evolved to keep down the cost of mobile phone text-messaging and emailing, speed up the response time and inject emotion into concise missives.
Teachers say that the new shorthand style associated with emails is making their job of improving literacy skills even harder.

EXAM PRACTICE
Part 3: Discussion

2 Discuss these points in pairs. Try to think of arguments both for and against. Before you start, refer to the *Useful language* on page 69, *On the whole*, etc.
• There are good reasons for children to carry mobile phones.
• It should be illegal for employers and educational establishments to search the internet for information on applicants.
• It's no longer important to learn correct spelling and punctuation.
• Email is the most efficient means of communication these days.

▶ *Focus on Academic Skills for IELTS* page 142, ex. F/G

Focus on listening 1 *Media survey*

Section 1: Note completion; multiple choice
EXAM PRACTICE

► *Focus on Academic Skills*
for *IELTS* page 87

Questions 1–3
Complete the form below.
*Write **NO MORE THAN THREE WORDS AND/OR A NUMBER** for each answer.*

> ## MEDIA SURVEY
> *Details of Respondents*
>
> **Respondent No: 6**
>
> Name: *Philip* **1** ....
>
> Age: **2** ....
>
> Occupation: **3** ....

Questions 4–6
*List **THREE** sections of the newspaper that Philip reads regularly.*
*Write **NO MORE THAN THREE WORDS** for each answer.*

4 ....

5 ....

6 ....

Questions 7–10
*Choose the correct letters, **A**, **B** or **C**.*

7 Philip's preferred TV programmes are
  A comedies.
  B documentaries.
  C dramas.

8 His main source of information is
  A radio.
  B TV.
  C newspaper.

9 Philip uses his computer mainly for
  A computer games.
  B coursework.
  C accounts.

10 He uses the internet mainly for
  A sending emails.
  B surfing the Web.
  C banking.

Focus on listening 2 *Couch potatoes*

Section 3: Labelling, multiple choice

TASK APPROACH

1 This exam question includes data in the form of graphs and charts. Read the following advice.

- Study the data and notice the key elements: e.g. **heading, scale** (percentages, years, etc.), **key.**
- Notice significant features and describe them in your mind.
  e.g. relative differences: 50% v 10%, *a quarter* v *a half*, etc.
  changes over time: *a steep fall, a steady rise*, etc.

EXAM PRACTICE

2 Complete questions 1–10 on this page and page 142.

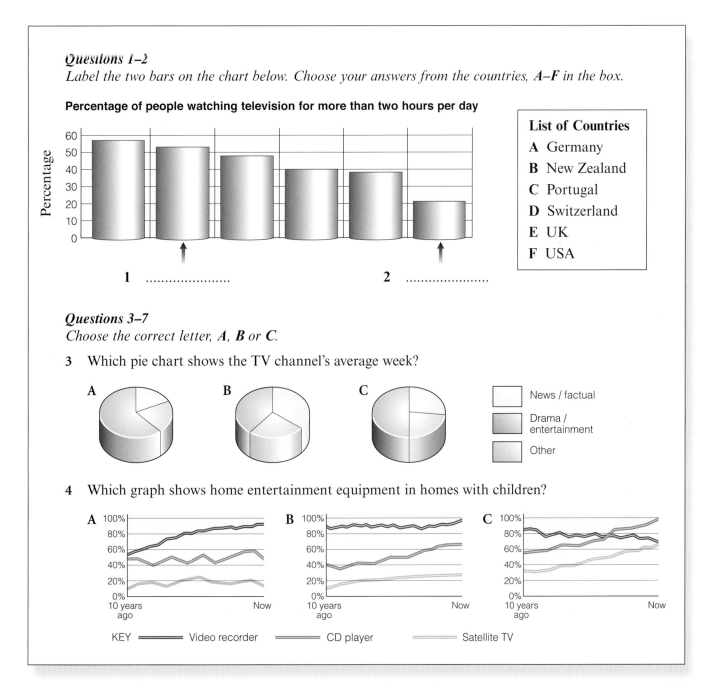

Questions 1–2
Label the two bars on the chart below. Choose your answers from the countries, A–F in the box.

Percentage of people watching television for more than two hours per day

List of Countries
A Germany
B New Zealand
C Portugal
D Switzerland
E UK
F USA

1 ....

2 ....

Questions 3–7
Choose the correct letter, A, B or C.

3 Which pie chart shows the TV channel's average week?

A   B   C

News / factual
Drama / entertainment
Other

4 Which graph shows home entertainment equipment in homes with children?

A   B   C

KEY ——— Video recorder ——— CD player ——— Satellite TV

5 Why does Jonathan think that television is so important to children?

A They don't have much else to do in their free time.

B They like to watch the same programmes as their friends.

C It's a way of escaping from their parents' demands.

6 How many British children have televisions in their bedrooms?

A less than half

B about half

C more than half

7 How many British children have access to computers in their bedrooms?

A less than half

B about half

C more than half

Questions 8–10
*Choose **THREE** letters, **A–G**.*
What **THREE** reasons did children give for not reading books?

A Not interesting

B Too expensive

C Parents don't buy books

D Not fashionable

E Information is out of date

F Too much effort

G Not enough pictures

Focus on writing 1 *Dealing with different data*

KEY LANGUAGE
Topic vocabulary: the media
▶ p. 229, ex. 26

▶ **EXAM BRIEFING**   Academic Writing: time management

It's important to spend no more than 20 minutes on Task 1, because it only carries one-third of the marks for the paper. You will need the full 40 minutes in order to do well in Task 2, which carries twice as many marks.

Task 1

1 **You will sometimes have to present information from more than one diagram. Read the following advice.**

TASK APPROACH

- Study each diagram so you are clear what information it contributes to the subject.
- Look for ways of comparing data *between* diagrams as well as *within* diagrams.
- Concentrate on describing the most significant information. It's a good idea to highlight key information on each diagram.
- Try not to use the exact words of the question. How else could you say *between 1987 and 1997* or *where people got news*, for example?

▶ *Focus on Academic Skills*
for IELTS page 96

You should spend about 20 minutes on this task.

The graphs below show where people first got their news, both about the world and about local events, between 1987 and 1997.

Summarise the information by selecting and reporting the main features, and make comparisons where relevant.

Write at least 150 words.

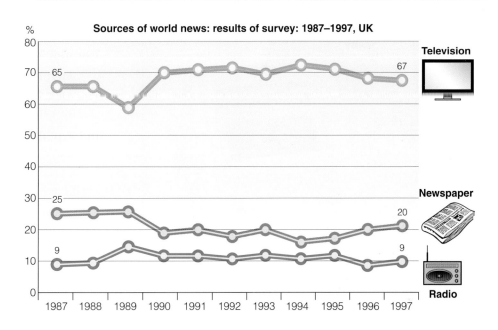

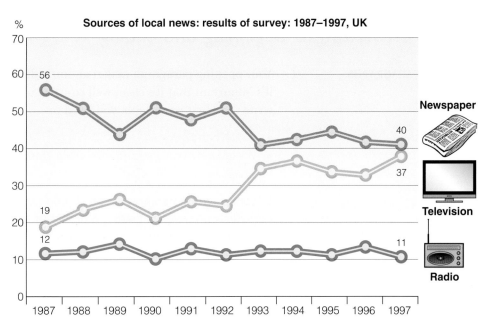

Focus on speaking 2 *The written word*

EXAM PRACTICE

Part 2: Long turn

▶ *Focus on Academic Skills for IELTS* page 95

Work in pairs, each taking one of the topics below.

1 Spend a few moments thinking about what you're going to say, perhaps using a mindplan to make notes. Then tell your partner about your topic for two minutes.

2 Listen carefully while your partner is speaking but don't interrupt. When your partner has finished, ask one or two brief questions.

A **Describe a website you visit regularly**

You should say:

what the website is
what features it has
how often you visit it

and explain why you are a regular visitor

B **Describe an important letter you received.**

You should say:

who the letter was from
what it was about
why it was important

and explain how you felt about it.

Focus on writing 2 *Beginning and ending*

OPENING PARAGRAPHS

1 Your opening paragraph makes an immediate impression on the examiner, so it's important that it's clear, well constructed and appropriate. Before you can write your first paragraph, you need to:

REMINDERS

- analyse the question
- decide how you are going to tackle your answer
- make a paragraph plan

In your opening paragraph, you should provide a general introduction to the topic for a non-expert reader. Whether or not you state your point of view here depends on the approach you choose: *evidence-led* (see page 65) *or thesis-led* (see page 122).

▶ *Focus on Academic Skills for IELTS* pages 91–93

INTRODUCING THE TOPIC

2 Look at the following topic and read three students' introductions A–C. Then answer Questions 1–3.

WRITING PRACTICE
Presenting and justifying an opinion (exam task)
▶ p. 247, ex. 14

Does television have a beneficial or a harmful influence on children?

A

Television was one of the most important inventions of the 20th century. Early sets only had small black and white screens, but later colour TVs became common, and nowadays you can even buy pocket-sized sets to carry with you.

B

Research shows that young people can be influenced by watching violence on television. For example, a 14-year-old killed a number of his classmates after watching the film Terminator.

C

It is undeniable that television, like the internet, can be a powerful educational tool. On the other hand, there are a number of reasons to be concerned about the effect it can have on children.

1 Which begins with a specific example rather than a general overview?
2 Which presents a balanced view of the issues involved?
3 Which fails to address the essay topic?

STATING YOUR POINT OF VIEW

3 In a thesis-led argument, you will need to give a clear indication of your general response to the topic in your opening paragraph. Which of the following, A–C, gives the clearest indication of the writer's overall opinion?

A

There are various conflicting views about the effects of television on the viewer, and I intend to give a brief outline of the main arguments.

B

Many people believe that television has a negative impact on children, but my view is that, like any other medium, it can have a positive and powerful effect.

C

One of the arguments in favour of television is that it can be a powerful educational tool, and there is certainly some evidence for this.

CLOSING PARAGRAPHS

4 Your final paragraph should briefly summarise the main points of your argument and give a conclusion that's clear and convincing to the reader. Read these closing paragraphs for the topic on page 144 and answer questions 1–3.

1 Which paragraph introduces unnecessary information?
2 Which paragraph brings the writing to an abrupt ending?
3 Which paragraph provides a thoughtful and balanced conclusion?

A

From my point of view, the government should also introduce more programmes specifically designed for children to watch.

B

In conclusion, TV sometimes brings good things for children to watch, such as general knowledge and news, but most children are not interested in these things.

Useful language

In conclusion, To sum up, To summarise, In the last analysis, On balance,

---

C

To sum up, children need to be exposed to television because it is part of our cultural life, but they should be supervised until they are old enough to make judgements about what they watch.

ERROR HIT LIST

news/media/press

✗	✔
The news are no better today.	The news <u>is</u> no better today.
There's a news that will interest you.	There's <u>a piece of</u> news that …
Television is a powerful media.	Television is a powerful <u>medium</u>.
Several reports have appeared in press.	… in <u>the</u> press.

- **the news** is an uncountable noun. To refer to specific information, use *a news item, a piece of news* or *an item of news.*

- **the media** refers to all the organisations which provide information, especially the newspapers, television and radio. It takes a definite article and can be followed by a singular or plural verb. The singular of **media** is **medium**.

- **the press** refers to all newspapers and reporters, considered as a single group. It takes a definite article and can be followed by a singular or plural verb. **in the press** = in the newspapers.

after all/finally

✗	✔
After all, I would like to sum up the arguments …	<u>Finally</u>, I would like to sum up …
They fought the case for years, but after all they lost.	… <u>in the end</u> they lost.

- Don't use **after all** to introduce the final point. Use *finally/lastly*.

- Don't use **after all** to mean 'after a long period of time'. Use *in the end/eventually*.

- **After all** can be used to remind someone of a fact they should consider, e.g. *I think we have every right to protest. **After all**, we live in a democracy.*

affect/effect

✗	✔
The ageing process effects the memory.	The ageing process <u>affects</u> …
Smoking can have a serious effect to the health.	… can have a serious effect <u>on</u> …

- **affect** is a verb meaning 'to have an effect on something'.

- The noun **effect**, meaning 'change' or 'result', takes the preposition **on**.

- The verb **effect** is very formal and means 'cause to happen', e.g. *The new law is designed to **effect** a change in employment.*

Reflective Learning 4 *Dealing with errors*

Introduction

There can be errors of **grammar**, **vocabulary**, **punctuation**, **spelling** and **pronunciation**. NB The words *error* and *mistake* are used interchangeably in this section.

How do you feel about errors?

1 **Discuss the following questions with a partner.**

1 Which of the following is closest to your attitude to errors? Which is most/least helpful?

A An error is a sign of failure. I'd rather say nothing than make a mistake.

B An error is a sign of incomplete learning. I can learn a lot from being corrected.

C I never worry about errors. The most important thing is to express myself.

2 Should teachers try to correct every mistake? Why/ Why not?

3 When do errors matter? What kind of errors are likely to matter most?

Proofreading

Proofreading is the process of reading through a finished text in order to find and correct any mistakes in it. The aim is to ensure that a piece of writing is of the highest standard possible.

These are typical correction symbols used by teachers to identify different **types of mistake**.

A Article	**Coh** Cohesion (eg which/that)
Prep Preposition	**P** Punctuation
Sp Spelling	**T** Tense
S ➔ V Subject/verb agreement	**WO** Word order
WW Wrong word	

2 **Each sentence 1–6 contains two mistakes which have been underlined. Match each one to a correction symbol from the list above and correct the mistake.**

1 There <u>has been</u> a sudden decrease <u>of</u> sales two years ago.

2 The car industry <u>have</u> received very little help from <u>_</u> government.

3 <u>Unfortunatly</u>, there's no such thing as an effective drug <u>_</u> has no side-effects.

4 Catches of food fish such as cod and tuna <u>has</u> decreased over <u>_</u> last fifty years.

5 Shanghai has increased <u>it's</u> population <u>until</u> almost 20 million.

6 Most accidents are due to <u>peoples</u> <u>incautiousness</u>.

3 **There are two mistakes in each sentence in the following text. Find and correct each mistake using the correction symbols as clues.**

1 Nowadays, one of major difficulties faced by parents and teachers are how to educate children suitably. (A, S ➔ V)

2 There are many people believe that encouragment is more effective than punishment. (Coh, Sp)

3 Moreover, this does not mean that discipline is unnecessary completely. (WW, WO)

4 Its important to start setting behaviour rules and boundaries with an early age. (P, Prep)

5 Children all want attention so worst punishment you can give is to ignore them when they misbehaved. (A,T)

> ### Ideas for dealing with errors
>
> - Look through your marked work and identify a few 'favourite' mistakes.
> - Revise this area of language. Ask your teacher for advice if necessary.
> - Make sure you're familiar with all the Error Hit Lists in this book.
> - Study your teacher's corrections – this is valuable personal feedback.
> - Correct your work carefully. Ask if you're unclear about anything.
> - Proofread your work carefully, especially in the exam. Look for:
>   – careless grammar mistakes, e.g. *Experts says …*
>   – careless spelling mistakes, e.g. *It's to expensive.*

Setting goals

4 How well do you proofread your work before handing it in? How carefully do you study your teacher's corrections? Give yourself a mark out of 10. Aim to continue doing what you already do well. Identify at least one favourite mistake and try to eliminate it from your next piece of work.

Reviewing goals

5 Work with a partner. Check the new vocabulary learning strategies you each noted on page 107. Discuss any success you've had or difficulties you've encountered. If you've made good progress, you may want to add another new vocabulary strategy to your learning goals.

15 ▶ Beyond gravity

gravity / ˈgræviti / *n* [U] **1** *technical* the force that causes something to fall to the ground or to be attracted to another planet: *the force of gravity* (Longman Exams Dictionary)

In this unit you will practise	Key Language	Exam Focus
• Discussing space exploration and science fiction topics • Predicting; skimming/scanning • Reading and sentence completion; Yes/No/Not Given; matching, multiple choice; labelling a diagram	Noun formation-*ing* forms vs infinitives Word partners	**Speaking:** Parts 2, 3 **Reading skills**

Lead-in

1 Work with another student to answer these questions.

1 The first artificial satellite was launched in

    a) 1948   b) 1957   c) 1961

2 Which event in 1969 was watched on television by one-third of the world's population?

3 By the year 2009, how many people had travelled into space?

    a) 100+   b) 250+   c) 500+

4 What is the longest continuous time a human being has spent in space so far?

    a) 212 days   b) 437 days   c) 803 days

Say whether you think the following statements are True or False.

5 Pegasus, at just 5 metres long, the smallest and cheapest US rocket to date, cost $10 million.

6 The amount spent by Americans on tobacco products annually is twice the NASA budget for space exploration.

7 A single NASA space shuttle launch produces 280 tons of carbon dioxide.

8 Aircraft flying in and out of Los Angeles International Airport emit about 800,000 tons of carbon dioxide each month.

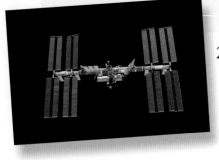

2 Check the Key on page 254 and and make any corrections necessary, then answer these questions. Look at the *Useful language* before you begin.

1 Did any of the facts surprise you? Explain which ones and why.
2 Which facts might be interesting to mention in an essay or discussion on the topic: 'Is space exploration a waste of money?' Make a note of these.

Useful language: Expressing surprise (Spoken English)

I didn't realise (that) …

I had no idea (that) …

It's (really) surprising/amazing/shocking (that) …

Focus on speaking I *The final frontier*

1   Read extracts A–D and discuss with a partner.

A   "My dream is too make space accessible to tens of thousands of people."
Sir Richard Branson, Virgin Galactic

B   **Big question: Is manned space travel a waste of time and money?**

C   **New Zealand enters space race**

D   The sheer beauty of it just brought tears to my eyes. If people could see Earth from up here, see it without those borders, see it without differences in race or religion, they would have a completely different perspective. All you see is one Earth …
Anousheh Ansari, Iranian-American space tourist

Anousheh Ansari

EXAM PRACTICE
Part 3: Discussion

2   Discussion topics in the interview can be quite challenging and it's often useful to begin with a brief introduction to give yourself a moment to think. Study the *Useful language* and then discuss the questions in pairs.

> **Useful Language: Answering difficult questions**
> That's an interesting question.
> That's (*quite*) **a difficult question to answer.** Let me think
> (*I think*) **it depends** on the situation …
> **It depends** what kind of … / what you mean by …

1   Would you like to be a space tourist? Why/Why not?
2   What qualities do you think a professional astronaut would need?
3   What is the space race, and why are countries keen to join it?
4   Some people say space exploration is a waste of government resources. Do you agree or not? If so, how do you think the money could be better spent?

▶ *Focus on Academic Skills for IELTS* page 116

Focus on reading 1 *Out of this world*

1 Skim the text for a general idea of the topic, then answer questions 1–12.

FOR THOSE TOURISTS who have visited every continent, or even every country, space has become the new destination. In 2001, American businessman, Dennis Tito, became the first private space adventurer and since then others have followed. US-based *Space Adventures* is now offering a lunar expedition for $100 million per person. "Experience the majesty and wonder of earthrise," and "explore and experience the far side of the moon," says the company's website, as if the prospect of a rocket trip around the moon is barely more extraordinary than a sunset cruise on the Nile.

Meanwhile, the British entrepreneur Sir Richard Branson has set up Virgin Galactic, which plans to offer sub-orbital[1] space travel on a commercial basis. For $200,000, any member of the paying public will be able to join five other passengers on SpaceShipTwo for a two-hour flight reaching an altitude of 110 km. Passengers will be able to leave their seats and float in zero gravity for up to 6 minutes and, according to the press factsheet "enjoy a view of space and Earth stretching for around 160 km in every direction".

Branson promotes space tourism as a means to save the planet. At the company's press launch, he spoke of the "transforming effect" a space flight will have on the thousands who would travel with the company: "Seeing the planet from out there, surrounded by the incredibly thin layer of atmosphere, helps one to appreciate the fragility of the small portion of the planet's mass that we inhabit and the importance of protecting our Earth."

Virgin Galactic has calculated the carbon emissions for a space flight as being "approximately 60 per cent of a per passenger return commercial London-New York flight", which equates to 1.5 tonnes of CO_2. Per Egstam, Managing Director of Tricorona Climate Partner, a major participant in the international carbon market, says with some understatement, that 1.5 tonnes "seems low for taking someone into space". But Branson insists that Virgin Galactic will be a force for good for the environment. A reusable spacecraft and unpowered re-entry and landing are two "environmental credentials" listed. In addition, the company has just announced that the spacecraft will be used to facilitate investigations into climate change by carrying research instruments for the US government's National Oceanic and Atmospheric Administration.

One of the first space tourists will be Professor James Lovelock, who, in a well-judged PR exercise, has been promised a free trip by Branson. "It will give me a chance to see the planet from the outside. It was that view from space that helped me see the Earth as a quasi-living entity that regulates its own composition and climate," says the scientist best known for formulating the controversial "Gaia theory". In Lovelock's view, space tourism is a valid scientific experiment that could play a part in the development of relatively low-emitting "coasting flights" to the other side of the world, ultimately replacing the present generation of jumbo jets.

According to psychologist and travel specialist Professor Robert Bor of London's Free Hospital, "Travel gives us a perspective on our place and size in the world, how and where we fit with others," he says. "It shines a light on our own lives in a way that we do not normally experience when at home. In this sense, travel is psychologically beneficial." He attributes the attraction of space travel to dissatisfaction with more simple pleasures. If we look at modern life, there is a drive to constantly work harder, to excel and be super-successful. "Ordinary" and "comfortable" may be too mundane. The same applies to some holidays. Space travel may be the ultimate expression of this."

Will high-spending amateur astronauts come back down to Earth transformed and inspired to save our fragile planet? Maybe a CEO[2] will cancel a logging concession[3]. Another will invest millions in carbon capture technology[4]. A celebrity might donate all her wealth to environmental causes. If so, might not the benefits of space tourism outweigh the environmental costs? Or would it be better for the planet if these high-flying tourists spent their $200,000 ticket money here on Earth? That can pay for a lot of good works.

Paul Miles, *the Ecologist*

Glossary 1 *sub-orbital*: without completing an orbit around the Earth
2 *CEO*: Chief Executive Officer
3 *logging concession*: a legal right to cut down trees
4 *carbon capture technology*: methods of reducing fossil fuel contributions to global warming

EXAM PRACTICE
Sentence completion

> **EXAM TIP** Don't make any changes to words from the text. Check spelling carefully.

REMINDERS

2 This task was introduced on page 33. In this version, you have to complete sentences by choosing words from the reading text. The instructions will tell you the number of words you can use for each answer. You'll lose marks if you write more than the maximum.

Read the following reminders.

- The questions appear in text order.
- Underline key words and phrases in the questions.
- Look for parallel expressions in the text.

Questions 1–4
Complete the sentences below.
*Choose no more than **TWO WORDS AND/OR A NUMBER** from the passage for each answer.*

1 Trips to the moon are available at a cost of ……....

2 Passengers on SpaceShipTwo are promised wonderful views from a height of ……... above Earth,

3 The Virgin Galactic company has undertaken to assist research into ………………..

4 Professor James Lovelock is famous as the originator of the ……...

Yes/No/Not given

3 Before you begin, study the *Task Approach* on page 14.

▶ *Focus on Academic Skills*
for IELTS pages 74–75

Questions 5–9
Do the following statements agree with the views of the writer in the passage?
Write

YES	*if the statement agrees with the view of the writer*
NO	*if the statement contradicts with the view of the writer*
NOT GIVEN	*if it is impossible to say what the writer thinks about this*

5 Dennis Tito is the only private individual to have experienced space travel so far.

6 Virgin Galactic is planning to set up a purpose-built commercial spaceport.

7 Per Egstam thinks that Virgin Galactic's figures for carbon emissions may not be accurate.

8 It makes no sense for Virgin Galactic to offer Professor Lovelock a free space flight.

9 Space tourism may not be the best way of saving the planet.

Matching

4 Before you begin, study the following reminders.

REMINDERS
- In the text, underline or highlight the experts listed.
- In the list of opinions, underline or highlight key words and phrases.

Questions 10–12
Look at the following opinions (10–12) and the list of people (A–E) below.
Match each opinion to the correct person.

10 Space tourism appeals to people's need for challenge and adventure.

11 Space tourism could help in the development of more environmentally-friendly transport on Earth.

12 Space tourism will help to change people's attitudes towards the world they live in.

A Dennis Tito	**B** Richard Branson	**C** Per Egstam
D Professor James Lovelock	**E** Professor Robert Bor	

Focus on speaking 2 *Sci-fi*

Part 2: Long turn

1 Work in pairs. Take it in turns to speak about the following topic for about two minutes. Before you begin, take a minute to think about what you're going to say and to make a few notes. Before you begin, look back at the *Useful language* for introducing a topic on page 85.

> **Describe a work of science fiction that you have read or seen.**
>
> **You should say:**
>
>> **what the book/film/programme was**
>> **what it was about**
>> **when you read/saw it**
>
> **and explain how you felt about it.**

Focus on reading 2 *Surviving in space*

KEY LANGUAGE
Word building: nouns
► p. 229, ex. 27

1 Read the headline and subtitle of the text below. Then discuss the possible health risks astronauts could face during long space missions.

2 Use skimming/scanning skills to find the general areas of risk that are mentioned. Compare answers with another student.

Surviving in Space

A voyage to Mars may be every astronaut's dream, but the health risks are formidable.

By MICHAEL E. LONG

Motion sickness afflicts more than two-thirds of all astronauts upon reaching orbit, even veteran test pilots who have never been airsick. Though everyone recovers after a few days in space, body systems
5 continue to change. Deprived of gravity information, a confused brain engenders visual illusions. Body fluids surge to chest and head. The heart enlarges slightly, as do other organs. Sensing too much fluid, the body begins to excrete it, including calcium, electrolytes and blood plasma. The
10 production of red blood cells decreases, rendering astronauts slightly anaemic. With the loss of fluid, legs shrink. Spinal discs expand, and so does the astronaut – who may gain five centimetres and suffer backache. Though the process may sound terrible, astronauts adjust to it, come to enjoy it and
15 seem no worse for wear – at least for short missions such as space shuttle flights that last a week or two.

During longer flights, however, physiology enters an unknown realm. As director of Russia's Institute for Biomedical Problems from 1968 to 1988, Oleg Gazenko
20 watched cosmonauts return from long flights unable to stand without fainting, needing to be carried from the spacecraft. "We are creatures of the Earth," Gazenko told me. "These changes are the price of a ticket to space."

Americans, returning from months-long flights on Mir, the Russian space station, also paid the price, suffering losses in weight, muscle mass and bone density. NASA geared up to see how – even if – humans would survive the most demanding of space ventures, a mission to Mars, which could last up to three years. "We don't even know if a broken bone will heal in space," said Daniel Goldin, NASA's administrator. To get answers, in 1997 Goldin established the National Space Biomedical Research Institute (NSBRI), a consortium of experts from a dozen leading universities and research institutes. NSBRI will study biomedical problems and by a given date will present NASA with a "go" or "no go" recommendation on a Mars mission.

Jeffrey Sutton, leader of the medical systems team at the NSBRI, has treated the head trauma, wounds, kidney stones and heart rhythm irregularities that one could encounter on the way to Mars. On the spacecraft he envisions, Mars-bound in the year, say, 2018, there may lurk harmful bacteria or carbon monoxide. No problem. The deadly substances will be detected by smart sensors – microprocessors no bigger than a thumbnail – that roam autonomously through the spacecraft, communicating their finds to a computer that warns the crew.

To cope with infection, Sutton plans a factory to make drugs, even new ones, to cope with possible organisms on Mars. Miniature optical and ultrasound devices will image body and brain, while a small X-ray machine keeps track of any bone loss. Smart sensors embedded in clothing will monitor an astronaut's vital functions. The crew will be able to craft body parts, Sutton says, precisely tooled to an astronaut's personal anatomy and genome stored in computer memory. Researchers are building artificial liver, bone and cartilage tissue right now.

Lying in wait beyond the Earth's atmosphere, solar radiation poses additional problems. Coronal mass ejections fling billions of tons of electrically charged gas into space, relegating Earth's volcanic eruptions to mere hiccups. Nevertheless, NASA officials are confident that accurate monitoring will warn astronauts of such events, allowing the crew to take refuge in an area where polyethylene shielding will absorb the radiation.

A second kind of radiation, cosmic rays from the Milky Way or other galaxies, is a more serious threat – possessing too much energy, too much speed for shielding to be effective. "There's no way you can avoid them," says Francis Cucinotta, manager of NASA's Johnson Space Centre. "They pass through tissue, striking cells and leaving them unstable, mutilated or dead. Understanding their biological effects is a priority."

Another major concern is the psychological health of astronauts. And there's a new stressor on a three-year Mars Mission – people, other members of the crew. NASA found that the stresses of isolation and confinement can be brought on rapidly simply by giving people few tasks. Mir astronaut Andrew Thomas described how six astronauts were confined in a 12-foot square room for a week. "If you give them little to do, stress can be achieved in a couple of days," says Thomas.

Will NSBRI meet Daniel Goldin's deadline for a decision on Mars? "Yes, we will, perhaps even before. We're very confident," says Laurence Young, the director of NSBRI. Meanwhile, some of NSBRI's research may bear fruit on Earth. The institute has made one discovery that promises to save many people at risk of sudden cardiac death, usually brought on by a heart-rhythm disturbance called ventricular fibrillation. This kills 225,000 people in the US each year.

Richard Cohen, head of the NSBRI cardiovascular team, explained that zero gravity may – emphasising "may" – incite this condition in astronauts. So the team invented a non-invasive diagnostic device that measures extremely tiny changes in heart rhythm. The team found that the device can be used as part of a standard stress test to identify patients at risk. Then pacemaker-like devices can be implanted to regulate the rhythm anomalies. "This technology has the potential to save hundreds of thousands of lives," says Cohen. "NASA can be proud."

Such discoveries are no accident, says Michael E. DeBakey, a cardiovascular surgeon who has saved many hearts himself. "The key word is research. When I was a medical student and a patient came to the hospital with a heart attack, things were mostly a matter of chance. Today there's a better than 95 per cent chance of surviving. Now that all comes from research. The unfortunate thing is that there are people, even some scientists, who look at the money that goes to NASA and say we could use that money to support our work. That's very short-sighted. The more research that's done in any area of science, the better off everyone is going to be."

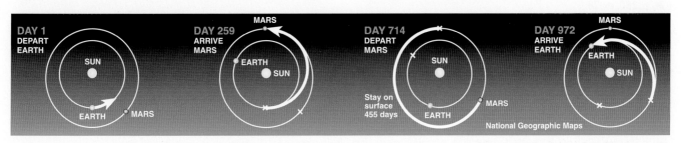

EXAM PRACTICE
True/False/Not Given

3 Now complete the four tasks in this section.

Questions 1–5

Do the following statements agree with the information in the reading passage?
Write

TRUE	*if the statement agrees with the information*
FALSE	*if the statement contradicts the information*
NOT GIVEN	*if there is no information*

1   Everyone who travels in space suffers from feelings of motion sickness initially.....................
2   Astronauts are likely to increase in height while in space.   ....
3   It's important for astronauts to exercise in order to keep their muscles fit.   ....
4   Scientists have found a way of protecting astronauts from solar radiation.   ....
5   If astronauts are given tasks to do, they quickly begin to suffer from stress.   ....

Multiple choice

REMINDER

● Make sure there is evidence in the text for the options you choose.

Questions 6–8

*Choose **THREE** letters, A–F.*
*According to the text, which **THREE** of the following are part of the role of the*
National Space Biomedical Research Institute (NSBRI)?

A   To develop technology for monitoring astronauts' health in space
B   To study the effects of weightlessness during short space missions
C   To advise NASA on whether to launch a future Mars mission or not
D   To improve the design of spacecraft in order to reduce the risk of injury to astronauts
E   To assess and select suitable astronauts for long space flights
F   To find ways of dealing with medical emergencies on board a spacecraft

---

KEY LANGUAGE
-ing forms vs infinitive
▶ p. 230, ex. 28

Labelling a diagram

In this task you name parts of a diagram using words from the passage. Look at the *Task Approach* below.

TASK APPROACH

● Study the instructions and the diagram, including any labels that are given. Think about the information which is missing. Can you make any guesses?
● Scan the text until you find each topic, and study the information carefully.
● Make sure you use exact words from the passage in your answers.

Questions 9–11
Label the diagram below.
*Choose **NO MORE THAN THREE WORDS** from the passage for each answer.*

A   B

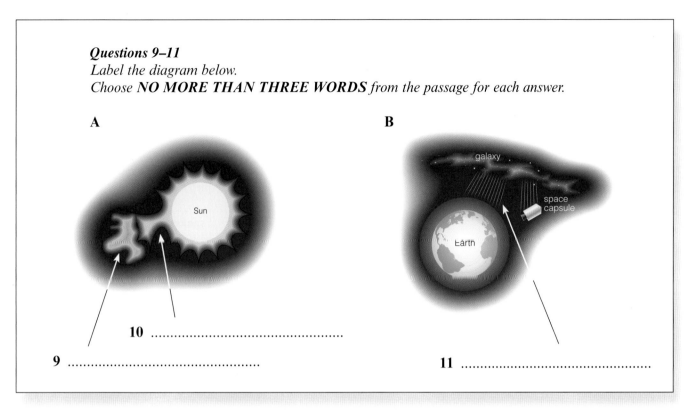

10 ....

9 ....   **11** ....

Matching

REMINDERS
- In the text, underline or highlight the experts listed.
- In the list of opinions, underline or highlight key words and phrases.

Questions 12–14
*Look at the following opinions (**12–14**) and the list of experts (**A–F**) below.*
Match each opinion to one of the experts.

12 A discovery made by NSBRI could prevent many deaths.

13 It is inevitable that astronauts will be subject to a range of biomedical changes.

14 Research carried out by NASA is ultimately beneficial for everyone.

Experts
A	Oleg Gazenko	**D**	Laurence Young
B	Jeffrey Sutton	**E**	Richard Cohen
C	Francis Cucinotta	**F**	Michael E. DeBakey

KEY LANGUAGE
Word partners
▶ p. 231, ex. 29
e.g. *aural stimulus*

Academic Style 8 *Nouns and Noun Phrases 3*

Introduction

Noun phrases often include several pieces of information about the headword (main noun) in a condensed form, which can make a text quite dense and difficult for the reader. Knowing how more complex noun phrases are formed will help you to read and understand academic texts better.

1 The main elements of the message in the sentence below are underlined. a) what is the message and b) what additional information is given?

Soaring <u>greenhouse gas emissions</u> *subject*, driven by a surge in coal use in countries such as China and India, <u>threaten</u> *verb* dramatic <u>temperature rises</u> *object*.

Adding information in a noun phrase

Additional information can be added **before** the headword (e.g. <u>dramatic</u> temperature rises) or **after** it (e.g. <u>greenhouse gas emission driven by a surge in coal use</u>).

2 One way of providing information **before** the headword is by adding another noun to make a **noun + noun combination** (see *Academic Style 3*, page 56). Find three examples in the sentence above.

3 Another way to add information **before** the headword is with determiners (*a, the, this, some*, etc.), adjectives and adverbs. Read the following extract and complete the table below.

Excavations in an open-pit coal mine in Colombia have uncovered the remains of several very large prehistoric snakes, thought to be the largest ever to have lived on Earth. The fossils, found in rock formations dating back 60m years, give scientists an unprecedented insight into the giant animals that ruled the tropics after the sudden disappearance of the dinosaurs 65m years ago.

Determiner	Adverb/adjective	Headword
	several very large prehistoric	a) ....
b)	c)	insight
d)	sudden	e) ....

4 There are also several ways of conveying information **after** the headword. Complete the examples in the table below using words from the text in exercise 3.

Type	Headword	Example
1 prepositional phrase (in, of, with, etc.) Says where, when, what for, etc.	excavations	a) in ....
2 past participle clause (*-ed*, etc.) = Short relative clause (passive meaning)	snakes	b) <u>thought</u> ....
3 present participle clause (*-ing*) = Short relative clause (active meaning)	rock formations	c) <u>dating</u> ....
4 relative clause (that, who, etc.)	animals	d) <u>that</u> ....

5 Match each underlined section a)–d) in the text below to one of the four constructions in exercise 4.

Gold bullion a) <u>said to be worth $1bn</u> has been located among the wreckage of the warship HMS Victory. According to the company b) <u>that led the search</u>, the ship was also carrying important naval artillery when it sank in 1744. A huge bronze cannon c) <u>weighing four tons</u> has already been recovered, and this is the only gun d) <u>of this size and type</u> still in existence.

Changing clauses into noun phrases

6 Academic English often prefers to use shorter noun phrases rather than longer relative clauses. Rewrite the underlined parts of these sentences as noun phrases.

1 Six <u>companies that supply energy</u> have announced <u>that they are reducing prices</u>.
2 <u>Scientists who are involved in the study</u> say that the process produces some <u>by-products that are not desirable</u>.
3 It is <u>an electronic thermometer which reacts fast</u> and <u>has a three digit LED screen</u>.
4 The company has paid millions of dollars in fines for <u>activities that were against the law</u>.

Academic Vocabulary 8

Meaning

1 Study the examples and match each academic word in bold to the correct meaning, A, B or C. Check your answers in a dictionary if necessary.

consistently/constantly

1 … there is a drive to **constantly** work harder, to excel.
2 Statistics have **consistently** shown that smoking causes lung cancer.
   A happening regularly or all the time
   B always behaving in the same way

visual/visible

3 The moon's craters are sometimes **visible** from Earth.
4 … a confused brain engenders **visual** illusions
   A relating to seeing
   B possible to see

aspect/prospect

5 … the **prospect** of a rocket trip around the moon
6 Salary is not the most important **aspect** of a person's job.
   A event that will probably happen
   B part of a situation

2 Complete these sentences using words from exercise 1.

1 Judges must be (consistent/constant) in their application of the law.
2 (Visual/Visible) perception is the ability to interpret information from (visual/visible) light reaching the eye.
3 A good essay should cover every key (aspect/prospect) of the subject.

Word Building

3 Choose the correct prefix to form the opposite of the following adjectives.

in-	il-	im-	un-

1 accessible
2 appropriate
3 consistent
4 legal
5 precise
6 specified
7 stable
8 valid

4 Complete these sentences with answers from exercise 3 above.

1 It is …………… to sell cigarettes to someone under 16.
2 It would be …………… to use idiomatic language in a formal essay.
3 The argument is …………… because it is not based on any evidence.

4 Unfortunately, the results of the tests have been …………… so far.
5 After the earthquake, many buildings were left dangerously …………… .

Grammar

5 Rewrite the following sentences using the academic words in brackets, so that the meaning is the same. Do not change the form of the word in brackets.

1 A solar charger is designed to recharge batteries using the sun's rays. (**device**)
2 Parents should talk to their children's teachers regularly. (**communicate**)
3 You may need to adjust the temperature slightly. (**adjustment**)
4 The spacecraft will be used to investigate climate change. (**investigation**)
5 Experts are very concerned about the psychological health of the astronauts. (**major**)
6 This technology could save thousands of lives. (**the potential**)

Revision

6 In each of the following sentences a wrong part of speech has been used. Cross out each wrong word and replace it with the correct part of speech.

1 According to a survey, IT is one of the most stress professions.
2 The article made a useful contribute to the discussion of climate change.
3 It's important to emphasis that further research is needed.
4 Learning is based on the interact between teacher and student.
5 He is an energy supporter of the Green Party.
6 The population has begun to expansion rapidly.

5 Choose five academic words from this page to learn or revise, and write personal examples to help you remember them.

1 ……………………………………………………………
2 ……………………………………………………………
3 ……………………………………………………………
4 ……………………………………………………………
5 ……………………………………………………………

16 ▶ Going forward

going forward in the near future – used
especially in business and economic
contexts: *Going forward, we will be able to
deliver better products to our customers and
better returns for our shareholders.*
(www.longmandictionariesonline.com)

In this unit you will practise	Key Language	Exam Focus
• Talking about the future; discussing personal goals • Listening and note completion; multiple choice; labelling a diagram; completing a table • Explaining how something works • Presenting an opinion; summarising sentences	Expressing probability **Writing Practice** Task 2: Presenting and justifying an opinion	**Speaking:** Parts 1–3 **Listening:** Sections 3, 4 **Writing:** Tasks 1, 2

Lead-in

1   Read predictions A–G below and answer the following questions.

1   Why were predictions A–D ill-advised?
2   Why are we bad at predicting the future? Look especially at predictions E–G.

A   ❝ He will never amount to anything. ❞
(Albert Einstein's high school report, c. 1890)

B   ❝ We have struck an iceberg, but there is no danger. The ship is unsinkable. ❞
(Captain's announcement to passengers, *Titanic*, 1912)

C   ❝ Man will never set foot on the Moon. ❞
(British astronomer, 1957)

D   ❝ I think there is a good market for about five computers. ❞
(IBM chief executive, 1958)

E   ❝ The Americans may have need of the telephone but we do not. We have plenty of messenger boys. ❞
(British official, 1876)

F   ❝ No mere machine can replace an honest and reliable clerk. ❞
(Remington company official, on turning down the rights to manufacture the typewriter, 1896)

G   ❝ There will probably be a mass market for no more than a thousand motor cars in Europe. There is, after all, a limit to the number of chauffeurs who could be found to drive them. ❞
(Spokesman for Daimler-Benz, 1900)

I never think of the future — it comes soon enough.
ALBERT EINSTEIN

2   The illustrations opposite show predictions about the future made during the 1950s. Discuss the following questions with a partner.

1   How accurate were these predictions?
2   Which aspects of modern life were not foreseen?

B You'll cook on a solar range.

C Because everything in her home is waterproof, the housewife of 2000 will do daily cleaning with a hose

A You'll eat food from sawdust.

D You'll shop by picture phone.

E You'll drive to work in an aero car.

Focus on speaking 1 *Predicting the future*

▶ *Focus on Academic Skills for IELTS pages 98–99*

1 Writing in 2001, the science-fiction writer, Brian Dana Akers, made a number of predictions for the 21st century. These he divided into four categories:

A Definite   B Almost certain   C Probable   D Possible

The list below represents some of Brian Dana Akers's predictions. Work in pairs to discuss which of the four categories A–D to put them in.

- Fewer species
- More countries
- Longer lives
- Global warming
- First contact with an alien civilisation
- More city dwellers
- Computers everywhere

- Massive, rapid change
- Nuclear war or meltdown
- Alternative energy replaces fossil fuels
- More people
- Space exploration and colonies in space
- Fewer languages

You will hear more about these predictions in *Focus on listening 1.*

KEY LANGUAGE

Expressing probability
▶ p. 232–233 ex. 30
It's (highly) likely/probable

▶ *Focus on Academic Skills for IELTS page 109, ex. 2*

EXAM PRACTICE

Part 3: Discussion

2 Discuss these points.

- Are you generally optimistic or pessimistic about the future?
- Do you believe that we will ever contact beings from other planets?
- Do you think computers will eventually replace human workers?
- Do you think that the environment will change dramatically because of global warming?

Focus on listening 1 *Reality or science fiction?*

Section 3: Note completion

Read the advice on note completion and study questions 1–10.

REMINDER

- Read through the notes and try to predict the answers – this will help you tune in to the topic and vocabulary so you will be able to listen more effectively.

Questions 1–10
*Complete the notes below. Write **NO MORE THAN THREE WORDS AND/OR A NUMBER** for each answer.*

- Immense changes – political, **1** .... , etc.
- Changes caused by forces of demography and **2** ....
- Species disappearing faster than they're coming **3** ....
- **4** .... languages spoken today expected to die out.
- Earth's long-term capacity estimated at **5** ....
- Trend will continue towards **6** .... countries.
- New energy economy theoretically possible by **7** ....
- Space exploration depends on **8** ....
- Countries likely to enter the space race: China, **9** ....
- Factors making nuclear war possible:
- availability of nuclear know-how
- number of **10** ....
- quantity of nuclear weapons

Focus on listening 2 *The techno-house*

Section 4: Multiple choice, labelling, table completion

REMINDERS

Read the advice on labelling a diagram and study qustions 1–10.

- Study the diagram and try and describe it in your mind. Think about topic vocabulary.
- Look at the labels and also the gaps. Can you guess any answers?

Questions 1–3
*Choose the correct letter, **A**, **B** or **C**.*

1 In Britain
   - **A** most new houses include the latest technology.
   - **B** the technology for high-tech houses is not available.
   - **C** few people are interested in buying high-tech houses.

2 An important concern for British homebuyers is that a house
   - **A** is in a suitable place.
   - **B** has a modern design.
   - **C** is environmentally friendly.

3 How do Integer Project buildings compare with conventional houses?
   - **A** They cost more to buy.
   - **B** They can be built more quickly.
   - **C** They are more complicated to construct.

Questions 4–6
*Label the diagram of the Millennium House. Write **NO MORE THAN THREE WORDS** for each answer.*

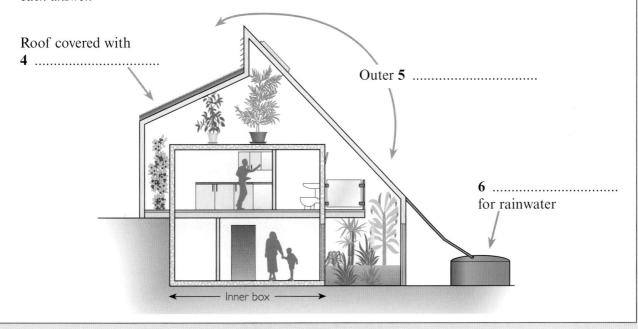

Roof covered with
4 ....

Outer **5** ....

6 ....
for rainwater

Inner box

Questions 7–10
Complete the table below. Write **NO MORE THAN THREE WORDS** *for each answer.*

Company	Building(s)	Features
Berkeley Homes	Housing development	• Computers control heating and lighting. • Water is recycled and heated by **7** ....
Laing Homes	**8**	• Heating, TV and security system can be operated from the **9** .... via a website.
Redrow Homes	'House for the Future'	• The **10** .... is moveable, so shape and size of rooms can be changed. • Water and waste are recycled.

Focus on writing 1 *Explaining how something works*

Task 1

1 In this task, you are given a diagram of a machine, device or process and you have to explain how it works. Read the following advice.

TASK APPROACH

▶ *Focus on Academic Skills for IELTS* pages 101–102

- Study the diagram and identify the key features and/or main stages.
- Begin with a brief overview of the equipment and its function.
- Continue by describing the main stages in the process, step by step.
- End with a brief concluding sentence if possible.

EXAM TIP: This language is also useful in the Interview when you don't know the exact word you need.

2 Study the *Useful language* and then do the exercises below.

> **Useful language: Describing function and structure**
>
> **Function**
>
> a system/a process
> a device/a tool/a machine
>
> (which is used) for + -*ing*
> which causes/allows/enables ... to + inf.
> which prevents/stops ... from + -*ing*
>
> **Structure**
> It consists of ... contains ... (is) called ... (is) divided into ... sections
> The ... (is / are) connected to ... by ...

1 Explain the function of the following.

   a) a burglar alarm   b) central heating   c) a photocopier

2 Explain the function and structure of the following.

   a) an umbrella   b) a hammer   c) sat-nav

3 Study the diagram and answer the questions below.

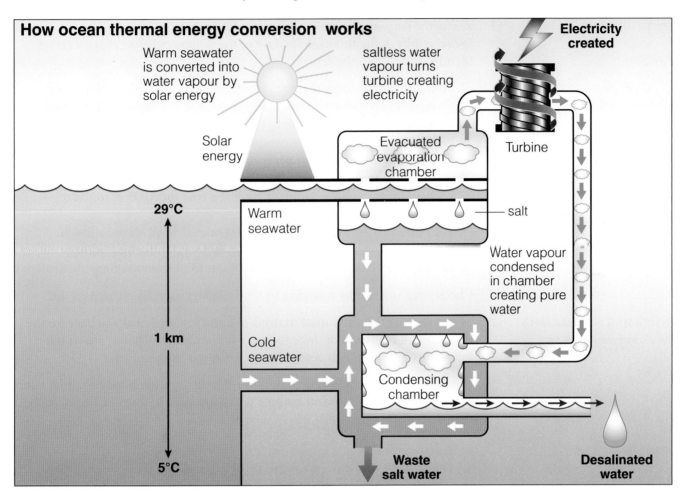

How ocean thermal energy conversion works

Warm seawater is converted into water vapour by solar energy

saltless water vapour turns turbine creating electricity

Electricity created

Solar energy

Evacuated evaporation chamber

Turbine

29°C

Warm seawater

salt

Water vapour condensed in chamber creating pure water

1 km

Cold seawater

Condensing chamber

5°C

Waste salt water

Desalinated water

1 What are the three main parts of the system?
2 What is the depth of the ocean at this point?
3 What other useful product does the system produce, apart from energy?

4 Complete the gapped model answer, using up to *THREE WORDS AND/OR A NUMBER.*

Ocean Thermal Energy Conversion OTEC is a system **1** ………. energy, using the difference **2** ……… between water at the surface of the sea, which can be up to **3** ……… Celsius, and water **4** ……… deep, which is only 5 degrees Celsius.

The system **5** ……… an evacuated evaporation chamber, which **6** ……… a turbine and a condensing chamber. Water at the surface of the sea **7** ……… by the sun and this warm water is introduced into the **8** ……… , where it boils. As it boils, salt is deposited and water vapour is generated. This water vapour causes a turbine **9** ……… and create electricity. **10** ……… the turbine, the water vapour **11** ……… a condensing chamber, which is cooled by **12** ……… from the depths of the ocean. The water vapour is condensed in this chamber, producing pure **13** ……… . Meanwhile, waste salt water **14** ……… to the ocean and the process can begin once more.

(Approximately 156 words)

Focus on speaking 2 *Personal goals*

SPOT THE ERROR

1 Revise the language for expressing probability that you practised in *Focus on speaking 1* by doing this exercise. Five of the sentences below contain errors. Identify and correct the errors.

1 I think it's highly likely that the tax on cigarettes will be increased.
2 If you don't complete your last assignment, you probably will fail the course.
3 They say there's 90% probability of snow later today.
4 What is the likelihood of the company making a profit, in your view?
5 There seems to be very little prospect of achieving a lasting peace in the area.
6 According to me, it's unlikely that the government will be re-elected.
7 I believe there is a high chance of finding a cure for AIDS in the next few years.
8 The possibility of a reduction in interest rates is small, in my opinion.
9 It's unlikely for a new form of energy to be found in the near future.
10 I don't think there's much likelihood of our local team reaching the finals.

Check your answers by referring to *Key language* exercise 30 on page 232.

DISCUSSING FUTURE GOALS
Part 2: Individual long turn

2 In this practice task, you need to think about a personal goal you have for the future. Work in groups of three to five. You should each choose one of the following topics. You will need to speak for about two minutes.

Describe one of the following topics. You should say what is special about your chosen goal and explain your reasons for choosing it. Before you begin, study these reminders.

REMINDERS

- Try using a mindmap to make notes.
- Think of as many aspects of your topic as possible.

- **The place** you would like to live
- **The job** or career you would like to have
- **A country** you would like to visit
- **Something** you would like to own
- **A skill** you would like to learn

► Focus on *Academic Skills for IELTS* pages 107, 111, ex. 4

Focus on writing 2 *Summarising sentences*

1   It is often helpful to summarise the main points you have made as a way of introducing the next stage of the argument. Look at the *Useful language* box below for examples of this language.

Useful language: Summarising

Having looked at a number of problems / benefits **we should now consider** … discussed

Given   the problems / factors which   **we can turn to the question of** …
        have been outlined,   **we need to ask** …

---

2   Summarising sentences are often used to 'signpost', that is to give the reader an indication of the direction your argument is taking.

Complete the following sentences in a logical way.

1   Having discussed the benefits of single-sex education, we should consider …
2   Given the expense of subsidising school lunches, we must ask …
3   Having examined the case for the death penalty, …
4   … we need to ask whether taking a gap year is such a good idea.
5   … we can now turn to the arguments of more traditional educators.
6   … we have to examine the case presented by those who oppose speed limits.

EXAM PRACTICE
Task 2

3   Read the following reminders and then write your answer to the task below.

REMINDERS

- Make notes before you begin, perhaps using a mindmap.
- Decide on your choice of approach, depending on your reaction to the point of view expressed.
- Revise ways of expressing disagreement by challenging a claim, pointing out a false conclusion or asking a rhetorical question (pages 83 and 84).
- Check your work, especially for your most frequent mistakes, before you finish.

WRITING PRACTICE
Presenting and justifying an opinion (example answer)
▶ page 248, ex. 15

You should spend about 40 minutes on this task.

Write about the following topic.

Advances in science and technology and other areas of society in the last 100 years have transformed the way we live as well as postponing the day we die. There is no better time to be alive than now.

To what extent do you agree or disagree with this opinion?

Give reasons for your answer and include any relevant examples from your own knowledge or experience.

Write at least 250 words.

ERROR HIT LIST

few/a few; little/a little

✗	✔
We need to discuss few problems that have arisen.	We need to discuss <u>a</u> few …
Unfortunately, there's a little that can be done.	… there's <u>a</u> <u>little</u> that can be done.

- Used with articles, **a few** and **a little** mean 'some', e.g. *Would you like a little soup? Have you got a few minutes to spare?*

- Used without articles, **few** and **little** have the meanings 'not many', 'not much', 'not enough', e.g. *There's little hope of finding survivors. Few places on Earth are as beautiful.*

- **very few** and **very little** give an even more negative meaning: 'hardly any', e.g. *Very few people speak my language. There's very little time left.*

middle position adverbs: *probably/definitely; always/usually,* etc.

✗	✔
You definitely should go there …	You <u>should definitely</u> …
I sometimes have been asked to give advice.	I <u>have sometimes</u> been asked …
There probably is an easy solution to the problem.	There <u>is probably</u> an easy solution …

- Middle position adverbs include *probably, definitely, even, really* and adverbs of **frequency** (*always, usually,* etc.); **time** (*already, still,* etc.); and **degree** (*almost, hardly,* etc.).

- These adverbs usually go in front of the main verb, e.g. *I already know the answer.*

- When the main verb is *be*, they go immediately after it, e.g. *We're always pleased to help.*

- When there is more than one auxiliary verb, they go immediately after the first one, e.g. *We'll soon be leaving. I have often been asked that question.*

in spite of/despite

✗	✔
Despite the economy is weak, some companies are still making a profit.	<u>Although</u> the economy is weak, …
	Despite the economy <u>being</u> weak, …
	Despite <u>the fact that</u> the economy is weak, …

- **In spite of** and **despite** are followed by a noun or *-ing* form. They mean the same as **although** + clause.

- They are prepositions (not conjunctions) and cannot introduce a clause.

nevertheless

✗	✔
The dangers of cigarettes are well known, nevertheless people continue to smoke.	The dangers … well known<u>.</u> <u>Nevertheless</u>, people continue …

- **nevertheless** is a formal word meaning 'despite the fact which has just been mentioned'. It's normally used at the beginning of a sentence.

Critical Thinking 4 *Evaluation*

Introduction

It's often not enough to describe a situation or to list facts in academic writing. You also need to make your personal attitude towards a topic clear to the reader. This is called **evaluation**. This section looks at some key ways of indicating evaluation through choice of language.

Adverbs

Example: **Interestingly,** *there were more female than male applicants for the job.*

Single adverbs are a common way of indicating evaluation in academic English. Typical adverbs used in this way include:

clearly	interestingly	surprisingly
correctly	naturally	unfortunately
fortunately	predictably	unusually
hopefully	significantly	worryingly

1 Choose the more suitable adverb from each pair to complete the following statements.

1 **Fortunately / Hopefully** a solution to the problem will be found in the near future.
2 Recent studies suggest that tea and coffee are **surprisingly / inevitably** good for our health.
3 Unusual weather suggests that the world's climate is **clearly / correctly** out of balance.
4 Death risks from smoking are **significantly / worryingly** reduced within five years of quitting.
5 The announcement of tax increases caused a(n) **predictably / unusually** negative reaction.

It + verb + adjective + that / to

Example: It was **difficult** *to establish the exact cause.*

This pattern is another way of indicating evaluation in academic English. Typical adjectives used in this way include:

adjectives followed by *that-clause*			
clear	notable	true	significant

adjectives followed by *to-infinitive clause*		
difficult	easy	hard

adjectives followed by either *that-* or *to-clause*		
disappointing	(im)possible	(un)necessary
essential	interesting	ridiculous
important	(un)likely	surprising

2 Add suitable *It* + verb + adjective constructions to the following statements.

1 … humans will be able to control the Earth's weather some day.
2 … distinguish between cancer cells and healthy tissue.
3 … think that wealth is the only mark of success in life.
4 … Experts reassured the public …… bird flu would reach Canada.
5 … over a third of the population didn't cast a vote in the last presidential election.

Emphasisers

Example: He's **highly** *qualified. Students pay* **just** *£1,200 in top-up fees*

Emphasisers are adverbs which affect the strength of a message. **Maximisers** (e.g. *highly*) increase the strength, while **minimisers** (e.g. *just*) weaken it.

Typical emphasisers in academic English include:

Maximisers	Minimisers
very, extremely, fully, highly, almost, strongly, entirely, completely, totally, really, significantly	relatively, quite, fairly, slightly, rather, only, somewhat, hardly, barely, just

3 Add minimisers to the following sentences.

1 e-commerce is a recent development.
2 The results of the enquiry have been delayed.
3 Forty-five per cent of exam candidates achieved a C grade or higher.
4 The operation was partially successful.
5 Over a fifth of the newspaper consists of advertising

4 Add maximisers to the following sentences.

1 Farming contributed to the region's wealth.
2 He was opposed to capital punishment.
3 The treatment is regarded as effective.
4 The situation is not clear yet.
5 This latest statement contradicts what was said earlier.

Critical Thinking for IELTS

- When planning for writing, think carefully about your attitude to the topic.
- Use a range of evaluative language to make this clear to the reader.

Critical Thinking 4 Evaluation

17 ▶ Avoiding gridlock

gridlock /ɡrɪdlɒk/ *n* [U] **1a** a situation in which streets in a city are so full of cars that they cannot move: *Only better public transport can save the city centres from the threat of gridlock.* (Longman Exams Dictionary)

In this unit you will practise

- Discussing traffic and transport topics
- Short-answer questions; classification; True/False/ Not Given
- Reading and locating information; sentence completion; flow-chart completion
- Reading and answering short-answer questions; classification; True/False/Not Given
- Vocabulary: verbs expressing increase and decrease

Key Language

British vs American vocabulary

Topic vocabulary: Cars and traffic

Talking about research

Writing Practice

Task 1: Presenting and comparing data

Exam Focus

Speaking: Part 3

Reading: Exam practice 1, 2

Lead-in

Walking*
Hundreds of kilometres per year per person

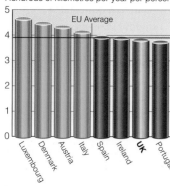

*Top and bottom four

Cycling*
Hundreds of kilometres per year per person

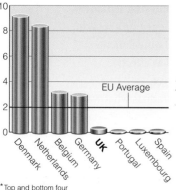

*Top and bottom four

1 In pairs, complete each sentence 1–8 by choosing the correct ending a–h.

1 Exhaust fumes from road transport now constitute
2 Road traffic is expected to increase
3 Urban rush-hour drivers are typically stuck in traffic
4 Riding a transit bus is 26 times
5 Seven out of ten journeys to work are
6 Industrial nations use 59% of global transportation energy, despite
7 Traffic congestion wastes
8 Car emissions cause

a by 50% by 2026.
b the early deaths of 30,000 people a year in the US.
c having just 19% of the world population.
d by car.
e over 70% of all emissions of carbon monoxide.
f safer than car travel.
g three billion gallons of gas a year in the US.
h for an average of 46 hours a year.

2 Choose suitable figures from the box below to complete each sentence.

1 A typical American family spends $ .... a year to own and run a car.
2 A good bicycle can be bought for $.........., lasts for years and costs almost nothing to operate.
3 The energy and resources needed to build one medium-sized car would produce .... bicycles.
4 It costs $.......... to build and maintain one space in a bike rack, while one car parking space in a multi-storey car park costs about $...........
5 .... bicycles typically fit into the road space used by one car.

| 7–12 | 50 | 100 | 300 | 8,000 | 8,500 |

EXAM TIP Relevant factual information can be useful for supporting an argument in the Interview or Writing paper.

3 Check the Key to exercises 1 and 2 on page 254 and make any corrections necessary, then answer these questions in pairs.

1 Explain which of the facts in exercise 1 or 2 surprised you most and why.
2 Choose two or three facts which might be interesting to mention in an essay or discussion on the topic of: '*The world would be a better place without private cars.*' Highlight or make a note of these.
3 Explain the advantages of a bicycle as a means of transport.

Focus on reading 1 *Avoiding gridlock*

KEY LANGUAGE
British vs American vocabulary
▶ p. 233, ex. 31
e.g. *automobile* (US), *car* (UK)

1 Work in pairs to answer the following questions before reading the text. Note this text comes from an American source and contains a number of American words and spellings.

1 What is 'gridlock'? Check the dictionary definition on page 168 if necessary.
2 What causes gridlock?
3 How can gridlock be avoided?

Avoiding Gridlock

A Beginning from the earliest sledges, people have sought ways to move themselves, messages and goods from place to place. By 1900, speeds of up to 120 miles per hour were possible on land. The spread of steamships, the introduction of railways and the development of bicycles were among the transforming innovations of the nineteenth century. The scope of transportation in industrial countries was further widened in the twentieth century with the mass production of the automobile and the development of air travel.

B Since the end of World War Two, motor vehicle production has risen almost linearly. As a result, the global car fleet now numbers more than 500 million. In the United States, the number of household vehicles increased at six times the rate of the population between 1969 and 1995. However, while road traffic dominates the transportation system, air transportation is the fastest growing segment. And as road

and air travel have grown, rail has become relatively less important. (See Figure 1.)

C Cities have spread out over larger expanses of land as builders have constructed wide expressways and ample parking to accommodate motor vehicles. Asked in a survey to identify the top influence shaping the American metropolis, a sampling of urban historians, social scientists and architects

chose the highway system and dominance of the automobile as the number-one influence. As cities sprawl, cars become essential while transit, bicycling and walking become less practical. In the Czech Republic, for instance, car use has surged and public transit use has fallen as the number of suburban hypermarkets ballooned from one to fifty-three between 1997 and 2000.

D Advances in transport technology have brought benefits, but growing vehicle fleets and escalating fuel use have also created problems. Researchers estimate that nearly a million people are killed on the world's roads each year, and most of them are pedestrians. Motor vehicles impede other forms of traffic and cause delays. Congested roads in São Paulo have prompted the wealthiest residents to take to the skies, boosting the city's helicopter fleet to the third largest in the world, after New York and Tokyo.

Roads also cause profound changes to ecosystems. A great deal of land in car-dependent cities is lost to roads and parking lots. Water quality and quantity both suffer in proportion to the amount of paved roads and parking that cover a watershed. Plants and animals are killed during road construction as well as by vehicles. And roads promote the dispersal of species that are not native to a given area, and alter the physical and chemical environment.

E The single largest contributor to the costs of transportation borne by society in many countries is illnesses and deaths from air pollution. One challenge, therefore, is to tackle immediate health threats from the most polluting vehicles. By adopting policies that promote cleaner technologies, governments can take one important step towards solving this problem.

F Today transportation planners increasingly recognize that building more roads does not necessarily solve traffic problems. Michael Replogle, a transportation specialist, came up with this analogy: "Adding highway capacity is like buying larger pants to deal with your weight problem." As new roads attract more cars, regions that have invested heavily in roads have fared no better at easing traffic than those that

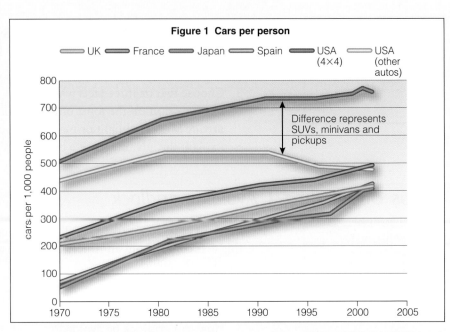

Figure 1 Cars per person

UK France Japan Spain USA (4×4) USA (other autos)

Difference represents SUVs, minivans and pickups

have invested less. Measures to diversify transportation options include regulations to curb car traffic, price incentives to reduce motor vehicle use and boost alternatives, and changes in urban design that enhance the viability of cycling, walking and public transit.

G Individuals make choices every day about different transportation modes, based, in part, on perceptions about safety and comfort. Poorly maintained cycling and public transport networks are therefore less appealing than the private car. High-income residents of Mexico City, surveyed in a recent study of travel behavior, said they feared robberies on buses and that they would use public transportation only if it were safe, well organized and comfortable.

People are also influenced by the car's image of freedom, power and modernity. To many young people, getting a driver's license is a rite of passage. In one survey in England, young adults were asked: "Imagine that you were only able to have one of the following two rights – the right to vote in an election, or the right to obtain a driving license – which would you

choose?" Some seventy-two per cent chose the license.

H But views and behaviors may change, as congested roads thwart the car's promise of individual freedom and power. The category "traffic congestion and urban sprawl" was the major concern of both urban and suburban Americans, and nationwide it tied with and violence" as the top worry according to five public-opinion surveys around the country.

I The automobile came to dominate the world's roads in the last century, the age of oil. Today, with the environmental and social costs of road traffic well documented, and with natural gas and renewable sources of energy beginning to replace oil, we can envision a new generation of transportation systems. Vehicles could be cleaner, and cities could be made more attractive and functional, with integrated networks for bicycles, bus, rail and new types of transit. People will need to work together to build this future, and to confront those in government and industry with vested interests in transportation systems that belong to the last century.

From *Making Better Transportation Choices* by Molly O'Meara Sheehan, Worldwatch Institute

EXAM PRACTICE
Locating information

2 **This task was introduced in Unit 13. Before you begin, read the reminders.**

REMINDERS

- Study the example, if there is one, to see how information from the text is expressed.
- Read through the questions and underline or highlight key words and phrases.

▶ *Focus on Academic Skills for IELTS* page 103

- Remember to look for parallel expressions when searching for each topic in the text.

Questions 1–5
The reading passage has nine sections labelled **A–I**.
Which section contains the following information?
*Write the correct letter, **A–I** next to each question **1–5**.*

Example	*Answer*
The importance of the manufacture of cars?	**A**

1 a description of the attraction of the car for young people?
2 a comparison of the growth of the population and car ownership?
3 a list of energy sources which have advantages over oil?
4 reasons why expanding the road network has failed to reduce traffic congestion?
5 a city where the rich have begun commuting by air?

Sentence completion

3 **Now complete the next task in this section. Refer the to task *Task Approach* on page 33 if necessary.**

Questions 6–9
*Complete each sentence with the correct ending, **A–H** from the box.*

6 The development of modern cities both reflects and contributes to

7 Animals and plants may spread to new areas as a result of

8 Possible strategies for reducing the use of private cars include

9 Improved standards of maintenance would increase the popularity of

A transport technology
B public transport
C motor vehicle production
D traffic congestion
E the dominance of the automobile
F changes in town planning
G road building
H new energy sources

Flow-chart completion

TASK APPROACH

▶ *Focus on Academic Skills for IELTS* page 128

4 Refer to the *General strategies* for this kind of task on page 91 if necessary.

- Information is in note form, not grammatically correct sentences.
- Answers may not be in passage order.
- Choose answers from the text. Check spelling carefully.

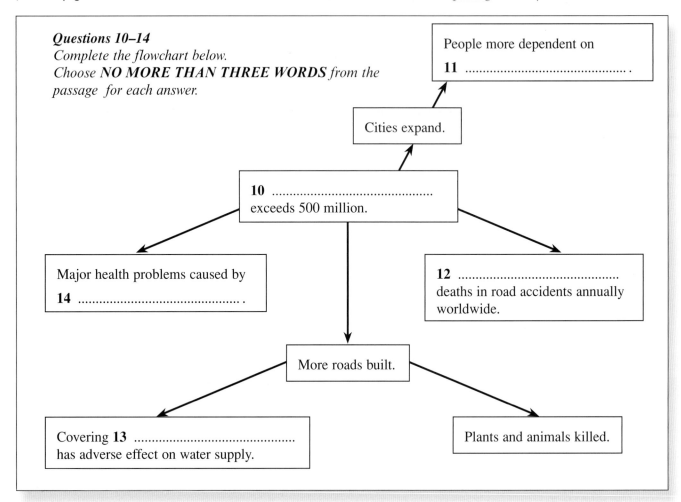

Questions 10–14
Complete the flowchart below.
Choose **NO MORE THAN THREE WORDS** *from the passage for each answer.*

People more dependent on
11 ....

Cities expand.

10 ....
exceeds 500 million.

Major health problems caused by
14 ....

12 ....
deaths in road accidents annually
worldwide.

More roads built.

Covering **13** ....
has adverse effect on water supply.

Plants and animals killed.

Focus on vocabulary *More or less?*

1 Several of the verbs below come from the reading text on pages 169–170. Decide whether the general meaning in each case is A or B.

A become or make more, wider or bigger
B become or make less or smaller

1 balloon	5 dwindle	9 rise	13 surge
2 boost	6 escalate	10 shrink	14 widen
3 diminish	7 fall	11 sprawl	15 restrict
4 drop	8 lessen	12 spread	

2 Complete the following sentences with the correct words from the list in exercise 1.

1 In winter, temperatures rarely .... above freezing.
2 We intend to .... class sizes to a maximum of 20 pupils.
3 Revenue is likely to .... from $98 million to $65 million.
4 They plan to .... the road from three lanes to four.
5 A win would help to .... the team's confidence.
6 Fire .... quickly through the building.
7 Exercise can significantly .... the risk of heart disease.
8 I'm afraid the present situation could .... and lead to war.

Focus on speaking *On four wheels*

Part 3: Discussion

KEY LANGUAGE
Topic vocabulary: Cars
and traffic
▶ p. 233, ex. 32

Work in pairs to discuss the following mini topics. Mention reasons for and against each point of view. Refer to the *Useful language* below before you start.

1 The world would be a better place without cars.
2 The best way to reduce traffic congestion is to build more motorways.
3 Anyone who breaks the law while driving should lose their licence.
4 The minimum age for driving should be 25.

Useful language: Balancing an argument		
In some ways I agree …	On the other hand	there are also arguments against …
It may seem an attractive idea …	but	I'm not sure it would work in practice …
I don't think so myself…	Having said that,	I can see why some people believe that …

Focus on reading 2 *Demolishing stereotypes*

1 Discuss the questions in exercises 1 and 2 before reading the text. Choose from the list of driver-types A–E below to answer these questions. Give reasons for your answers.

1 Who is **the safest** driver?
2 Who is **the most dangerous** driver?
3 Who is **most likely to drink and drive**?

KEY LANGUAGE
Talking about research 2
▶ p. 233, ex. 33
e.g. *Demolishing stereotypes*

WRITING PRACTICE
Presenting and comparing
data (guided practice)
▶ p. 249, ex. 16

A Male driver under 25 years old   D Female driver more than 35 years old
B Female driver under 25 years old   E Older driver (55+)
C Middle-aged male driver

2 Now answer this question.

Which is a more significant factor in road accidents: Gender or Age?
You will find answers to most questions in the text on page 174.

3 Now read the text to find answers to most of these questions.

Demolishing Stereotypes

In a study titled Male and Female Drivers: How different are they? Professor Frank McKenna of the University of Reading looked at the accident risk between men and women. He found that men drive faster, commit more driving violations, and are more inclined to drink and drive. They look for thrills behind the wheel, while women seek independence. And, although anecdotal evidence might suggest otherwise, women are not starting to drive as aggressively as men.

The question of whether, as drivers, women differ from men is important, because it could affect insurance premiums, which are closely geared to accident statistics.

Despite the increase in women drivers, McKenna's researchers found no evidence that this is changing accident patterns. It seems that age is far more important than gender in the car. It is the biggest single factor in accident patterns, and, while inexperienced new drivers of both sexes are more likely to be involved in accidents, the study found striking new evidence to confirm that young men drive less safely than any other group.

The survey shows that men and women aged 17 to 20 are most likely to be involved in bend accidents – men almost twice as often – but the difference decreases as drivers mature.

Nearly half of all accidents involving young men and one-third of those involving young women take place when it is dark. Again, there is a steady decrease in such accidents as drivers grow older, but gender differences remain significant until drivers reach the age of 55.

Although there is little difference between men and women in the distance they keep from the car in front, there are differences across age groups. Young drivers show less regard for the danger of following more closely, and young men are likely to 'close the gap' as an aggressive signal to the driver in front to speed up or get out of the way.

Men consistently choose higher speeds than women of the same age and driving experience. "This could be because men seek a thrill when they drive," says McKenna. "Speed choice is one of the most important causes of accidents. But breaking the speed limits is regarded by men as a minor offence."

Contrary to public belief, young drivers, as a group, are more likely to avoid drinking alcohol if they are driving, while men in the 30 to 50 age group admitted to drinking the most alcohol before driving.

Men are most likely to nod off, probably because they are willing to drive for longer periods without a break – driver fatigue is another important factor in accidents.

According to Andrew Howard, of the Automobile Association, "We have to combat the group that speeds for thrills. The key is how men are brought up to look at the car. It is this which needs to be addressed."

Short-answer questions   Refer to the *Task Approach* on page 70 if necessary before you begin.

Questions 1–4

*Answer the questions below. Write **NO MORE THAN THREE WORDS AND/OR A NUMBER** for each answer.*

1 What is women's motivation for driving? ....

2 Which group of drivers has grown in number in recent years? ....

3 What is the most significant factor in accident patterns? ....

4 After what age do men and women drive equally safely at night? ....

Classification

▶ *Focus on Academic Skills for IELTS* page 90

TASK APPROACH

In this task you classify events, characteristics or other pieces of information into specific categories. This tests your ability to see connections between facts in the passage.

- Underline or highlight key words in the question
- Skim or scan to locate relevant information, then read for detail.
- The answers are not in text order.

Questions 5–9
According to information in the passage, classify the following characteristics (5–9) as applying to:

> **A** men in general
> **B** young men in particular
> **C** both young men and young women

Example	*Answer*
They are the most likely to have accidents while driving.	**B**

5   They may follow another car closely to make the driver go faster.   ....

6   They are more likely to have accidents due to tiredness.   ....

7   They are the least likely to drink and drive.   ....

8   Driving gives them a feeling of excitement.   ....

9   They are the most likely to have accidents on bends.   ....

True/False/Not Given

Refer to the notes on True vs Not Given answers on page 72 if necessary, then complete the final task of the exam practice.

Questions 10–14
Do the following statements agree with the information in the reading passage?
Write

TRUE	*if the statement agrees with the information*
FALSE	*if the statement contradicts the information*
NOT GIVEN	*if there is no information*

10   There is a common belief that women are becoming more aggressive drivers. ....

11   The results of the study may influence the cost of motor insurance.   ....

12   Young women are most likely to have accidents when driving at night.   ....

13   Men do not consider it very serious to exceed the speed limit.   ....

14   Women are more prone to accidents at junctions than men.   ....

Academic Style 9 *Being Impersonal*

Introduction

Academic Style 2 advised you to avoid using personal pronouns, like *I*, or *you*, *me* or *my*. This section looks at ways of writing clearly without using these pronouns.

Talking about the organisation of your text

1 Here is the opening of a student's essay. Underline the personal pronouns the student has used.

> *My essay is a comparison of two methods of producing energy. I'm comparing energy produced from fossil fuels, such as oil, with what is called renewable energy, that is, energy produced from natural resources. I'm going to write about two aspects of renewable energy production. To begin with let's start with wind energy.*

Academic writers avoid using these pronouns by referring to what the text will do rather than what the writer will do. This is because the reader wants to know about the text and the topic, not the person who wrote it.

2 Which of the words below are names of a) types of texts b) parts of a text? c) illustrations in a text?

report	graph	section	paragraph
essay	introduction	table	conclusion
figure	list	article	diagram

3 a Coursebook writers often use words like *unit*, or *section module* to avoid using *I*. Look at the introduction at the top of this page and underline the two verbs that represent what a *section* can 'do'.

b Match the opening phrases 1–4, with a suitable ending, a)–e). Endings may match more than one opening.

c Underline the main verb in each sentence.

    1   This essay   3   This problem
    2   The graph   4   Diagram 2a

    a) … illustrates the structure of a typical flowering plant.

    b) … will be discussed in the next section.

    c) … shows participation in a sport or physical activity by different age groups in the UK.

    d) … reveals that UK households with home access to the internet increased from 2006 to 2010.

    e) … will argue that investing money in education brings social and economic benefits to a company

4 Now try to rewrite the opening of the student's essay from exercise 1 in a more impersonal style. Make any changes you think are necessary.

Presenting your own opinion

As pointed out in *Academic Style 2* it is not usual to use phrases like *In my opinion*, or *I think* in academic writing. Instead, opinion is often expressed less directly, using this pattern:

> **Present simple + evaluative nouns, verbs, adjectives or adverbs**

Using the simple present means that the writer believes that this statement is true: expressions like *It is a fact that* or *Indeed* are not needed. In addition, writers often use general nouns such as *problem, solution, issue, benefit* to show they think something is a good or bad thing.

    e.g. It *is important…* (**present simple + evaluative adjective**)
        A *serious problem is*….(**evaluative adjective+ general noun + present simple**)

In the conclusion of an essay, you may need to summarise the solution to a problem, or make recommendations based on the argument you have presented. This is generally done very simply, using the modal verb *should*, or the pattern

> *It is* + evaluative adjective + recommendation.

5 Underline the words used in these examples to show the writers' opinions.

    1 Governments should invest in research into natural energy sources and encourage people to use public transportation instead of travelling by car.

    2 Houses where people mostly spend their time must be well designed to supply comfort for the occupants. A house has to be able to counteract the main disadvantages of the local climate.

    3 The best way to save money and energy is to try to reduce power consumption.

    4 It is essential to reduce global warming in order to avoid an economic and humanitarian catastrophe.

6 Rewrite this extract from a student's essay to make it more impersonal and academic, using all the formal types of language you have studied in these sections.

> *I think that energy is very important in our life. I come from a country with very cheap electricity but in the UK it is very expensive. We should try to save as much as we can. We must turn on the light only in the room that we are using and try to use the washing machine as little as we can to save electricity.*

Language Fact
In an electronic corpus, containing over 1 million words of University Management Studies texts, the phrase *In my opinion* occurred only once.

Academic Vocabulary 9

Meaning

1 The extracts below come from Unit 17. The numbers in brackets show which reading text they are from. Choose the answer A or B which best matches the meaning of the academic words in bold.

1   Road traffic **dominates** the transportation system. (1)
    A   is the most important form (of)
    B   is in control of

2   Air pollution is the single largest **contributor** to the costs of transportation (1)
    A   somebody who gives money to
    B   something which helps to cause

3   … regions that have **invested** heavily in roads … (1)
    A   spent money on   B   studied

4   … (government) policies that **promote** cleaner technologies. (1)
    A   encourage   B   control

5   different **modes** of transport … (1)
    A   manufacturers   B   methods

6   The question of whether men differ from women as drivers could **affect** insurance premiums. (2)
    A   cause to change   B   cause strong emotions

7   Men seek a thrill when they drive, while women **seek** independence. (2)
    A   try to avoid   B   try to achieve

8   Men drive faster and commit more traffic **violations**. (2)
    A   jams   B   offences

Word partners

2 Choose an appropriate verb from the box to combine with each academic word

make	do	give	reach	have

1   an impact (on)   4   a contribution   7   a conclusion
2   an error   5   a consequence   8   a target
3   a lecture (on)   6   a job   9   a prediction (about)

Word Building

3 Use the word in capitals at the end of each line to form a word that fits the space. Think about the part of speech which is needed in each case.

1   The test measures children's …………… in reading. ACHIEVE

2   …………… thinking is needed to solve the problem. CREATE

3   A drop-in class requires no long-term …………… from students.   COMMIT

4   A successful manager needs to be …………… as well as efficient.   COMMUNICATE

5   You need to bring some form of …………… with you to the exam.   IDENTIFY

6   People who do badly at school may …………… themselves as failures.   PERCEPTION

7   There is more than one possible …………… of the data.   INTERPRET

8   Foreign …………… in the country rose by 50% last year.   INVEST

Pronunciation

4 Examples A–C show three different word stress patterns. Identify one word from each group which has a different word stress pattern from the rest. When you've checked your answers, practise saying the other words with the correct stress.

A   oOoo e.g. *economy* communicate, psychology, statistics, technology

B   ooOo e.g *economic* academic, generation, perception, violation

C   ooOoo e.g *economical* analytical, psychological, significant, technological

Revision: *Grammar*

5 There is one grammar mistake in each sentence. Underline the mistakes and correct them. Page numbers are given in brackets for you to check your answers if necessary.

1   The calculation has an error. (37)
2   The company has been founded since 1900. (37)
3   He's hoping to gain work experience in overseas. (37)
4   The driving test is consisted of two parts, theory and practical. (77)
5   It's a job which is involved a great deal of travel. (117)
6   Despite of the high cost of a university education, enrolments are rising. (117 *Error Hit List* 166)

6 Choose five academic words from this page to learn or revise and write personal examples to help you remember them.

1   ……………………………………………………………………
2   ……………………………………………………………………
3   ……………………………………………………………………
4   ……………………………………………………………………
5   ……………………………………………………………………

18 ▶ Small world

It's a small world *coll* used when one meets a person who has an unexpected connection with someone or something in one's past: *When I was introduced to the new boss I realized that we'd both been to the same school. It's a small world.* (Longman Dictionary of English Idioms)

In this unit you will practise	Writing Practice	Exam Focus
• Discussing travel and the tourism industry • Listening and short-answer questions; completing a table and flow-chart; sentence completion; labelling a diagram; multiple choice • Dealing with different data • Presenting the solution to a problem • Topic vocabulary: pronunciation: sounds	Task 2: Comparing data	**Speaking:** Parts 1–3 **Writing:** Tasks 1, 2 **Listening:** Sections 2, 3

Lead-in

1 In pairs, look at the picture and discuss the questions.
   1 Would you like to be there. Why/Why not?
   2 What positive and negative aspects of tourism does it illustrate?

2 Choose countries from the list to answer questions 1 and 2 below.

Canada	Germany	Mexico	Spain
China	Italy	Russia	UK
France	Japan	South Korea	USA

1 Over the last 50 years cheap air fares have made long-distance travel common. Which **three** countries are the most visited tourist destinations in the world?

2 Tourism has been marketed as a universal benefit. But not everyone can afford to travel. Which **three** countries spend most on tourism?

Check your answers on page 255.

'This hotel is renowned for its peace and solitude. In fact, crowds from all over the world flock here to enjoy its solitude.'

AN ITALIAN HOTEL BROCHURE

Focus on speaking 1 *Tourism*

TOPIC VOCABULARY

1 Complete the sentences below with words from the box, making any changes required. Check the meaning in a dictionary if necessary.

attraction	*class*	*destination*	*industry*	*resort*	*office*

1 Oxford is one of the most popular tourist .... in England.
2 For a simple tourist .... hotel it's very comfortable.
3 Call at the tourist .... in town for information on sightseeing tours.
4 The majority of Turkey's wealth is generated by the tourist ....
5 Many luxury tourist .... have been developed along the Emerald Coast.
6 The Eiffel Tower is probably the best known tourist .... in France.

PRONUNCIATION: DIPHTHONGS

2 When two vowels are pronounced together quickly, they form a combined sound called a *diphthong*. For example, /e/ + /ɪ/ produce the diphthong /eɪ/ as in *Spain*.

Put the following words in the correct group, according to their pronunciation.

buy	*eight*	*freer*	*freight*	*grey*	*height*	*light*
we're	*sphere*	*weigh*	*while*	*year*		

1 /eɪ/ as in US**A**, Austr**a**lia ....
2 /aɪ/ as in Ch**i**na, Dub**ai** ....
3 /ɪə/ as in Kor**ea**, Kashm**ir** ....

▶ *Focus on Academic Skills for IELTS* page 123, ex. 4

3 Work in pairs. Imagine that foreign tourists regularly visit your local area. Which of the following would you object to most, and why? Number them 1 (most) – 6 (least). Compare your answers with the results of a survey on page 255.

a) Group of tourists take photographs of the local people without asking permission.	....
b) Prices in your local shops double during the tourist season.	....
c) Tourists are disrespectful or inappropriately dressed at an important cultural event.	....
d) Tourists expect you to speak their language.	....
e) Tourists criticise your home and country in front of you.	....
f) Most of the money tourists spend goes to companies based in another country.	....

4 Make three suggestions about ways of making tourism fairer and more acceptable for local people.

Focus on listening 1 *Worldwide student projects*

Section 2: Short-answer questions, table/flow-chart completion

Before you listen, read the following advice on completing flow charts.

TASK APPROACH

- Study the questions so that you know the topic and understand the sequence.
- Think about the kind of information needed in each space.
- Remember to check the spelling carefully.

Question 1
Answer the question below.
Write **NO MORE THAN THREE WORDS** *for your answer.*

1   What does WSP aim to promote?

Questions 2–7
Complete the table below.
Write **NO MORE THAN THREE WORDS AND/OR A NUMBER** *for each answer.*

LIST OF PROJECTS		
Country	**Project**	**Special information**
Japan	Village 2	Some knowledge of 3 .... required
Poland	Renovating children's 4	
Mexico	Sea turtle conservation	Accommodation in school with 5 ....
China	Architecture: planning and design	US$ 6 .... payable on arrival
India	Medicine: centre for 7 .... children	

Questions 8–10
Complete the flow-chart. Write **NO MORE THAN THREE WORDS AND/OR A NUMBER** *for each answer.*

You complete an application and send it with 8 ....

↓

We send 'Welcome Pack' with: • General information
                                • Formal 9 ....
                                • A questionnaire for you to return

↓

We use the questionnaire to match you to your job.

↓

10 .... before departure we send full details of your placement.

Focus on writing 1 *Presenting the solution to a problem*

KEY LANGUAGE
Conditionals
▶ p. 220–221, ex. 15
Expressing probability
▶ p. 232, ex. 30

EXAM PRACTICE
Task 2

WRITING PRACTICE
Problem/solution (example answer)
▶ p. 236, ex. 2

▶ *Focus on Academic Skills for IELTS pages 53–55*

1 In some questions, you have to consider a problem and either evaluate possible solutions or suggest a solution of your own. The best way to answer this question is to follow the evidence-led approach described on page 65. Study the paragraph plan.

NB Conditional structures and expressions of probability are both useful for this task.

2 Now answer this exam question.

> **PARAGRAPH PLAN**
>
> <u>Opening paragraph</u>
> • Outline the problem in your own words.
> • Discuss its implications.
>
> <u>Middle sections</u>
> • Evaluate a number of possible solutions.
> • Include the pros and cons in each case.
>
> <u>Closing paragraph</u>
> • Sum up your argument.
> • Give your view as to the best solution(s).

You should spend about 40 minutes on this task.

Write about the following topic.

> *Most of the world's poor live in countries where tourism is a growing industry. The issue is that tourism does not benefit the poorest.*
>   *How can the income generated by tourism benefit the poor? And how can we ensure that tourism does not destroy traditional cultures and ways of life?*

Give reasons for your answer and include any relevant examples from your own knowledge or experience.

Write at least 250 words.

Focus on speaking 2 *Time off*

TOPIC VOCABULARY

1 Study the table. The example shows three possible noun-noun combinations with 'tour'. Write three words from the list in each space to form other common combinations.

| agent | air | ~~bus~~ | camping | expenses | ~~guide~~ | job | ~~operator~~ |
| package | pay | rail | season | sickness | skiing | space | |

tour	e.g. *operator, guide, bus*
holiday	a)
travel	b)
c)	holiday
d)	travel

2 What do you think the following expressions mean? Discuss your ideas.

a) armchair traveller   b) tourist trap   c) eco tourism

- What are the advantages of being an armchair traveller?
- Describe a tourist trap you have experienced.
- What kind of holidays would qualify as 'eco-tourism'?

EXAM PRACTICE
Part 1: Interview

3 Work in pairs to ask and answer the following questions.

REMINDER

- Notice the **tense** or **verb form** in the examiner's questions as this can help to guide your reply.

1 How do you usually spend your holidays?
2 What's the best holiday you've ever had?
3 How do you prefer to travel, by road, rail or air?
4 Would you rather go on holiday with one or two friends, or in a group?

Part 2: Long turn

4 Work in pairs. Take it in turns to tell each other about the topics below. Speak for one to two minutes. Your partner should listen carefully and ask the 'closing questions' to finish.

REMINDERS

- Take a few moments to make brief notes before you begin, perhaps using a mindmap.
- Make sure you cover all the points on the topic card.

TOPIC 1

Describe a tourist attraction you have visited. **You should say:** **what the attraction was** **when you visited it** **what you saw and did there** **and explain what you thought of it.**

Closing questions
Would you recommend other people to go there?
Do you enjoy sightseeing in general?

TOPIC 2

Describe a tourist attraction you would like to visit. **You should say:** **what the attraction is** **what you can see and do there** **how you know about it** **and explain why you would particularly like to go there.**

Closing questions
Have you been to a place like that before?
Do you like travelling in general?

Part 3: Discussion

REMINDERS

5 Discuss questions 1–5 below. Before you begin read these reminders.

- Don't give one-word answers – this is a chance to demonstrate your fluency.
- Be prepared to express a variety of opinions and to give reasons for them.
- Try to use a range of structures and vocabulary, and to use linking expressions, e.g. *Because, as, since* (reason); *and, as well as, besides* (addition); *although, even though, despite* (concession), etc.

> **KEY LANGUAGE**
> Names of tenses
> ▶ p. 211, ex. 2

1 What changes have there been in the last 50 years or so in the way people travel?
2 Have all the developments in travel and transport been for the better?
3 Some young people nowadays have a 'gap year' between school and university, when they travel or work in another country. Is this a good idea?
4 How should people prepare before visiting another country?
5 What new developments will there be in tourism in future, do you think?

Focus on listening 2 *The end of oil*

EXAM PRACTICE
Section 3: Sentence completion, labelling a diagram, multiple choice

You are going to hear a discussion between a student called Andrew and his tutor. Before you listen study questions 1–10.

Questions 1–3
Complete the sentences.
*Write **NO MORE THAN TWO WORDS AND OR A NUMBER** for each answer.*

1 Andrew's tutor thinks he can achieve a .... if he maintains his progress.
2 His tutor advises him to avoid the subject of ....
3 The assignment needs to be .... words long.

Questions 4–6
Label the pie chart.
*Write **NO MORE THAN ONE WORD** for each answer.*

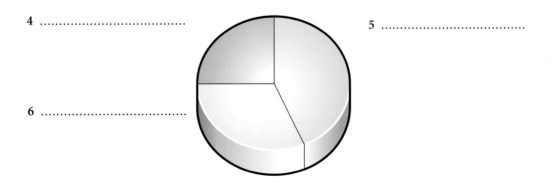

4 ....

5 ....

6 ....

Questions 7–9
Complete the sentences below.
*Write **NO MORE THAN THREE WORDS** for each answer.*

7 The former .... and .... are both producing less oil, now than in the past.

8 The ...., Canada, ... and .... use the most gasoline per head.

9 .... and .... are increasing their gasoline use most rapidly.

Question 10
*Choose the correct letter **A**, **B** or **C**.*

10 Which solution does Andrew favour?

    A finding new sources of oil

    B developing an alternative to oil

    C imposing taxes on the use of oil

Focus on writing 2 *Dealing with different data*

1 Complete the following reminders about presenting and comparing. You can check your answers on page 253.

REMINDERS

DON'T
- try to describe every detail. Concentrate on a) ....
- speculate about reasons. Stick to the b) ....
- spend longer than c) .... on Task 1 in the exam. Task 2 carries d) .... marks.

DO
- begin with a(n) e) .... and end with a concluding comment about f) ....
- think about the g) .... way to describe data, e.g. *one in three, twice as many*, etc.
- try to h) .... points together logically.

When there is more than one set of data:
- be clear about what each contributes to the overall i) ....
- look for opportunities to j) .... information, **between** diagrams as well as **within** them.

2 **Study the bar charts below and answer these questions before you do the exam task.**

1 What is the focus of each bar chart?
2 What are the main parameters in each case?
3 How many countries are compared? What does the additional bar represent?
4 Which countries have the highest and lowest car use? What is the difference between them?
5 Which country makes greatest use of alternative transport (bus, tram, metro, bike)? How does this compare with the EU average, and with the UK?
6 How long do British drivers spend commuting to work each day?
7 Take the two countries which make most use of alternative transport, and look at their positions on the commuting time bar chart. What conclusions can you draw?

EXAM PRACTICE
Task I

You should spend about 20 minutes on this task.

The bar charts below give information on road transport in a number of European countries.

Summarise the information by selecting and reporting the main features, and make comparisons where relevant.

Write at least 150 words.

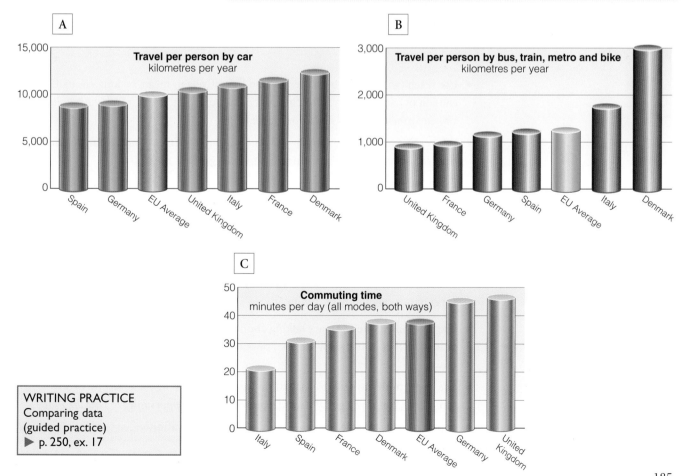

WRITING PRACTICE
Comparing data
(guided practice)
▶ p. 250, ex. 17

ERROR HIT LIST

✗	✔
You can make journeys to local places of interest.	You can <u>take trips</u> to …
We've done several journeys in Asia.	We've <u>made/been on</u> several journeys …
The travel to college takes about an hour.	The <u>journey</u> to college …
I enjoy foreign travelling.	I enjoy foreign <u>travel~~ling~~</u>.

- **a journey** is the period of travel between two places, especially over a long distance. Use **go on** or **make a journey** (not *do*), e.g. *Take some food with you for the **journey**. Every year the Atlantic salmon makes a 2,000-mile journey to warmer zones.*

- **a trip** is a return journey, especially for a short visit. Use **go on, make** or **take a trip**. It occurs in compound nouns such as *day trip, business trip,* etc.

- **travel** (uncountable) is the general activity of moving from place to place, e.g. ***Travel** broadens the mind.* It occurs in compound nouns such as *air travel, travel sickness,* etc.

reach/arrive

✗	✔
The ladder didn't reach to the window.	The ladder didn't reach ~~to~~ the window.
I first reached this country in 1984.	I first <u>arrived in</u> this country …
The best way to reach your purpose is to persevere.	… to <u>achieve</u> your purpose …

- Use **reach** (without *to*) both literally and figuratively to mean 'be long enough, high enough or large enough to reach a particular point', e.g. *I can't **reach** the top shelf. Unemployment **reached** a peak in March.*

- You **reach** a place after a long or difficult journey, e.g. *It was midnight by the time we reached the capital.* Otherwise **arrive (at/in)** or **get to** is more usual.

- Use **achieve** to mean 'succeed in doing something' or 'get the result that you want'.

possibility/opportunity

✗	✔
I'm considering the possibility to buy a car.	I'm considering the possibility <u>of buying</u> …
You will have a possibility of joining in.	… an <u>opportunity for</u> joining in.

- Use **possibility** when you are talking about something that may happen, e.g. *There's a **possibility** that it may snow later on.* **possibility** is followed by *of* + *-ing*, or a *that* clause.

- Use **opportunity** to refer to a situation where it is possible for someone to do something, e.g. *If you go to Madrid, you will have an **opportunity** to visit the Prado.*

- **opportunity** is followed by *for* or *of* + *-ing* or by *to* + infinitive, e.g. *an **opportunity** of making money/to make money.*

Reflective Learning 5 *Time management*

Introduction

Good time management is essential for study and exam success, and is also valued by employers. It describes the techniques we use to complete specific tasks and to achieve personal, academic or professional goals.

Key time management skills include:

- **Planning** – deciding what needs to be done, and how/when/where best to do it
- **Subdividing tasks** – breaking tasks into smaller, more manageable parts
- **Prioritising** – putting tasks in order of importance so as to make best use of your time
- **Setting goals** – deciding what you can realistically aim to achieve in a set time
- **Allotting work time** – predicting how much time is needed for a task
- **Analysing results** – tracking your progress and adjusting your programme as necessary

Private study

1 Discuss these questions in pairs.

1 What time of day do you study best? Are you a morning or an evening person?

2 Where do you prefer to study? What makes it a suitable place?

3 Do you study at a regular time every day? Or whenever you find time?

4 How long is a typical lesson at school/college? How long is it before you feel restless?

5 What kind of things distract you from your work? How can you avoid these?

6 Do you often find reasons to delay starting work? If so, how can you avoid this?

The exam

2 How prepared are you? Discuss in pairs.

1 How much time should you allow for each of the following tasks in the IELTS test?

   1 to read one text and answer the questions on it? (Academic Reading) _____

   2 to complete Task 1? (Academic Writing) _____

   3 to complete Task 2? (Academic Writing) _____

   4 to transfer answers to the answer sheet (Listening) _____

   5 to read through the instructions on the task card and make notes (Speaking, Part 2) _____

   6 to speak about a topic (Speaking, Part 2) _____

2 Tick those tasks you have practised and know you can complete within the exam time limit. Put a cross by those you haven't practised or can't yet complete within the exam time limit. What can you do to improve your performance in these?

Ideas for managing study time

- **Keep a Study Diary**

List all your study commitments, including classes and hand-in dates for assignments. Set specific times for private study. Review your study programme each week and adjust as necessary.

- **Make a To-Do List**

At the start of each study period, make a list of the tasks you want to achieve and put them in order of priority. Begin immediately with the most important.

- **Monitor your progress**

Become more aware of how you use time. In your Study Diary note when you begin and end each study period, and any breaks you take. Record how much you achieve each time.

- **Build in some time for yourself**

Plan regular times to relax, see friends, take exercise. You deserve it! You will study more effectively as a result.

Setting goals

3 How well do you manage your time for private study and/or in an exam situation? Give yourself a mark out of 10. Aim to continue doing what you already do well. Make a point of:

- trying one or two new time management strategies.
- practising timed exam tasks

Reviewing goals

4 Work with a partner. Check the 'favourite' mistake you each identified on page 147. Discuss how much success you've had in eliminating this. If you've made good progress, choose another 'favourite' mistake for elimination. If not, what more can you do to tackle the problem?

Remember the **Plan/Do/Review** cycle followed in these sections. For really effective learning, continue to set new learning goals and monitor your progress as you continue your academic career.

19 ▶ Face value

take something at face value to accept a situation or accept what someone says, without thinking that there might be a hidden meaning: *You shouldn't always take his remarks at face value.* (Longman Exams Dictionary)

In this unit you will practise

- Discussing facial expressions and gesture
- Reading and answering short-answer questions; table completion; multiple choice
- Long turn and two-way discussion
- Vocabulary: word families, dependent prepositions

Key Language
Modal verbs

Exam Focus

Speaking skills

Speaking: Parts 1–3

Lead-in

1 It is generally agreed that there are a number of basic universally recognised facial expressions including *anger, contempt, disgust, fear, happiness, sadness* and *surprise*. Work in pairs to identify five basic emotions shown below.

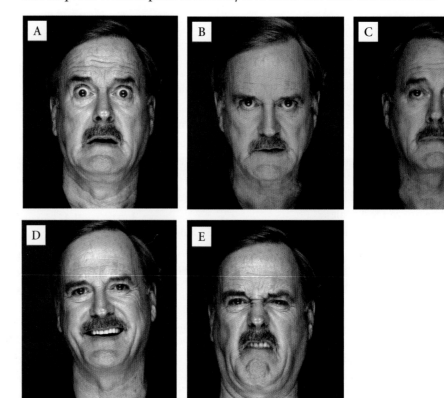

You can check your answers on page 253.

2 With your partner, discuss the following questions.

1 Which of the expressions were easiest, and which most difficult to identify?
2 What other signals (e.g. gestures) might accompany these facial expressions? Are they equally universal?
3 On what occasions would you try to hide the following feelings? Why?

Anger   Fear   Disgust

Focus on speaking 1 *Face the facts 1*

Part 3: Discussion

Discuss the following questions in pairs.

1 How do facial expressions help in everyday communication?
2 What kind of difficulties can arise when people communicate without being able to see each other, by telephone or email for example?
3 Why is it better for children to play with friends than play on a computer?
4 How can you tell if someone is embarrassed? What kind of situations make you feel embarrassed?

Focus on reading 1 *Face the facts 2*

SKIMMING AND SCANNING

1 Each of the extracts (A–D) relates to one of the questions (1–4) above. Read the extracts quickly and answer the following questions.

1 Which extract below relates to each question above? Write the letters next to the questions.
2 Which words or phrases helped you identify the correct extract?

A

When two pedestrians collide, there's none of that anger we see when motorists cross one another's path. The experts say that we don't see aggression when people collide because they're liable to exchange little signs of apology, which you are unable to do when you're trapped inside a car.

The same kind of misunderstandings can easily happen on email. The style of email is terse but informal, so people get annoyed where no rudeness is intended, because they can't see the expression on the face of the person they're communicating with. If they could, the problem would instantly disappear.

B

Facial movements associated with embarrassment act as an apology, with the gaze averted and the eyes moving downwards. A brief smile flickers across the face and the hand often moves to the cheek. This may be accompanied by blushing. The whole response takes about five seconds.

Studies done in court rooms in the United States prove that of the defendants found guilty in court, the ones who blushed and looked embarrassed after the verdicts were read out received shorter sentences than those who appeared unrepentant. Embarrassment on the face is the equivalent of apologising. It helps to show people that you know you've transgressed the rules.

Interestingly, embarrassment seems only to appear at the age of eighteen months, much later than other expressions. It's at this age that a child first gets an awareness of people around it and a social sense.

C

Eye contact and head nods are crucial to our conversations. The single head nod indicates that the nodder has understood what is being said and wishes the speaker to continue. Rapid and repeated head nods indicate that the speaker wishes to speak. Eye contact is also vital, and we spend up to 75 per cent of the time looking at the person we're talking to. We can underline the points we are making by raising our eyebrows or pursing our lips. The eyebrows can also be raised in a kind of visual question mark at the end of a sentence.

D

Most children learn to express themselves naturally through face-to-face communication with their parents and their peers. But in the modern world this kind of contact is diminishing. Instead of playing football and fighting, children are spending increasing amounts of time in front of computers. Numerous studies have shown that this can cause relationship problems later in life. Without the feedback of another's emotions, children risk becoming withdrawn and depressed.

For more information on this subject
see www.bbc.co.uk/science/humanbody

READING FOR DETAIL

2 Do the extracts on page 189 confirm your answers in *Focus on speaking 1* or not? What additional points do they make?

REFERENCE LINKS

3 Say what the words in italics below refer to in the extracts.

> **KEY LANGUAGE**
> Reference links
> ▶ p.217–218, ex. 10

▶ *Focus on Academic Skills for IELTS* page 45, ex. 4

1 The *same* kind of misunderstandings … (Text A)
2 If they *could* … (Text A)
3 *This* may be accompanied … (Text B)
4 … *those* who appeared unrepentant. (Text B)
5 … an awareness of people around *it* (Text B)
6 … *this* kind of contact (Text D)

DEALING WITH UNKNOWN VOCABULARY

4 You may not be familiar with the following words, but it's possible to work out the general meaning from the context. Explain the general meaning in your own words.

A 1 collide   B 4 unrepentant   C 6 crucial   D 7 peers
  2 liable   5 transgressed   8 feedback
  3 terse

Focus on reading 2 *Face*

Answer questions 1–6 which are based on the reading passage opposite.

Questions 1–5
*Answer the questions below using **NO MORE THAN THREE WORDS** for each answer.*

1 How does facial skin differ from other human skin?
2 Which **TWO** facial muscles are employed when we are afraid?
3 When can human beings first show an expression of happiness?
4 Which part of the face has a limited role as an indicator of mood?
5 Which subject did Gottfried Leibnitz have an important insight into?

Questions 6–10
*Complete the table below. Choose **NO MORE THAN THREE WORDS** from the passage for each answer.*

	Sadness	Fear	Anger	Surprise
Eyebrows	6	Rise	Descend	7 ....
Mouth/Lips		8	9	Open
Eyes	Look 10	Widen		Open

FACE
by Daniel McNeil

A We rely on facial signals constantly, yet we cannot define them. We are reading a language we cannot articulate and may not consciously notice. Good face-reading can provide an insight into a person's true feelings. As always, real skill demands practice but anyone can learn a few basics.

B We have twenty-two facial muscles on each side, more than any animal on earth. In common with most muscles, they anchor in bone. Unlike most, they attach to skin, making the face more mobile than the skin on other parts of the body. These muscles form a complex skein, as shown in Figure 1, but some stand out in particular. The *zygomatic major* is the smile-maker. It runs across the cheek to the corner of the mouth, which it pulls upwards. The *corrugator* knits the eyebrows together, causing vertical furrows in between. Most pleasant expressions involve the *zygomatic major*, most unpleasant ones the *corrugator*.

C Other muscles also play important roles. The busiest is the *frontalis*, the curtain-like muscle of the forehead, which causes the eyebrows to rise in expressions of fear or for emphasis. Its opposite number, the *procerus*, causes the eyebrows to descend in sadness. When the mouth is retracted horizontally in fear, we employ the *risorius*. These signals emerge in infancy and on a reliable timetable. The smile and surprise appear at birth, disgust and distress (sadness) between zero and three months, the 'social smile' at one and a half to three months, anger at three to seven months, and fear at five to nine months.

D Anger is a dark look of concentration. The eyebrows descend and the lips tighten. An angry face is a warning. Fear has almost the opposite characteristics. The eyes widen and the eyebrows rise. Surprise resembles fear and often precedes it. Both the eyes and mouth fly open and the eyebrows rise and arch. Disgust centres on the nose, not otherwise a very expressive facial feature. It may partly turn up, wrinkle and contract, as when we sense a bad smell.

E What about telling lies? On the whole we are not very good at detecting lies. Even individuals one would expect to be skilled – judges, policemen and psychiatrists – fail here and score only slightly above average. Prisoners spot lies fairly well, possibly because they live in a world of deceit and must become expert.

What is the secret? In the eighteenth century, Gottfried Leibnitz suggested that studying the face and voice could improve lie detection – and he was right.

F First, a warning: there is no sure give-away of a lie. Anyone who relies on a lone cue will often be misled, so good lie-spotters seek out several. One key involves smiling. The liar shows fewer genuine smiles and more masking or cover-up smiles and these, along with higher vocal pitch, are the best evidence of deception. True smiles make little starburst crinkles in the skin near the eyes; false smiles tend not to. The phoney smiles may occur too early or too late for the context, halt instantly instead of dying away, or show a slight asymmetry.

Figure 1

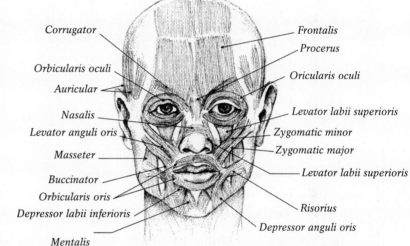

Corrugator
Frontalis
Procerus
Orbicularis oculi
Oricularis oculi
Auricular
Nasalis
Levator labii superioris
Levator anguli oris
Zygomatic minor
Masseter
Zygomatic major
Buccinator
Levator labii superioris
Orbicularis oris
Depressor labii inferioris
Risorius
Depressor anguli oris
Mentalis

G Honest expressions that are more than ten seconds long, and most that last longer than five, are probably fake. Intense displays – rage, ecstasy, depression – are exceptions, but even they usually appear as a series of short bursts. Surprise is especially brief. It always lasts less than a second; if it goes on longer, the person is counterfeiting. Unlike other expressions, it also begins and ends abruptly. Many people can mimic the look of surprise, but few capture its flick-switch start and end.

H According to folk wisdom, rapid blinking is a key to lying. While this is true of some lies, unfortunately blinking is a general response to arousal. It can signal excitement, anxiety or other strong emotions. What about averted eyes? We do tend to look down and away out of guilt or shame – as we look straight down with sadness and to the side with disgust. But the eye gaze is an unreliable clue. Liars know some people rely on it and exploit the fact. Curiously, probing for truth can actually blind us to lies. When pressed, some liars increase eye contact and facial animation, convincing questioners of their honesty.

I One secret of facial truth, known to few people, is the micro expression. For an instant or two, the face flashes the emotion it is hiding. Untrained people rarely notice micro expressions, although they spot them on slow-motion videotape. But clinicians detect them readily, and most individuals can learn to recognise them with an hour of training. While the micro is fairly rare, a messier phenomenon, known as the squelch, is much more common. A damning expression starts to emerge, the person senses it and covers it rapidly, usually with a smile. A squelch can occur quickly enough to hide the underlying emotion, but it usually lasts longer than the micro, and even when we cannot see the emotion, we often sense the squelch itself.

J Scientists have now identified six basic expressions – enjoyment, anger, fear, surprise, disgust and sadness. By 'basic expressions', scientists mean expressions that people all over the world can identify from photographs. Movement signals, like those of the eyes, are more difficult to study and have tended to elude research. Even so, numerous expressions spin off from the basic models. Some are matters of degree, like annoyance, which is mild anger. Others are fusions, like contemptuous enjoyment.

K Practice enhances face-reading, and a person may attain varying levels of success with it. But there is one sure path to error: the pseudo-science called physiognomy, which purports to divine character from large chins, long noses and the like. No evidence supports it, modern experts laugh at it. So watch the play of expressions on the face, not the structure. It is a lot more interesting.

Adapted from *Times Weekend*

Questions 11–13
Choose **THREE** letters, *A–F.*
*Which **THREE** of the following signals are considered to be unreliable as signs of lying?*

A cover-up smiles

B higher vocal pitch

C rapid blinking

D averted eyes

E intense displays of emotion

F facial animation

Questions 14–16
Choose the correct letter, *A, B, C or D.*

14 One way in which an expression of surprise differs from other emotions is that
    A it often appears in short bursts.
    B it disappears suddenly.
    C it lasts a short time.
    D it is easy to imitate.

15 What do micro expressions and squelches have in common?
    A They are both equally difficult to detect.
    B They are both unusual occurrences.
    C They are both connected with concealing an emotion.
    D They are both the subject of current research.

16 Which aspect of the subject have scientists not yet been able to study in detail?
    A face-reading
    B physiognomy
    C basic expressions
    D movement signals

KEY LANGUAGE
Modal verbs
▶ p.234, ex. 34
e.g. *The phoney smile may appear too early*

Focus on vocabulary *World building*

WORD FAMILIES

1 Complete the following table by writing in the missing parts of speech.

Verb	Noun	Adjective
appear	1	2
collide	2	
communicate	4	5
deceive	6	7
8	emphasis	9
enjoy	10	11
exist	12	13
identify	14	15
intend	16	17
18	response	19
20	21	wide

2 Complete the following sentences with words from the table.

1 Advertisements should not contain untrue or …… information.
2 The organisation has been in …… for 25 years.
3 A new law was passed in …… to public pressure.
4 There was a(n) … vote of no confidence in the government.
5 The two countries are on a(n) …… course which could lead to war.
6 The gap between income and expenditure has begun to …… .
7 It was …… from the study that the drug had serious side effects.
8 Differences in languages can lead to a breakdown in …… .
9 He was heavily fined for his mistake even though it was not …… .
10 It's easy to …… members of staff by the uniform they wear.

DEPENDENT PREPOSITIONS

3 Fill in the missing prepositions. You can check your answers by referring to similar examples in the reading passage on page 191 as indicated.

1 This research provides an insight ………… the causes of crime. (paragraph A)
2 There are points to be made ………… both sides of the argument. (B)
3 ………… common with many other countries, we're entering a recession. (B)
4 A recent photograph must be attached ……… to the application. (B)
5 One example stands out ……… particular. (B)
6 The 'social smile' generally appears ………… the age of two months. (C)
7 Eyebrows rise ………… expressions of fear, or ………… emphasis. (C)
8 In the past, many children died ………… infancy. (C)
9 The police investigation centred ………… the victim's friends. (D)
10 ………… the whole, we are not good ………… detecting lies. (E)
11 I'm not convinced ………… the truth of that argument. (H)
12 The government is deeply unpopular, according ……… a recent poll. (H)

Focus on speaking 2 *Dress the part*

EXAM PRACTICE
Part 2: Long turn

REMINDERS
▶ *Focus on Academic Skills
for IELTS* pages 39–41, 107

1 Remember that in Part 2 you need to be able to speak about a topic clearly and fluently. This means using appropriate language and organising your ideas well.

- Jot down key words or phrases to jog your memory. Don't write whole sentences.
- Make sure you cover both elements on the topic card: **description** and **explanation**.
- Try to make your subject interesting. Don't be afraid to use humour!

2 Work in pairs as 'examiner' and 'candidate'. When you've finished Topic 1, change roles for Topic 2.

The examiner should:

1 Read out the instructions below.
2 Allow the candidate one minute to prepare (use a watch if possible).
3 Listen to the candidate's talk without interrupting, and make sure it doesn't exceed two minutes.
4 Ask the closing questions.

> **Instructions to the candidate**
> - *Read the topic below carefully. You will have to talk about it for one to two minutes.*
> - *You have one minute to think about what you're going to say.*
> - *You can make some notes to help you if you wish.*

TOPIC 1

> **Describe your favourite style of dress.**
>
>   **You should say:**
>
>   **what kind of clothes you like to wear**
>   **what fabrics and colours you prefer**
>   **what (or who) influences you in your choice of clothes**
>
>   **and explain whether clothes are important to you or not.**

Closing questions

What kind of clothes do you feel least comfortable in?
Do you enjoy shopping for clothes?

TOPIC 2

> **Describe a film, theatre or TV performer you admire.**
>
>   **You should say:**
>
>   **what they look like**
>   **what they do**
>   **where and when you saw them**
>
>   **and explain why you admire this person.**

Closing questions

Do you see a lot of films/go to many plays/watch a lot of TV? Would you recommend the performance you mentioned to a friend?

Part 3: Discussion

3 Remember that in Part 3 of the Interview you need to be able to express and justify opinions, to analyse, discuss and speculate about more general issues. Study the following Reminders.

REMINDERS

- Give full answers with reasons and examples, as appropriate.
- Try to link your ideas to make longer, more complex sentences.
- This is an opportunity to demonstrate your fluency, and your range of vocabulary and grammar.

4 Work in pairs to discuss the following points. Look back at the *Useful language* for answering difficult questions on page 149 before you begin.

Topic 1: Clothes

1 Do you think it's important to wear formal clothes for a job interview? Why/ Why not?
2 How much can you judge a person by their appearance, in your opinion?
3 Do you think people should be free to wear whatever they like at work?
4 What do you think about school uniforms? Are they a good idea?
5 Do you think the fashion industry has a bad influence on young people?

Topic 2: Performers

1 Do you think that acting is a good profession for young people to enter? Why/ Why not?
2 What would be the advantages and disadvantages of being a famous actor or actress?
3 Do you think there is too much interest in the private lives of famous people?
4 What do you think about well-known TV and movie celebrities appearing in advertisements?
5 How can celebrities use their fame to do good in the world?

Academic Style 10 Review

Introduction

Previous sections looked at important aspects of academic style. This final section gives you an opportunity to review what you have learnt.

Key terms

1 Complete the explanations using words from the list below.

1 **Functions** are a basic a) .... of any text. They represent the writer's b) .... in writing, for example to put forward a(n) c) .... or describe a(n) d) ....

2 A **noun phrase** is a group of words containing a(n) e) .... noun together with additional f) .... Using nouns, (e.g. *belief*) rather than verbs (*believe*) helps to make academic writing more formal and g) ....

3 Writers use **hedging** language to make it absolutely clear how h) .... or common they believe something to be. Hedging language includes i) .... auxiliaries (*will*, *might*, etc.), and j) .... adverbs (*always*, *sometimes*, etc.).

4 **Attributive adjectives** like *simple* or *political*, which are used k) .... a noun, are particularly k) .... in academic writing.

argument	feature	information	probable
before	frequency	main	process
common	impersonal	modal	purpose

Formality

2 Write a short formal paragraph of advice based on the information below.

Begin *There are a number of simple steps …*

ATTENTION OFFICE WORKERS: 3 WAYS TO SAVE THE PLANET
1 Turn everything off before you leave the office, from printers to coffee machines. So simple, yet so effective! That way you'll save energy and money. Who doesn't want to do that?

2 Email more. No, I'm not joking! Email may be annoying when it's nothing but spam. But all the same, it saves tons of paper and also lets you access a lot of data and keep it safe.

3 Cut down on travel. Use a video conferencing system (e.g. Skype) to contact colleagues and hold meetings. The best thing about Skype is that' it's absolutely free!

Signposting

3 Use linking expressions to rewrite the following text in about four sentences.

Bad waste practices are costing the UK at least £15 bn a year. A recent estimate said so. 70 per cent of office waste is recyclable. Only 7.5 per cent on average reaches a recycling facility. Educating your staff as to what can be recycled will help the environment. It will also save your business money. Recycled ink cartridges save natural resources. They reduce the amount of toxic waste created. They represent substantial savings on the cost of new ink cartridges.

Presenting your own opinion

4 In examples 1–4, language that expresses the writer's opinion is underlined. Add each of these words to the correct category A–C below.

1 It <u>is</u> widely believed that a <u>major</u> <u>cause</u> of crime in the UK <u>is</u> alcohol consumption.

2 Many students <u>find</u> writing a <u>difficult</u> skill to master.

3 Concrete is <u>an extremely</u> <u>important</u> building material because without it most constructions <u>are</u> <u>impossible</u>.

4 An <u>advantage</u> of this method of producing energy <u>is</u> that the production process <u>generates</u> very little pollution.

A **Present simple verbs**
   (7 words) ....

B **Evaluative general nouns**
   (2 words) ....

C **Evaluative adjectives**
   (4 words) ....

Language facts

5 Choose the correct answer a), b) or c).

1 Which of the following is used in 25 per cent of all verb phrases in academic writing? (36)
   a) The present perfect   b) The passive
   c) The second conditional

2 Which are most common in academic English? (56)
   a) verbs   b) nouns   c) adjectives

3 What is the most common word in English after *the*? (76)
   a) *a(n)*   b) *and*   c) *of*

4 What do most modal verbs in academic English express? (96)
   a) possibility   b) permission   c) obligation

5 The most common way of showing you believe a statement is true in academic writing is by using (176)
   a) the phrase *It is a fact that …*   b) The adverb *Honestly!*
   c) the present simple tense

Academic Vocabulary 10

Meaning

1 Study these examples of academic words used in texts in Unit 19. Think about the part of speech in each case, and match each one with a meaning a)–f) below.

1 These signals **emerge** in infancy.
2 Practice **enhances** face reading.
3 Embarrassment on the face is the **equivalent** of apologising.
4 Liars **exploit** the fact that some people rely on the eye gaze as a sign of honesty.
5 The nose is not a very expressive facial **feature**.
6 Surprise resembles fear and often **precedes** it.

a)	go before	d)	make use of
b)	improve	e)	(roughly) the same as
c)	appear	f)	significant or interesting part

2 Complete these sentences using words from exercise 1. Make any changes necessary.

1 Windmills are characteristic .... of the landscape in the area.
2 The rainforest has been .... for timber for many years.
3 The course will enable people to .... their existing skills.
4 The pronunciation of 'the' changes when it .... a vowel.
5 A dolphin's brain is roughly .... in size to a human brain.
6 In April Colorado's bears .... from their winter hibernation.

Revision: Meaning

3 Circle the correct word in brackets in each sentence below. Page references are given in brackets.

1 China has experienced a marked social and (economic/economical) change. (97)
2 The NHS was founded on the (principal/principle) that healthcare should be free to all. (117)
3 Sleep may be the most important (factor/function) in achieving peak athletic performance. (117)
4 There have been major changes in social (structure/construction) since the 1950s. (117)
5 Microbes are too small to be (visual/visible) to the human eye. (157)
6 Echolocation gives bats (consistent/constant) feedback about their position. (157)

Revision: Word building

4 Use the word in capitals at the end of each line to form a word that fits the space. Make sure your answer fits grammatically as well as logically.

1 Unfortunately, many of the villages are .... in winter.   ACCESS
2 The summit meeting reached a .... yesterday.   CONCLUDE
3 There was an .... vote of no confidence in the government.   EMPHASISE
4 Many people are opposed to the .... of the airport.   EXPAND
5 For effective management it's essential to .... your tasks.   PRIORITY
6 Fortunately the condition is .... to drug therapy.   RESPOND
7 Hunting is threatening the .... of the species.   SURVIVE
8 Slight .... in temperature are normal.   VARY

Revision: Round-up

5 There is one mistake in each sentence. This could be related to any aspect of vocabulary knowledge. Underline the mistakes and correct them. Page references are given in brackets.

1 The Earth is unsignificant compared to many other planets in the universe. (57)
2 Not everyone accepts that written exams make a good indication of a student's ability. (137)
3 There was opposition to the new motorway which is currently on construction. (37)
4 After you collect the surveys, you will need to analysis the data carefully. (57)
5 Many countries are currently experiencing unnormal weather conditions. (57)
6 This distance learning course is involved study for 6–7 hours a week. (117)
7 Responsible tourism enables local communities to benefit about tourist developments. (117)
8 The report says that many more states are potential for becoming nuclear powers. (157)
9 It's important for restaurants to be aware of the regulates concerning food safety. (97)
10 There are an estimation of 600 million cars on the world's roads today. (37)

20 ▶ Through the lens

photography /fətɒgrəfi/ n [U] the art, profession, or method of producing photographs or the scenes in films: *He did fashion photography for Vogue magazine.* (Longman Dictionary of Contemporary English)

In this unit you will practise

- Interview; long turn; two-way discussion
- Listening and note, table and flow-chart completion
- Describing an object
- Pronunciation: word stress

Writing Practice

Task 1: Describing objects

Task 2: Presenting and justifying an opinion

Exam Focus

Speaking: Parts 1–3

Listening: Sections 1, 4

Writing: Task 1

Lead-in

1 In pairs, discuss the following questions.

1 Which medium A–D would you choose for the following purposes, and why?

A drawing   B painting
C photograph   D video recording

1 to take with you on a week's holiday in the countryside
2 to provide a record of a wedding
3 to keep a child occupied
4 for a portrait of a special person
5 as a subject to study at an evening class

2 Which uses of photography do the following pictures illustrate? Can you think of any more?

€242,750 Traditional Normandy house with three bedrooms, kitchen, living room and …

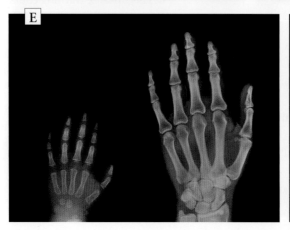

F C023

PRONUNCIATION:
WORD STRESS

2 Examples A–D below show four different word stress patterns.

A oOoo photography ....

B Ooo studio ....

C oOo equipment ....

D Oo subject ....

Put the following words in the correct group A–D, according to their stress pattern. There should be five words in each group. Check any meanings you're not sure of.

accessory	commercial	landscape	photographer	technology
advertise	develop	negative	portrait	tripod
advertisement	digital	perspective	programme	transparency
cinema	enlargement	photograph	projector	wildlife

Focus on listening 1 *Photography courses*

GENERAL REMINDERS

- **Completion:** Study the questions and think about possible answers. Remember that correct spelling is essential.
- **Table/flowchart:** look carefully at the layout and any headings, so you know how the information is organised.
- **Multiple choice:** read through the items silently. Thinking about meaning and pronunciation will help you identify answers when you hear them.

Section 1

Questions 1–6
Complete the table below.
Write **NO MORE THAN THREE WORDS AND/OR A NUMBER** for each answer.

PHOTOGRAPHY COURSES			
Course title	**Level**	**Day/Time**	**Length**
Introducing photography	1	Monday 6.30–9.30	10 weeks
Black and white photography	2	Tuesday 3	10 weeks
Landscape photography	Advanced	Tuesday 6.30–9.00	4 ....
The art of digital photography	Advanced	Wednesday 5	6 ....

Question 7
*Choose **TWO** letters, **A–G**.*
Which **TWO** of the following subjects are covered in the
Introducing photography course?

A film types   E composition

B camera controls   F night photography

C camera accessories G printing

D lighting

Questions 8–10
*Choose the correct letters, **A**, **B** or **C**.*

8 What is the fee for the *Black and white photography* course?

   A £85

   B £95

   C £140

9 What does the fee for the *Landscape photography* course include?

   A materials

   B field trip

   C examination fee

10 Which course is it especially important to apply for early?

   A *Introducing photography*

   B *Black and white photography*

   C *The art of digital photography*

Focus on listening 2 *History of cinema*

1 Discuss the quiz questions below with another student.

Film Quiz

1 Where did the history of the camera begin?
   A Arabia   B France   C USA

2 When was the first Oscar ceremony?
   A 1929   B 1949   C 1969

3 Which city has held an international film festival every
   year since 1946?
   A Amsterdam (Netherlands)
   B Barcelona (Spain)
   C Cannes (France)

4 Which film actor became President of the USA?

5 Which country has the biggest film industry in
   the world?

The answers to
the quiz are on
page 255.

2 Now listen to the recording and answer these questions.

Questions 1–3
*Complete the table below. Write **NO MORE THAN THREE WORDS** for each answer.*

PRE-HISTORY OF THE MOVIE		
Name of device	**Dating from**	**Details**
Camera obscura	11th century	Originally used to observe solar eclipses. Later used as a **1** .... tool.
Magic lantern	17th century	Ancestor of modern film projector. Mainly used for **2** ....
'Kinetoscope'	1894	Also known as 'peep-hole machine'. Only **3** .... could view film.

Questions 4–7
*Complete the flow-chart below. Write **NO MORE THAN THREE WORDS** for each answer.*

LANDMARKS IN CINEMATOGRAPHY

1895   First **4** .... demonstrated in Paris.

↓

1903   First Western screened, 'The Great **5** ....'.

↓

1927   'The Jazz Singer' was the first **6** .... film.

↓

1932   Technicolor introduced and used in a **7** ....

Questions 8–10
List three more factors which made California attractive to film makers.
*Write **NO MORE THAN THREE WORDS** for each answer.*

Constant sunshine

8 ....

9 ....

10 ....

Focus on speaking *Practice interview*

▶ *Focus on Academic Skills for IELTS pages 132–133*

This section allows you to practise all three parts of the interview.

Work in pairs as 'examiner' and 'candidate'. Do the tasks for Candidate A in each part first. When you've finished, change roles and do the tasks for Candidate B. Try to simulate exam conditions as much as possible. Read the instructions for each part before you begin

Part 1: Interview

▶ *Focus on Academic Skills for IELTS page 132*

The *Introduction and Interview* stage should take four to five minutes.

Examiner: Greet the candidate. Read out the questions below.
Candidate: Close your book and listen carefully to the questions.

Questions for Candidate A

Let's talk first about what you do in your free time.
- Do you have any special hobbies or interests?
- How long have you been interested in .... ?
- What do you enjoy about it?

Moving on now to talk about your studies.
- How long have you been studying English?
- What do you enjoy most about your studies?
- How do you expect to use English in future?

Questions for Candidate B

Let's talk first about your country.
- You come from .... What's the best thing about living there?
- How do people enjoy themselves in their free time in .... ?
- What places are there for a tourist to visit in .... ?

Let's move on to your future plans.
- What are you planning to do after the IELTS Test?
- And what about longer term? Do you have any long-term plans for work or study?
- Where would you like to be living in five years?

Part 2: Long turn

The *long turn* should take three to four minutes including one minute for preparation.

Examiner: Read out the top line of the topic card and give the candidate one minute to prepare. Then ask him/her to start speaking. Don't interrupt during the candidate's speaking time. After two minutes, ask the closing questions.

Candidate: Read the topic card. You have one minute to prepare. Make notes on a piece of a paper if you wish. You will need to speak for one to two minutes.

Topic for Candidate A

> **Describe a photograph you have taken which is important to you.**
>
> **You should say:**
>
>> **what the picture shows**
>> **when and why you took it**
>> **where you keep it**
>
> **and explain what is special about it.**

Topic for Candidate B

> **Describe a film you have enjoyed.**
>
> **You should say:**
>
>> **what it was about**
>> **when and why you saw it**
>> **what special features it had**
>
> **and explain what you especially liked about it.**

Closing questions
Are you a keen photographer?
Do you like looking at other people's photographs?

Closing questions
Do you often watch films?
Do you prefer watching films in the cinema or on video?

Part 3: Discussion

The two-way discussion should take four to five minutes.

Examiner: Begin by asking the following questions. Listen to the candidate's answers carefully. Be prepared to react and ask appropriate follow-up questions.

Candidate: Listen carefully to the examiner. Answer the questions as fully as possible.

Questions for Candidate A
- Is photography becoming more or less popular these days, in your experience?
- Would you agree with the saying: 'The camera never lies'?
- Would you say that photography is an art?

Follow-up questions
- News photographers sometimes take pictures of people in distress, after a disaster, for example. Do you think this is justified?
- Do you think advertising can have harmful effects?

Questions for Candidate B
- Are film stars paid too much money, in your opinion?
- Do you think there's too much violence in modern movies?
- What do you feel about film censorship? Is it necessary?

Follow-up questions
- Do you think television and video will kill the cinema?
- Special cameras are sometimes used to film everything that goes on in the street and in shops. Do you think this is a good idea?

> **WRITING PRACTICE**
> Presenting and justifying an opinion (exam task)
> ▶ p. 250, ex. 18

Focus on writing *Describing an object*

Task 1

1 In the exam task on page 205, you have to describe a number of developments in camera design over the years. Read the *Exam Briefing* and *Task Approach* below.

> ▶ **EXAM BRIEFING** Academic Writing: Task 1
>
> One possible task in this section is to describe *an object,* event or *sequence of events.*
> - You are not expected to have technical knowledge or to use specialist vocabulary.
> - Your task is description – don't try to give reasons for developments.
> - Don't try to describe every detail – concentrate on significant features.

TASK APPROACH
- Start with a brief overview, outlining the common features, for example: *The basic design of all the cameras shown is the same. They consist of …*
- Look for significant similarities and differences between examples. Try to vary your language whenever possible.
- End with a summarising statement.

VARYING YOUR LANGUAGE 2 In tasks where you have to describe a development process, try to avoid repeating the verbs you use to introduce each stage. Think of at least three other ways **to** say *was invented.*

> *Focus on Academic Skills for IELTS* page 135, ex. 2

3 Study the *Useful language* for describing objects below.

Useful language: Describing objects

shape

… is   *(basically / roughly) square / rectangular / cylindrical* **in shape**
           shaped like a cube / rectangle / cylinder

structure

           consists of …   *contains …*
…   *is divided into … sections / parts*   *(is) connected to …*
           is made of …

size

… is 1 metre   *long / wide / high*
… has   *a length / width / height / diameter of 1 metre*

                   (slightly / considerably) **bigger / heavier / more complex than** *…*
… is   *(approximately / less than)* **half the size of** *…*
                   (only) **a fraction of the size of** *…*

---

4 Use the expressions above to describe and contrast the following:

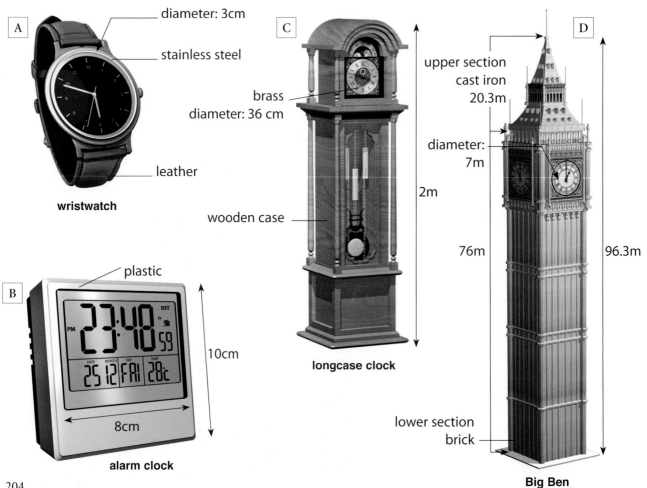

A — wristwatch
diameter: 3cm
stainless steel
leather

B — alarm clock
plastic
10cm
8cm

C — longcase clock
brass
diameter: 36 cm
wooden case
2m

D — Big Ben
upper section
cast iron
20.3m
diameter: 7m
76m
96.3m
lower section
brick

EXAM PRACTICE

5 Now complete the exam task.

WRITING PRACTICE
Describing objects (guided
practice and exam task)
▶ p. 251–252, ex. 19 and 20

You should spend about 20 minutes on this task.

The diagrams below show stages in the development of the camera since its invention in 1839.

Summarise the information by selecting and reporting the main features, and make comparisons where relevant.

Write at least 150 words.

1839 Daguerrotype

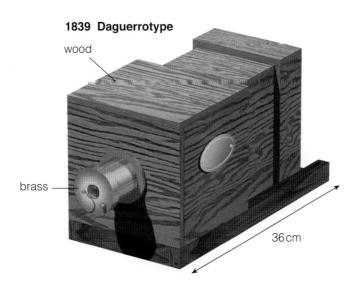

wood

brass

36 cm

1888 Kodak No. 1

metal

16 cm

1925 Leica 1

metal

14 cm

2000 Digital camera

plastic

zoom lens

LCD screen

internet connection

8 cm

205

ERROR HIT LIST

contain/consist/include

✗	✔
Essays should include no more than 200 words.	Essays should <u>contain</u> …
The exam is consisted of a written test and an oral.	The exam <u>consists of</u> …
The wallet was containing £150.	The wallet <u>contained</u> …

- These verbs cannot be used in progressive tenses.
- Use **contain** to refer to the contents of something, e.g. *The bag **contained** a wallet and car keys. This product **contains** nuts.*
- Use **consist of / be made up of** to describe all the parts of something, e.g. *The population **is made up of** three ethnic groups.* The verb *comprise* can also be used, though this is more formal in style.
- Use **include** to mention one or more (but not all) of the parts of a thing, e.g. *The book **includes** a chapter on recent economic trends.*

surely/certainly

✗	✔
Scientists say that temperatures are surely rising.	… are <u>definitely/certainly</u> rising …
Unemployment will surely increase as a result.	Unemployment <u>is bound/sure</u> to …

- **surely** is used, especially in spoken English, as a way of inviting someone to agree with your point of view, e.g. ***Surely** you don't accept that argument, do you?*
- Use **certainly** or **definitely** to emphasise that something is true.
- To say you are confident that something will happen, use **is/are bound to / sure to** or **there is no doubt that**, e.g. *The polls show that the Prime Minister **is bound to** win the election. **There is no doubt that** the Prime Minister will win the election.*

a great deal of/a great many

✗	✔
There have been a great deal of problems.	… <u>a large number of/a great many</u> …

- The phrase **a great deal of** means 'a large amount' and is followed by an uncountable noun, e.g. *It's taken **a great deal of** time to reorganise the office.*
- If there is no need to emphasise the size of a number, use *many* or (informally) *a lot of.*

older/elder/elderly

✗	✔
This type of music is popular with elder people.	… with <u>older</u> people.
The job requires an elderly, more experienced person.	… requires an <u>older</u>, more …

- Only use **elder** and **eldest** to refer to members of a family, e.g. *my **elder** brother.*
- **elderly** is a polite word meaning 'old'; **the elderly** = old people, e.g. *a home for the elderly.*

Critical Thinking 5 *Presenting another point of view*

Introduction

An effectve argument depends on good supporting evidence in the form of relevant ideas and information. This is particularly important in academic writing, where you will be expected to read widely and show your understanding of the main lines of thought on a subject.

When mentioning other people's ideas, it's essential to describe these accurately and to say where they come from. Sources may be quite general in an IELTS writing task, but they need to be very specific in academic writing. If you do not give the source, the ideas will appear to be your own. This is called plagiarism and it is taken very seriously in the academic world.

Reporting language

1 In the sentences below, underline the phrases which are used to show that the writer is referring to someone else's idea(s). Which one is not appropriate for an IELTS task? Why?

1 Some people believe that the movement of the stars can influence life on Earth.
2 Fourteen per cent of young children are not physically active (Nelson, 2004).
3 "The Internet is becoming the town square for the global village of tomorrow," according to Bill Gates.

2 Use suitable expressions from the table to report the ideas in 1–5 below.

General sources	From what I've read/heard … (Some) people/experts say/think/believe (that) … It is generally thought/believed (that) … (Some) studies have shown (that)….
Specific sources e.g. a person, journal, website, etc.	According to … As reported in … As … says, … … says/states (that) …

1 "Poverty is the worst form of violence". (Gandhi)
2 A period of bed rest can cause the heart to shrink in size. (an article in the New Scientist)
3 "To every action there is an equal and opposite reaction." (Newton's Third Law of Motion)
4 Football is a matter of life and death.
5 Nicotine can be as addictive as heroin.

Indicating attitude

According to your choice of language, you can indicate your own attitude to a point of view, or simply report it without judgement. For example the use of *As* at the beginning of a clause suggests that you agree with an idea, whereas *According to* simply reports something without judgement.

3 Underline the reporting verbs in these statements, then match each one to a use, A, B or C.

1 The company claims that its new software will make computers more secure.
2 The author argues that the time for debate about climate change is over.
3 Research reveals that boys do worse at English when there are girls in the class.

A reports something which you **accept as true**
B reports something which **may or may not be true**. No opinion expressed
C reports something which **you do not believe** or do not think there is proof for

Reporting verbs
argue   believe   claim   find   indicate   point out, prove   report   reveal   say   show   state   suggest

4 Find three other verbs from the list in exercise 3 which match use A and five which match use B.

5 Use suitable reporting verbs to complete the sentences below, making any grammatical changes necessary.

1 Some scientists …………… that global warming may not result from human activities.
2 Researchers ……… people on low pay suffer more ill health than high earners.
3 The makers of nicotine gum …………… their product makes it easy to give up smoking.
4 The article …………… the US and Canada have a very close economic interrelationship.
5 Researchers ……… a clear link between smoking and cancer by the 1960s.

> **Critical Thinking for IELTS**
>
> • In writing tasks, try to mention a range of relevant ideas you've read or heard about.
>
> • Use relevant language to show how far you agree with these ideas.

See also Key Language, pages 219 and 233, ex. 12, 33

The Academic Word List

The Academic Word List (AWL) is a list of 570 word families that are commonly found in academic texts. It was developed by Averil Coxhead in 2000 as a reference for students who are studying or preparing to study at college or university in English. The AWL focuses on non-subject-specific vocabulary that students of any discipline will need to master in order to study at tertiary level. For more information go to: www.victoria.ac.nz/lals/staff/Averil-Coxhead/awl

The list below contains all the AWL words in the Academic Vocabulary sections.

WORD	AV section				
academic	9	community	2	economic	
(in)accessible	8, 10	complex	7, 9	(*v* economical)	5, 9, 10
(in)accurate	3, 6, 7	component	2	economical	
achieve /-ment	5, 9	concept	1, 2	(*v* economic)	5, 9, 10
adequate	2	conclude /		emerge	10
adjustment	7, 8	conclusion	4, 9, 10	emphasis / -ise /	
affect	9	conduct	1	-emphatic	3, 7, 8, 10
aid	4	connect / -tion / -ed	3	enable	2, 5
alter / -ation	2, 7	consequence	9	energy / -tic	8
alternative (*to*)	4, 5	consist (of)	4, 9	enhance	10
analyse / -lysis /		(in)consistent / -ly		environment / -al	2, 4, 5, 7
-lytical	3, 4, 9, 10	(*v* constant / -ly)	4, 7, 8, 10	equipment	7
(in)appropriate		construction		equivalent	10
/ -ly	7, 8	(*v* structure)	2, 6, 10	error	2, 9
area	2	consume / consumer /		estimate / -ion / -ed	2, 5, 10
aspect (*v* prospect)	8	consumption	4, 5, 6	evidence	6
assign	3	contribute / -or /		expand / expansion	5, 8, 10
assistance	4, 7	-ution	5, 7, 8, 9	exploit	10
attach / -ment	3	create / -ive	9	factor (*v* function)	2, 6, 10
(un)available /		credit	4	feature	10
-ability	1, 2, 3	criteria	7	finalise	4
(un)aware (*of*)	3, 4	decline (*in*)	1, 2, 5	financial	2, 4
benefit (*from*) /		define (*as*)	6	focus (on)	1
beneficial	1, 6, 10	demonstrate / -tion /		found / -ed	2, 9
(in)capable (*of*)	3, 5	-ed (*by*)	1, 2, 7	function (*v* factor)	6, 10
category / categorise	4, 7	depression	1	generation	9
challenge	3	despite	6, 9	global	2, 4
commence	2	device	7, 8	goal	2
commit / -ment	7, 9	dominate / -inant	7, 9	identify (*as*) /	
communicate / -ative	8. 9	economy	4, 9	identification	6, 9

208

WORD	AV section				
impact (*on*)	3, 4, 6, 9	occur	1, 2, 6	reveal	1
incident	7	overall	1	role	2, 5
indicate / -indication	7, 10	overseas	2, 9	(in)secure / -rity	3, 4
initial (*v* prime)	5	participate (*in*) /		seek	9
innovation	7	-ation	1, 4, 5	sequence	7
institution	4	perceive / perception	9	(in)significant / -ance	1, 2, 3, 9, 10
interact / -ion / -ive	3, 8	physical	1, 2	site	2
interpret / -ation	9	policy	4	source (*v* resource)	5
invest / -ment	9	positive	2	specific	2, 7
investigate / -ation	8	potential	8, 10	(un)specified	8
involve (*in*)	6, 9, 10	precede /		(un)stable	8
issue	3, 4, 7	unprecedented	3, 10	statistic	9
item	7	(im)precise / -ion	8	stress / -ful	3, 8
job	9	prediction	9	structure	
lecture	9	previous	1, 7	(*v* construction)	6, 10
(il)legal	2, 8	prime (*v* initial)	5	substitute (*for*)	6
link (*between*)	6	principal (*v* principle)	6, 10	summarise	4
locate / -ion	1, 5, 6	principle (*v* principal)	6, 10	survive / -al	5, 10
maintain / enance	1, 2	priority / -itise	4, 7, 10	symbolise	4
major	8	process	6, 7	target	9
maximise	4	promote	9	task	7
mechanism	3, 7	prospect (*v* aspect)	8	technology / -ical	9
medical	2	psychology / -ical	9	transport	1
medium	7	purchase	1, 2, 6	trend	2
mental	1, 2	regional	2	ultimately	3
method	1	regulate / -ion	5, 10	(in)valid	8
minimise / -al	2, 4	reinforce	4, 7	vary / -iation / -iable	
mode	9	rely / (un)reliable	3, 6, 10	/ -ied	3, 10
network	1	require / -ment / -ed	3, 6	violation	9
(ab)normal	3, 6, 10	research	1, 7	visible (*v* visual)	8, 10
nuclear	3	resource (*v* source)	5	visual (*v* visible)	2, 8, 10
obtain	1, 6	respond (*to*) /			
		response	1, 6, 10		

▶ Key language bank

Grammatical terms

You need to be familiar with the names for the different parts of speech in English in order to follow the notes in this section, and also to make effective use of a dictionary or grammar reference book.

PARTS OF SPEECH

1 Read the following definitions (1–8) and then choose the correct group of examples (a–h).

1 **noun**
refers to a person, place, thing or an abstract idea, e.g. …

2 **pronoun**
can be used to replace a noun, e.g. …

3 **verb**
refers to an action or a state, e.g. …

4 **adjective**
describes people, things and events, e.g. …

5 **adverb**
used to say when, how or where something happens, e.g. …

6 **article**
has no meaning on its own, and is used before a noun/noun phrase, e.g. …

7 **preposition**
used before a noun or pronoun to indicate place, direction, time, etc., e.g. …

8 **conjunction**
used to join clauses together to make a sentence, e.g. …

a) *well, quickly, yesterday, there*
b) *and, because, although, if*
c) *he, it, her, myself*
d) *Maria, Cairo, train, honesty*
e) *walk, play, decide*
f) *in, at, over, by*
g) *the, a(n)*
h) *easy, expensive, necessary*

OTHER TERMS

2 Match each grammatical term with the correct definition below.

1 auxiliary ...... 5 participle ......
2 modal auxiliary ...... 6 phrase ......
3 phrasal verb ...... 7 clause ......
4 infinitive ...... 8 sentence ......

a) the 'base' form of the verb that you find in a dictionary, usually used after *to*
b) a verb with two parts: a main verb and an adverbial particle, e.g. *cut off, take over*
c) a verb used with a main verb to form tenses, negatives, questions: *be, do, have*
d) part of a sentence containing a subject and verb, e.g. *They left* (because) *it was late.*
e) a group of words with a subject and verb that express a complete statement, question, etc. *Dinner is ready. Have you booked the ticket?*
f) an auxiliary verb which is used with a main verb to show a particular attitude such as possibility or obligation, e.g. *may, might, could, should*
g) a form of the verb that can be used to form tenses or as an adjective, e.g. *working, moving; damaged, cooked*
h) a group of words which do not form a complete clause or sentence, e.g. *a box of chocolates, on holiday, going to the bank*

Exercise 2 (Unit 2)

Names of key tenses

The following table is a brief summary of the main tenses that you need to be aware of in preparing for IELTS. For more comprehensive information look in a good student grammar reference book.

PRESENT SIMPLE base form/base form + -s
- refers to established knowledge e.g. *The sun rises in the east. Research shows …*
- refers to permanent situations and regular events e.g. *They live in Paris. Meetings take place on Mondays.*

Important IELTS use: describing tables and diagrams: *As the graph indicates … The X then passes to the next stage …* (Writing)

PRESENT PROGRESSIVE *is/are* + present participle
- refers to things that are happening now or in the general present, e.g. *I'm applying for various jobs.*
- refers to future arrangements, e.g. *He's leaving on Monday.*

Important IELTS use: describing change and development, *e.g. The population is decreasing rapidly.* (Writing)

PRESENT PERFECT SIMPLE *have/has* + past participle
PRESENT PERFECT PROGRESSIVE *have/has* + been + past participle.
- refers to situations which began in the past and are still continuing, e.g. *I've lived here all my life. Scientists have been studying the problem for many years.*
- refers to a recent past event, e.g. *I've just heard the news. It's been raining.*
- Refers to a past event when time is not important, e.g. *I've had a tetanus injection.*

Important IELTS use: talking about past events which are still valid, e.g. *Experiments have shown that …* (Writing)

PAST SIMPLE base form + -ed (or irregular)
- refers to a completed past event or a series of events, e.g. *Nobel invented dynamite in 1867.*

Important IELTS use: mentioning past experience to support an argument, e.g. *I had one teacher in particular who inspired me.* (Speaking/Writing)

PAST PROGRESSIVE *was/were* + present participle
- refers to something which was going on at a particular time in the past, e.g. *The economy was booming when the government came to power.*

PAST PERFECT SIMPLE *had* + past participle
- refers to an event which happened before another past event, e.g. *When the police arrived, the thieves had already left the scene.*

Important IELTS use: describing graphs, e.g. *By the year X, the price of Y had fallen.* (Writing)

FUTURE SIMPLE *will* + base form
- gives information about the future or makes a prediction, e.g. *The company will make a loss this year. I think the Democrats will win the election.*

Important IELTS use: talking about the future, e.g. *I hope I'll pass the exam.* (Speaking)

Name the tense in italics in each of the following sentences.

1 The cost of borrowing *has increased* over the last year.
2 The number of people out of work *had doubled* by 1989.
3 If management doesn't improve its offer, there *will be* a strike.
4 The price of fuel *fell* again in January.
5 More and more people *are taking* short breaks nowadays.
6 When winter *comes*, the situation will only get worse.
7 At the beginning of the year sales of luxury goods *were declining*.
8 Literacy rates *have been rising* for several years.

Language Fact
80% of all verb phrases in English are in the **present** or **past**.
90% of all verb phrases in English are **simple**.

211

Exercise 3 (Unit 2)

Adjectives describing change

The following adjectives can be used to describe changes in line graphs, e.g. *a sharp rise, a gradual increase.* Categorise each one A or B according to whether they describe:
A a big/fast change
B a small/slow change

dramatic	*marginal*	*sharp*	*steady*
gradual	*marked*	*significant*	*steep*
limited	*rapid*	*slight*	*substantial*

Exercise 4 (Unit 2)

Reporting tenses

When you are describing graphs or tables of statistics, it's important to establish the time frame and use an appropriate tense.

1 Which of the tenses listed below is most likely to be used with these expressions?

1 Since last summer …
2 During the period from June to December last year …
3 Over the next few years, …
4 For the time being, …
5 By the year 2000, …
6 Between 1958 and 1988 …
7 For nearly twenty years now …
8 In about 1900, …

Present	*Prices fall/are falling.*
Present perfect	*Prices have fallen/have been falling.*
Past	*Prices fell.*
Past perfect	*Prices had fallen.*
Future	*Prices will fall.*

2 Choosing an appropriate tense is also important in other types of writing. Complete the following sentences by putting the verbs in the correct tense.

1 This company (specialise) in microtechnology for over a decade.
2 By the time the war was over, almost a million people (lose) their lives.
3 We are confident that during the coming months we (see) an increase in profits.
4 Between May and June each year, thousands of students (receive) their exam results.
5 The regulations (not/exist) prior to 2005.
6 The president collapsed while he (jog).
7 The latest statistics on child poverty (show) a need for urgent action.
8 During the last recession, a large number of companies (cease) trading
9 At the moment we (do) everything in out power to solve the problem,
10 The internet (become) an increasingly important study tool in recent years.

Exercise 5 (Unit 3)

The passive

Look at these examples:

Active: *Tigers often kill livestock.*
Passive: *Livestock is often killed (by tigers).*

1 Complete these descriptions of the form and use of the passive.

> **Form:** To make an active sentence passive, the 1 .... (*the shop windows*) must become the 2 .... of the sentence, and be followed by a passive form. The passive is formed with various tenses of 3 .... followed by 4 ....
>
> **Use:** Using the passive places the 5 .... on an action rather than on the agent that 6 .... the action.
>
> In a **short passive** the agent is not expressed (e.g. *The shop windows were broken*). In a long passive the agent (*armed soldiers*) is expressed.

2 Look back at the four descriptions of cities on pages 28–29 and underline any examples of the passive.

3 Complete the following texts by putting the verbs in brackets into an appropriate tense of the passive.

Aluminium cans – what a waste

In 1963, when aluminium **1** .... (first/use) for disposable beverage cans, one billion **2** .... (produce) in the USA – about five per person. By 1985, up to 66 billion cans **3** .... (sell) annually. Huge amounts of energy **4** .... (require) for aluminium production. Added to this, most aluminium comes from bauxite deposits in the tropics; huge areas of rainforest **5** .... (destroy) not only to make room for open bauxite mining but also for hydroelectric dams and reservoirs to power the mining operations.

Waste food

Waste food should ideally **6** .... (return) to farms and **7** .... (feed) to livestock, or **8** .... (use) to fertilise garden soil, but very few city dwellers are able to do this. Most of the food which **9** .... (eat) in cities **10** .... (package) in plastics and cardboard, further contributing to the waste problem.

Language Fact

The passive

- There are passives in 25% of all verb phrases in academic English (compared with only 2% in conversation).
- The **short passive** (without an expressed agent) is much more common than the long passive, especially in academic writing, which is concerned with generalisations rather than the agent who carried out the action, e.g. *Radium was discovered in 1898.*

Exercise 6 (Unit 3)

Geographical positions

Read the following notes and answer the questions.

north/northern, etc.

The adjective *north*, etc. is generally used for fairly specific positions and *northern* for more general areas.

- *the **south** side of the house; the **north** face of the mountain*
- *the **northern** hemisphere; the **western** part of the island*

1 How do you make the comparative and superlative of *north*, etc?

2 What do the adjectives *northernmost/southernmost* mean? Complete this sentence:
Reykjavik is the .... capital city in the world.

in the north/to the north

3 Look at these examples, and say when you should use the preposition *in* + geographical position and when you should use *to*.
*Florida is **in** the south-east of the USA.*
*Cuba is **to** the south of Florida.*

Capital letters

4 Look at these examples and say when you should use capital letters at the beginning of geographical positions.
*He's gone to **North** America.*
*The **Southern** Alps are in New Zealand.*
*It's near the **northern** border of the country.*
*Some birds migrate **south** for the winter.*

5 Describe the position of the following places, according to this map of Australia.

1 Perth
2 Kakadu National Park
3 Great Barrier Reef
4 Tasmania
5 Great Sandy Desert and Gibson Desert
6 Canberra in relation to Sydney
7 South Australia in relation to Victoria
8 Cape York in relation to Australia

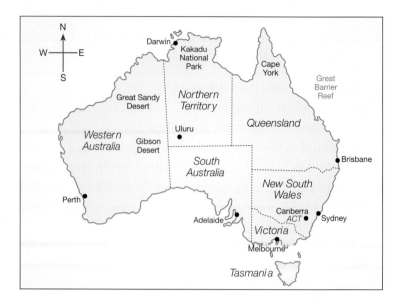

Exercise 7 (Unit 4)

Comparison 1: numerical and other comparative expressions

1 Study the following information.

half/twice/three times, etc. *as … as*

nearly/just under about/approximately exactly more than/over	half twice three times, etc.	as	much/many X tall/expensive, etc.	as

three/four times, etc. / 50% + comparative
With expressions like *three/four times*, etc. and with **percentages**, it's also possible to use a comparative:

*The computer system was **three times more expensive than** we'd expected.*
*Prices are 25% **cheaper** on the Internet **than** in the shops.*

NB It's not possible to use a comparative after *half* or *twice*.

2 Write sentences comparing the information in the following tables.

1 This table shows the earnings of some of the richest football clubs in the world (2000).

	Turnover in £ million
Manchester United	110.9
Bayern Munich	83.5
Real Madrid	76.1
Chelsea	59.1
Barcelona	55.7
Lazio	50
Liverpool	45.3
AS Roma	39.4
Leeds United	37
Celtic	33.4

2 This table shows how children aged seven to fifteen spend their money in the UK. The figures are percentages.

Children's expenditure by gender and type of purchase		
	Males	Females
Food and soft drinks	37	36
Leisure goods	29	17
Clothing and footwear	8	16
Household goods and services	5	8
Transport and fares	7	4

Exercise 8 (Unit 4)

Comparison 2: forming comparatives and superlatives

1 Study the examples and complete the notes relating to the comparison of adjectives.

ADJECTIVES

long, longer, longest	grey, greyer, greyest
fine, finer, finest	flat, flatter, flattest
dry, drier, driest	neat, neater, neatest

- Adjectives of one syllable add -(e)r or -(e)st. If the adjective ends in a 1 .... followed by y, this changes to ier or iest.
- If the adjective ends in a single consonant after a single 2 .... , the consonant is doubled.
- The following have irregular forms: good, better, best; bad, worse, worst; far, 3 ....
- The following determiners also have irregular forms: much/many, more, most; little, less, least.

secure, more secure, most secure
easy, easier, easiest
simple, simpler/more simple, simplest/most simple

- Most two-syllable adjectives take 4 ....
- Two-syllable adjectives ending in 5 .... add -ier and -iest.
- The following adjectives can take 6 .... :

common	narrow	polite	simple
likely	pleasant	quiet	stupid

interesting, more interesting, most interesting

- Adjectives of 7 .... take more and most.

ADVERBS

easily, more easily, most easily

- Most adverbs form comparatives and superlatives with 8 ....
- Adverbs with the same form as adjectives form comparatives and superlatives in the same way as adjectives, e.g. fast, faster, fastest; hard, harder, hardest; early, earlier, earliest.
- The following have irregular forms:
  well, 9 .... , ... ;
  badly, 10 .... , ...

2 Complete the following short texts by writing the appropriate form of the adjective or adverb and adding any other necessary words.

South America, the fourth (**1** large) continent in the world, stretches from Point Gallinas on the Caribbean coast to Cape Horn, (**2** southerly) point of Horn Island. Among its features are the Andes mountain range which, at over 7,000 kilometres, is (**3** long) the distance from London to Bombay, the world's (**4** high) city, La Paz in Bolivia, and one of the world's (**5** important) resources – the Amazonian rainforest. With an area of seven million square kilometres, this is twelve times (**6** big) than France. It is a major source of oxygen and is home to half of all known living species, including the anaconda, the world's (**7** heavy) snake, and the two-toed sloth, (**8** slow) animal. The continent experiences extremes of weather. Parts of Columbia are among (**9** wet) in the world, while the Atacama Desert in Chile, which has an average of only 0.5mm of rain a year, is (**10** dry) place on Earth. Spanish is (**11** widely spoken) language.

Railways have several advantages over road transport. Running on tracks, they use (**12** little) fuel than cars or lorries and allow heavy loads to be moved (**13** efficiently). Trains can also transport goods and passengers at (**14** great) average speeds and with (**15** few) hold-ups than road transport, making journeys (**16** short) and (**17** stressful). Rail networks are (**18** commonly) used in Japan and Europe than in the USA, and Russia has (**19** high) passenger railway usage of all. The (**20** fast) scheduled train service in the world is the French TGV's 254kph journey between Massy and St Pierre.

215

Exercise 9 (Unit 5)

Word Building: Affixes

Afffixes are groups of letters which can be added to a word to create a new word with a different meaning or word class. Prefixes are added at the beginning of a word (e.g. *lock/unlock*). Suffixes are added at the end (e.g. *solid/solidify*). It's important to understand affixes because they can help you to work out the meaning of unknown words in texts.

PREFIXES:

1 Study the list of common prefixes with examples, then choose a general meaning for each one from the box below.

NB Some prefixes have the same meanings and these are repeated in the box.

again	against	against	bad(ly)	before
between	extreme	opposite or negative		
opposite or negative	outside/beyond	self		
too little	too much	with/together	wrong	

PREFIX	EXAMPLE	MEANING
1 **anti-**	(*antibiotic, antinuclear*)	
2 **auto-**	(*autobiography, autonomy*)	
3 **co-**	(*co-operate, co-worker*)	
4 **counter-**	(*counterproductive, counterattack*)	
5 **dis-**	(*discomfort, disconnect*)	
6 **extra-**	(*extracurricular, extraordinary*)	
7 **hyper-**	(*hypersensitive, hypermarket*)	
8 **in-**	(*Independent, indecision*)	
9 **Inter-**	(*interaction, intergovernmental*)	
10 **mal-**	(*malformation, malnourished*)	
11 **mis-**	(*mislead, misinform*)	
12 **over-**	(*overload, overflow*)	
13 **pre-**	(*pre-school, predominant*)	
14 **re-**	(*rebuild, reunion*)	
15 **under-**	(*underweight, underused*)	

2 Use the tables in exercise 1 to work out and explain the meanings of the following words.

1	antisocial (*adj*)	8	interdependent (*adj*)
2	autopilot (*n*)	9	malfunction (*n/v*)
3	counteract (*v*)	10	misconception (*n*)
4	disqualify (*v*)	11	overstatement (*n*)
5	extraterrestrial (*adj*)	12	prejudge (*v*)
6	hyperinflation (*n*)	13	restructure (*n*)
7	inattention (*n*)	14	underfunding (*n*)

3 Use words from the list above to complete the following sentences. Make any changes necessary.

1 Drivers who exceed the speed limits in towns risk being ....
2 It would be a(n) .... to say that the news is disastrous, but it's certainly serious.
3 He takes drugs to .... the side effects of his cancer treatment.
4 The crash was caused by a .... in the port engine.
5 Any attempts to .... the company will lead to redundancies.
6 The new laws aim to tackle loud parties, graffiti and other .... behaviour
7 A jury must not .... a case, especially when there is heavy media coverage.
8 .... to detail could lead to serious errors in the overall calculation.
9 There is a popular .... that the more exercise you do, the better.
10 Our bodies' immune and nervous systems are ....

SUFFIXES

4 Suffixes can be categorised according to whether they are used to form nouns, verbs or adjectives. Choose suffixes from the lists A–C to complete sentences 1–10 opposite.

A	B	C
Noun forming	**Verb forming**	**Adjective forming**
-hood	-ate/iate	-able
-ism	-en	-al
-ity	-ify	-ful
-ment	-ise/ize	-ive
-ness		-less
-ship		
-tion/sion		

1 Some people believe friend………. is more important than love.
2 Cheap tools may not be as effect………. as better quality ones.
3 It is often said that child………. is the best period of one's life.
4 Many accidents that occur in the home are entirely avoid……….
5 It's important to different………. between fact and opinion.
6 The appearance of the dove is used to symbol………. peace.
7 It's a good idea if the punish………. fits the crime in some way.

8 There is a certain similar………. between the two situations.
9 I was able to study Spanish as an option………. extra subject.
10 Are there any circumstances that can just………. murder?

Language Fact
Adding affixes to form new words is common in academic English.
- The most common prefix used to form verbs in academic English is *re-*, and the most common suffix is *-ise*.
- The most common prefix used to form nouns in academic English is *co-*, and the most common suffix is *-tion*.

Exercise 10 (Unit 6)

Cohesion: reference links

A text is cohesive if the sentences are well constructed and well linked together, and there are no unnecessary repetitions. One of the main ways of making a text cohesive is the use of *reference links*.

REFERENCE LINKS

- **Pronouns**, e.g. *he, she, it, they; himself, herself; this, that, these; what, who, where; one/any*

Many <u>people</u> wrote to complain. | <u>They</u> particularly objected to …
We receive about <u>twenty calls</u> a day. | <u>These</u> range from requests for …
The hospital receives <u>insufficient funding</u>. | <u>This</u> is a major problem.
He asked if I could lend him <u>a torch</u>. | Unfortunately, I didn't have <u>one</u>.

- **Auxiliary verbs**, e.g. *do/did; have/had; can/could; will/would*

We all <u>tell white lies</u> occasionally. | Life would be difficult if we <u>didn't</u>.
You need <u>to pay the fee now</u>. | If you <u>can't</u>, please let us know.
They asked me <u>to help</u>. | I said I <u>would</u>.

- *there/then, so/not, such*

At the beginning of the 19th century … | Things were very different <u>then</u>.
I expect <u>I'll see you at the meeting</u>. | If <u>not</u>, I'll call you over the weekend.
… you may experience <u>symptoms of nausea</u>. | <u>Such symptoms</u> are not uncommon.

- **Parallel expressions**

<u>his fellow mathematicians</u> | <u>his colleagues</u>
<u>feelings of anger and betrayal</u> | <u>strong emotions</u>

- **Articles**

<u>A</u> survey … (first reference) | <u>The</u> survey … (later reference)

- **Names/titles**

<u>Peter</u> Barclay (first reference) | <u>Mr Barclay</u> … (later reference)
Professor <u>John Lewis</u> of UCLA (first reference) | <u>Professor Lewis</u> (later reference)

217

1 Say what each of the reference links in bold in the following text refers to.

> Each year, some 270,000 UK workers take time off because of work-related stress, at a cost to **the nation** in sick pay, lost production and medical bills of about £7 billion. **These figures**, the most recent from the Institute of Management, would be **much higher** if the true toll of stress could be measured. **Its** effect on our personal lives is even **more profound**.

The IOM's survey confirmed **what stress experts have long suspected**: bosses suffer less from stress than **their** subordinates. Only nine per cent of junior managers looked forward to going to work, and only seven per cent felt **they** were in control of **their** jobs. **A similar situation** was found in a recent study of civil servants.

> **The control factor** is crucial. It has been demonstrated repeatedly that **those** who feel in control of **their** lives are usually able to control the ill-effects of stress. **That is** why 'empowerment' has become such a buzz word.

2 Underline the reference links in the following text, and say what they refer to.

> My research into workaholism shows that the workaholic whose physical and emotional health suffers from working long hours was someone who wanted to be unavailable emotionally. They would find a way of being so even if they weren't in paid employment, perhaps by taking up an obsessive hobby. But people who work long hours because they love what they are doing are physically and mentally uplifted by their work.
>
> For unwilling workaholics, forced to stay at their desks for fear of losing their jobs, long hours can be a killer. For those to whom work is a pleasure, being forced into unsought leisure time can adversely affect their health. Such people, I found, were the ones most likely to fall ill on holiday.

3 Fill in the missing reference links in the following advice about reducing stress.

- Enjoy what you are doing. If you 1 ...., write down why you 2 .... and see if you can make any changes to the things 3 .... block your enjoyment. If you 4 ...., take steps to do 5 .... If 6 ...., change your job!

- If you suffer from a lack of feeling in control, try to figure out how to overcome 7 .... One idea might be to suggest to your boss that 8 .... delegates more decision-making to you. 9 .... might be to join the management committee or become active in the union.

- While you may think that smoking, drinking coffee or comfort eating help you to deal with stress, 10 .... actually add to 11 .... So try to find other 12 .... of relaxing, like taking a walk, going for a swim, or reading a book.

4 Make any necessary corrections or improvements to the cohesion of the following short texts.

1 We live in a global economy. In a global economy there are ever-increasing opportunities for people to leave its native land and live abroad.

2 Culture shock is a term is used to describe the impact of moving to an unfamiliar culture. A term comes originally from Professor John H Schumann's *Theory of Acculturation*. In there, Professor John H Schumann explained the stages for an immigrant goes through from arrival in a new country to one's eventual assimilation.

3 Culture shock can be experienced by anyone which travels abroad to work, live or study, that may include business people and international students. These suffering from culture shock may experience some feelings as surprise, disorientation, uncertainty and confusion.

Exercise 11 (Unit 7)

Linking expressions

1 Put the linking expressions below into one of the four groups according to meaning.

> *also   although   as   as a result   as well*
> *consequently   despite/in spite of   due to*
> *for this reason   furthermore   however*
> *in addition   in view of   moreover*
> *on the other hand   since   so*
> *this means that   thus   whereas/while*

a) words meaning 'and'	c) words meaning 'because'
b) words meaning 'but'	d) words meaning 'therefore'

2 Complete the sentences with suitable linking expressions.

1 Smoking causes lung cancer and it has …….…….. been linked to other diseases.
2 Fish populations are declining …….…….. large scale marine pollution.
3 Many people are worried about GM crops …….…….. research findings that they are no more dangerous than ordinary plant varieties.
4 The major banks stopped lending money and …….…….. many developers went out of business.
5 Some drivers obey the rules of the road …….…….. others regularly disregard them.
6 Credit cards are a convenient method of payment. …….…….. they offer insurance cover on purchases.
7 It's hard to understand why people still smoke, …….…….. of all the evidence that smoking causes cancer.
8 If children arrive late, …….…….. a large part of the lesson time is wasted.

For more information on linking expressions, see *Academic Style 6*, page 116.

Exercise 12 (Unit 7)

Talking about research 1

1 Study these examples from the text on page 73. The expressions in bold are commonly used to discuss the results of research.

According to a study published in the Journal of Consumer Research …

Professor Berns' brain scans show how … .

methods for evaluating scientific findings …

Music constantly emerges in surveys as the most popular form of art.

The research was carried out at the Institute of Education.

2 Complete the following passages using each of the words below just once.

> *findings   shows/reveals/indicates   emerge*
> *according to   carried out   published*

A study of moral sensibility in four-year-olds, recently 1 …………… in *The British Journal of Psychology*, 2 …………… that, even at an early age, girls have a better understanding of other people's feelings than boys. It is hoped that the 3 …………… may help shed light on the way pre-school children socialise. 4 …………… to the authors, the study may also provide teachers and parents with invaluable help when trying to teach discipline to youngsters in their care.

Senior executives and directors commonly 5 …………… in polls as 'fat cats', who award themselves huge pay rises each year. However, research 6 …………… for the Institute of Management 7 …………… that last year's pay rise of 5.7% was the lowest for four years. The research also 8 …………… that the average director is forty-seven years old, earns £109,000 a year and has been with the company for thirteen years.

Exercise 13 (Unit 7)

Noun + noun combinations

e.g. **brain scan, self image**

1 Choose words from the box to make noun + noun combinations related to business and commerce which match the definitions below. The first one is done for you.

chain	label	poll	store
customer	mail	research	window
designer	market	service	
junk	opinion	shopping	

1 expensive type of product with a fashionable name: *designer brand*
2 unwanted letters in the post advertising things:
3 collecting information about what people buy and why:
4 looking at goods in shop displays without intending to buy them:
5 the part of a business that deals with clients' questions or problems:
6 the process of finding out what most people think about a topic:
7 one of a group of shops all owned by the same organization:

For more information about noun + noun combinations, see *Academic Style 3*, page 56.

Exercise 14 (Unit 8)

Cohesion: avoiding repetition

The following sentences contain unnecessary repetition. Replace the underlined sections with a suitable word or phrase chosen from the box below, and make any changes necessary. You can use any expression more than once.

this	*these*	*one*	*the former … the latter*	
that	*those*	*did so*	*respectively*	

1 Whereas only 34% of adults said they went to the cinema in 1987–88, more than half said that they <u>went to the cinema</u> in 1997–98.
2 Some museums introduced admission charges and <u>introducing admissions charges</u> affected the number of visits made.
3 A higher proportion of people aged 35 and over said they attended classical music concerts than <u>people</u> aged fifteen to 34.
4 We were shown a number of good videos in the Life and Culture course, but the <u>video</u> I liked best was *Fawlty Towers*.
5 *Titanic* was the top box-office film of 1998 in the United Kingdom. <u>*Titanic*</u> was followed by *The Full Monty* and *Saving Private Ryan*.
6 The two most popular cultural events after the cinema were plays and art galleries/exhibitions with attendances of 24% and 22% <u>for plays and art galleries/exhibitions in that order</u>.
7 Excursions to Stratford-upon-Avon and Oxford have been arranged for this term. <u>The excursion to Stratford-upon-Avon</u> will be on the 16th of April and <u>the excursion to Oxford</u> will be on the 2nd of July.
8 Approximately 25% of visitors made purchases in the museum shop. Of <u>the 25% of visitors who made purchases in the museum shop</u>, most spent less than £5.
9 In 1998, the number of visits made to the Tate Gallery rose to more than double <u>the number of visits made</u> in 1981.

220

Exercise 15 (Unit 8)

Conditionals

Conditional clauses are often used to introduce or develop arguments in academic writing, e.g. *If we continue to burn fossil fuels at current rates, our economies may be at risk from rising seas, more severe storms and more intense droughts.*

Conditional clauses can be categorised according to how probable the condition is.

1 Match descriptions A, B and C below with Types 1, 2 or 3.

   A The condition is either impossible or unlikely to happen in the present or future. Type …

   B The condition is always true, or is possible in the present or future. Type …

   C The condition is impossible. Type …

   Type 1: Real

   If we don't offer good service, we'll go out of business.

   When it rains, the roof leaks.

   If you have any information, let me know.

If + present form + future form / *may/might/could* / imperative
If / When + present form + present form/imperative

   Type 2: Hypothetical

   If we started using cleaner fuels, air quality would improve.

   If I had any choice in the matter, I wouldn't take part.

If + past simple or past continuous   *would/could/might* + infinitive

   Type 3: Hypothetical (past)

   If you had dealt with the situation earlier, it wouldn't have become so serious.

If + past perfect simple or continuous   *would/could/might have* + past participle

MIXED CONDITIONALS

2 In the following examples, does the *if* clause refer to the past or the present? Does the main clause refer to the past or the present?

   If you had dealt with the situation earlier, you wouldn't be facing a major problem now.

   We would be rich now if you hadn't lost the lottery ticket.

PUNCTUATION

3 Look at these two examples and complete the rule about punctuation.

   When the *if* clause comes first in a sentence, it is followed by ....

   When the main clause comes first, ...

CONDITIONAL LINKS

In addition to *if,* the following expressions can be used to introduce conditional clauses:

unless	*provided (that)*
as/so long as	*suppose/supposing (that)*
on condition (that)	

4 Rewrite the following as conditional sentences.

1 A hold-up on the motorway made me late for work. *If …*

2 We need to take immediate steps to prevent further redundancies.
Unless …

3 To avoid cancellation fees, reservations must be cancelled at least seven days in advance.
Provided that …

4 Our flight was delayed because of ice on the runway.

5 My lack of overseas experience makes it difficult for me to further my career.

6 The professor agreed to come, but insisted that we put him up in a five-star hotel.

7 Operations are having to be cancelled because of a shortage of medical supplies.

8 It's easy to get lost in the desert, so you should only go with an experienced guide.

9 A computer would enable me to get through my workload twice as fast.

10 The restaurant is very popular, so it's essential that you book in advance.

11 There was a poor harvest this year which is likely to cause winter food shortages.

12 Increased interest rates have made it difficult for people to buy their own homes.

Exercise 16 (Unit 9)

Relative clauses

Relative clauses are a way of providing additional information within a single sentence, using relative pronouns, *who, that, which, where, when, why, whose.*
There are two kinds of relative clause:
Defining relative clauses contain information which is essential to the meaning of the sentence, e.g. *The film which won the award was called the White Ribbon.*
Notes:

- commas are not used before the relative pronoun.
- *that* is often used instead of *who* or *which.*
- The relative pronoun can be left out when it refers to the object of the sentence, e.g. *The biggest problem * we face is ignorance. (*which/that)*

Non-defining relative clauses contain extra information, which is not essential to the meaning of the sentence, e.g. *The White Ribbon, which is over two hours long, won the award.*
Notes:

- Commas are used to separate the relative clause from the rest of the sentence.
- *that* cannot be used.
- The relative pronoun cannot be left out.

1 Say whether the relative clauses in the following sentences are Defining (D) or non-Defining (ND).

1 Los Angeles has become a sprawling urban fantasy, which many people feel should not really exist.

2 The city is dependent on the State Water Project, which supplies more than a trillion gallons of water per year.

3 This removes half the water that would otherwise flow into the San Francisco Bay.

4 The flood control system destroyed the areas which provided an important staging area for migratory birds.

2 Complete the following sentences by adding a relative pronoun if necessary.

Antarctica is positioned over the South Pole, 1 ……… means it receives less of the Sun's energy than any other continent. In addition, about 80 percent of the energy 2 ……… does reach the region is reflected by the icy surface. Antarctica is separated from the rest of the globe by the huge Southern Ocean, 3 ……… surrounds it with water and sea ice, while the steep coastline acts as a barrier to the cyclones 4 ……… would otherwise bring warmer air inland. As a result, Antarctica has become a huge polar desert, 5 ……… surface is 98 per cent covered by ice, 6 ……… only cold-adapted plants and animals can survive. The concern 7 ……… scientists have is the rate at 8 ……… Antarctic ice sheets are melting.

3 Rewrite the following information, including the information in brackets as a relative clause.

1 Consumption of pork has doubled in the last ten years in China. (Pork is the China's most popular meat)

2 Admissions to museums have fallen. (They charge an entrance fee)

3 Marine parks have become more common. (Fishing and other commercial activity is banned there)

4 Businesses must have a licence to export any products like TVs. (they contain cathode-ray tubes)

5 Dwight D. Eisenhower was the 34th president of the United States. (His nickname was 'Ike'.)

5 .... , the concrete flood-control system had disastrous ecological consequences, destroying wetland areas which provided an important staging area for migratory birds. (Text 2)

For more information on introducing sentences, see *Critical Thinking 4*, page 167.

Check your answers by referring to the texts in Unit 9 (pages 90 and 92–93).

Exercise 17 (Unit 9)

Introducing sentences

1 **Put the expressions below under one of the following headings, according to meaning.**

> *Typically, Paradoxically, As a general rule, Surprisingly, Inevitably, By and large, Not surprisingly, In the normal course of events, Predictably,*

Usually true	*Expected outcome*	*Unusual/unexpected outcome*

2 **Choose one of the expressions above to complete the extracts.**

It is thought that 1.3 billion people worldwide do not have safe drinking water.
1 .... , the problem is much worse in rural areas than in towns. (Text 1)

2 .... , 80 litres of water per person per day are enough for a reasonable quality of life. (Text 1)

LA has nine million cars, and 40 per cent of the population suffer from respiratory problems due to vehicle emissions. 3 .... , the city is now becoming the forum for some of the most progressive environmental thought in the USA. (Text 2)

The city is often seen as the essence of anti-nature. 4 .... , people often move to Los Angeles because of nature. (Text 2)

Exercise 18 (Unit 9)

Word building: nouns

What are the nouns derived from the following words? They all appear in the texts in Unit 9 (*Water, water …*).

1	clear	6	emit	11	propose
2	complete	7	expand	12	provide
3	consume	8	extend	13	restore
4	despair	9	inhabit	14	diverse
5	destroy	10	oppose	15	sustainable

> **Language Fact**
> *-ion* is by far the most common suffix used to form nouns in academic English, occurring more than twice as often as its nearest rival *-ity*. The suffix *-ion* is used to form numerous common nouns and also to form new words like *computerisation* and *politicisation*.

Exercise 19 (Unit 10)

Expressing cause and result

1 Read the following text and look at the example sentences.

> The most violent tornado in recorded history struck in 1925, killing 689 people, injuring 1980 others, destroying four towns, severely damaging six others and leaving 11,000 people homeless across Missouri, Indiana and Illinois.

Cause		Result
• The tornado	caused/resulted in	the deaths of 689 people.
• The damage	led to	people losing their homes.

Result		Cause
• 689 people were killed	as a result of	the tornado.
• 689 deaths	resulted from	the tornado.

Grammar notes

- Look at these two ways of using the verb **cause**: *to cause a problem* (+ object); *to cause a problem to occur* (+ object + *to* + verb)

- **result from**, **result in** and **lead to** are phrasal verbs, which are followed by an object or an object + *-ing*.
  The swelling resulted from an insect bite.
  The illness led to him resigning.
  Lead to is used with results which happened after some time.

- **as a result of** is used as a preposition before a noun or noun phrase:
  As a result of the drought, the harvest failed.
  The harvest failed as a result of the drought.

---

2 Make three sentences about the other results of the tornado, using *result in, result from* and *as a result of.*

3 Rewrite the following sentences using the expressions in brackets.

1 In New York in 1988 the temperature stayed above 32°C for 32 days, and the murder rate soared by 75 per cent.

   A heatwave in New York … (result in)

2 When the Fohn wind blows in Geneva, traffic accidents rise by 50 per cent.

   There is … (as a result of)

3 During the severe winter of 1962–63, economic activity in the UK dropped by about seven per cent.

   (result from)

4 It has been estimated that by 2030, sea levels will rise 18cm with global warming.

   (cause)

5 Following recent coastal flooding, insurance companies may increase premiums for homes and businesses.

   (lead to)

6 Floods worldwide cost about $16 billion a year in damage.

   (result from)

7 By 2030, warmer winters could melt the snow at many ski resorts around the world.

   (cause)

8 Changes in atmospheric pressure can make swollen joints more painful for arthritis sufferers.

   (as a result of)

Exercise 20 (Unit 11)

The suffix -en
e.g. less ➔ lessen

1 Each of the adjectives in the box below can be made into a verb by adding the suffix -en. Two of them need further changes of spelling – which are they?

bright	dark	deep	hard	long	loose
weak	broad	fast	less	light	short
strong	wide				

2 Complete the following sentences by adding verbs formed by adding -en to adjectives in the box above. Make any other changes necessary.

1 Next year they plan to .... the course from four to six weeks.

2 The word 'examination' is often .... to 'exam'.

3 The council is proposing to .... this road to three lanes instead of two.

4 These exercises are specifically designed to .... the abdominal muscles.

5 It takes two hours for the glue to .... and the repair to be complete.

6 The danger of developing lung cancer .... as soon as you give up smoking.

7 The harbour was .... to make it suitable for larger boats.

8 The case for the defence was .... when a key witness failed to appear.

Language Fact
-en is the second most common verb suffix after -ise (-ize in American English).

Exercise 21 (Unit 11)

Articles

The **indefinite article** (a/an) is used with countable nouns:

• to mention a particular person or thing for the first time:
There was a fire in a local warehouse.
• to refer to something general rather than particular:
I'm looking for a job.
• to refer to one example of a general class:
My sister is an engineer.

The **zero article** is used with uncountable nouns and plurals:

• to refer to an indefinite number or amount:
Drink plenty of water.
The investigation will take months.
• with proper names and place names, including countries, cities, streets and public buildings:
Professor Jordan, Asia, Peru, Texas, Paris, Oxford Street, Heathrow Airport
• to refer to single mountains and lakes:
Everest, Lake Como
• in certain phrases:
have breakfast/lunch/dinner
(See also *Special cases* on page 200.)

The **definite article** (the) is used with countable and uncountable nouns to refer to:

• something which has already been mentioned:
There was a fire in a local warehouse. The fire is thought to have been started deliberately.
• a specific example of a general concept:
The water in the well was polluted. (Compare: *Water is essential for life.*)
The heat was unbearable. (Compare: *Heat kills insect larvae.*)
• things which are unique:
the Sun, the Moon, the Earth, the Internet
• oceans, seas, rivers, mountain ranges:
the Pacific, the Nile, the Himalayas
• something which is clear in the context:
The director has resigned. The library is closing.
• superlatives:
the longest river, the highest crime rate

225

SPECIAL CASES

	ZERO ARTICLE	DEFINITE ARTICLE
Transport	*travel by* **sea/boat/train/air/car**, etc.	*We took **the train** to the airport.* *You can buy a ticket on **the bus**.*
Communications	*contact by* **phone**; *send by* **post**	*He's on **the phone**.* ***The post** is late today.*
Times of day	*at* **dawn/daybreak/midday/lunchtime/** **sunset/night**	*The telephone rang in the middle of **the** **night**.* *We met **in the morning/afternoon/** **evening**.*
Days, months, seasons	*on* **Sunday**, *in* **September**, *in* **summer**	*on **the third Sunday** of the month* *in **the summer** of 2001*
Countries	**Jordan, Switzerland**	Plural countries and countries with a word like *republic* or *state* in their name take the definite article: **the Philippines,** **the Czech Republic**
Institutions	With zero article the focus is on the general purpose of the institution: *He's **at** **school/college/university**. (studying)* *She's been taken **to hospital**. (for treatment)* *He spent a year **in prison**. (as punishment)*	With an article, the focus is on some other aspect of the institution: *He's a caretaker at **the university**.* ***The hospital** is opposite **the school**.* ***The prison** was built last century.*

Complete the following texts by adding *a/an*, *the* or leaving a blank (zero article).

---

1 .... Maldives is 2 .... archipelago of 1,190 small coral islands situated in
3 .... Indian Ocean south-west of 4 .... Sri Lanka. None of 5 ....
islands rises above 1.8m, making 6 .... country 7 .... lowest place on Earth.
As 8 .... result, 9 .... country is threatened by 10 .... rise in sea level
caused by 11 .... global warming, and 12 .... sea wall has been built
around 13 .... capital island, 14 .... Male.

---

15 .... world's most easy-going prison system is about to be reformed after
16 .... protests that convicts frequently leave 17 .... jail richer than when
they arrived. 18 .... Prisoners in Greenland are allowed to go out to
19 .... work in 20 .... local community, and 21 .... wages they earn
are paid into their bank accounts. 22 .... regime, which emphasises
23 .... rehabilitation above 24 .... punishment, is becoming increasingly
unpopular among 25 .... public, according to 26 .... John Meyer, director
general of 27 .... island's police force. 28 .... team of judges and
magistrates is working on 29 .... reform plans which will be presented by
30 .... end of 31 .... year.

32 .... Symptoms of jet lag are well known.
33 .... Tiredness, and with it 34 .... lack of
35 .... energy, 36 .... enthusiasm and
37 .... concentration, is commonplace. Jet lag
is much worse for people who live by
38 .... strict timetable – those, for instance,
who must have 39 .... breakfast at eight a.m. or
who always go to 40 .... bed at 41 ....
same time and need 42 .... precise amount of
sleep each night. 43 .... Westward journeys
induce less jetlag than 44 .... eastern journeys,
partly because 45 .... sleep is easier when
travelling with 46 .... sun. 47 ....
Experienced travellers always try to travel westward
so they have 48 .... advantage of 49 ....
alertness and 50 .... mental agility after
51 .... good night's sleep.

Exercise 22 (Unit 12)

Vocabulary: collocations

Complete the following sentences with one of the verbs in the box. Make any changes necessary. You may use any verb more than once.

make	do	draw	play	set
have	give	take	pay	

1 He didn't .... the slightest notice of my advice.

2 He .... a serious error of judgement.

3 Every applicant must .... a spelling test.

4 You need to .... this matter your full attention.

5 We have to .... a distinction between private and state education.

6 More research into the causes of truancy needs to be ....

7 I expect you to .... an example for the others.

8 Your state of mind .... an important part in your ability to listen effectively.

9 You won't .... any progress unless you study.

10 Stress .... a negative effect on learning.

11 Please .... careful attention to what I'm going to say.

12 Two hundred people .... part in the survey.

Exercise 23 (Unit 12)

The ... the ... (comparatives)

Look at this sentence from Listening Task 2.

The older you are, the more likely this is to happen.

This structure is a common way of showing how two things develop in relation to each other. Here are some more examples.

The harder I work, the less progress I seem to make!
The more experienced the salesperson, the more money they make.
The earlier you arrive, the better.

Notice that:

1 *the* can be followed by both **adjectives** (e.g. *earlier, more experienced*) and **adverbs** (e.g. *harder, more quickly*);

2 the normal rules of forming comparisons apply;

3 a short form can be used with sentences which end *the better*.

1 Complete the following examples.

1 The more words you try to learn in one go, the .... (*likely*) you are to remember them.

2 The .... (*motivated*) you are when you start learning a language, ... (*fast*) you'll progress.

3 The .... you work, ... mistakes you'll make.

4 .... (*thoroughly*) you revise, ... you'll feel.

5 .... (*far*) you travel, ... everywhere seems to be.

6 .... the dictionary, ... the information it will provide.

2 Now compare the following.

1 Price/Quality

2 Education/Opportunity

3 Age/Wisdom

Exercise 24 (Unit 13)

Common verbs in -ed and -ing clauses

According to the *Longman Corpus of Written and Spoken English*, only a small number of verbs are really common in -ed and -ing clauses in academic prose. These verbs are shown in the following boxes.

1 In each group, three of the verbs are the most common. Can you guess the top three in each case?

> **-ing clauses**
> *having, being, using, concerning, involving, containing*

> **-ed clauses**
> *made, based, used, taken, caused, given, concerned, obtained, produced*

2 Complete the following sentences with verbs chosen from the lists above.

1 A number of problems .... with health and safety issues remain to be solved.

2 It's a long and complicated rail journey .... several changes.

3 A new drug .... on ginseng is undergoing clinical trials at the moment.

4 A memo .... highly confidential information has been leaked to the newspapers.

5 Farmers are keen to promote fruit and vegetables .... in this country.

6 Drugs .... illegally are not subject to quality control.

7 He was the ideal candidate for the job, ... both well qualified and experienced.

8 A shortage of Atlantic cod .... by overfishing has led to massive price rises.

9 He managed to slip out of the country .... a false passport.

10 The measures .... by the government to reduce unemployment have failed.

Exercise 25 (Unit 13)

The verb *doubt*

Doubt is used in various expressions, both as a noun and verb, to express degrees of certainty. Look at the following sentence: *I doubt very much that any form of media we have today will survive that long.* (*Bones to phones*, section A page 130)

Tick the correct uses of *doubt* in the following sentences, and correct any errors. Check your answers by referring to the notes below.

1 I doubt if anyone can look forward to a career for life these days.
2 It could have been a genuine mistake, but I doubt so.
3 If I doubt how to spell a word, I check it in a dictionary.
4 It is no doubt that there is still great inequality in the world.
5 This is without doubt one of the most challenging problems we face.
6 After yet another injury, his football career looks in doubts.
7 There seems little doubt that interests rates will rise.
8 Many people still doubt about the benefit of alternative medicine.

> **Grammar notes**
> • **there is little/some/no doubt (that)** (expresses how certain you are about something) e.g. *There is no doubt that one day this disease will be curable.*
> • **without doubt** (used to emphasise an opinion) e.g. *He is without doubt the best candidate.*
> • **have (some/any) doubts (about)** (= feel uncertain) e.g. *Some people have doubts about the method of research.*
> • **be/look in doubt** (= may not happen) e.g. *Without funding, the future of the project is in doubt.*
> • **doubt if/whether/that** (= think unlikely) e.g. *I doubt if anything we can do now will prevent global warming.*
> • **I doubt it** (= I don't think so) e.g. *I may become a famous scientist but I doubt it!*

Exercise 26 (Unit 14)

Topic vocabulary: the media

1 Match the following words or phrases (1–10) to the correct meaning (a–j).

1	(the) press	....	6	copy (*n*)	....
2	(the) media	....	7	journalist	....
3	to broadcast	....	8	correspondent	....
4	coverage	....	9	readership	....
5	edition	....	10	circulation	....

a) someone who writes or talks about a particular subject, especially a serious one, for a newspaper or news programme

b) the number of copies of a newspaper or magazine that are sold in a particular period

c) send out radio or television programmes so that people can hear them

d) all the organisations that are involved in providing information to the public, especially newspapers, television and radio

e) a single newspaper or magazine

f) newspapers and the people who write for them

g) the number of people or type of people who regularly read a particular newspaper or magazine

h) the way an event or subject is reported in the news, especially how much space or time is given to reporting it

i) someone who writes for a newspaper or magazine, or who appears on news programmes on television or radio

j) the version of a newspaper of magazine that is printed on a particular occasion

2 Complete the following sentences with the correct word or phrase.

1 There was an interesting letter in the Saturday .... of *The Times*.

2 And now for a report on bullying in schools from our education .... , Tim Low.

3 The magazine is aimed at a .... of mainly eighteen- to 30-year-olds

4 During his long career as a .... , he won many awards.

5 You haven't by any chance got a .... of yesterday's paper, have you?

6 The president's speech is due to be .... on Channel 8 tonight.

7 The resignation of the Foreign Minister received widespread media ....

8 There's going to be a debate in parliament on the subject of the freedom of ....

Exercise 27 (Unit 15)

Word building: nouns

1 Complete the table by adding the noun form of the following verbs.

Verb	Noun	Verb	Noun
1 adapt		7 invest	
2 adjust		8 isolate	
3 dense		9 lose	
4 discover		10 recommend	
5 disturb		11 renew	
6 expand		12 survive	

2 Complete the following sentences with words from exercise 1.

1 Illegal hunting is threatening the .... of the species.

2 The rapid .... of cities can cause many social problems.

3 The island of Macao has the highest population .... in the world.

4 .... is the process by which an organism becomes better suited to its habitat.

5 After the accident he suffered temporary memory ....

6 Astronomers in the USA have announced the .... of a new planet.

7 The life of a hill farmer is one of considerable social ....

8 The school inspector made several .... in her report.

Exercise 28 (Unit 15)

-ing forms and infinitives

Main uses of –ing forms

A in **verb forms**, with auxiliary verbs, e.g. *Crime levels are rising.*

B like **nouns**, e.g. *Swimming is prohibited.*

C after certain **verbs**, e.g. *The job involves working long hours. Most people dislike queuing.*

D after **all** prepositions, e.g. *You can be fined for speeding. The party is capable of winning an election.*

E in **participle clauses**, e.g. *The company introduced a new service, offering greater flexibility.*

-ing forms and infinitives are common grammatical patterns in English. Recognising and understanding them is an important tool in following the meaning in a difficult reading text.

1 Match each sentence below with one of the uses above by labelling it A, B, C, D or E.

1 .... Today there is a better than 95% chance of surviving a heart attack.

2 .... Understanding the biological effects of cosmic rays is a priority.

3 .... Lying in wait beyond the Earth's atmosphere, solar radiation poses additional problems.

4 .... Researchers are building artificial liver, bone and cartilage tissue right now.

5 .... Dennis Tito's plans involve spending a week on the Mir space station.

Main uses of infinitives

with *to*

A to express purpose, e.g. *You use a shredder to destroy documents.*

B after certain verbs, e.g. *Sales tend to fall in January. Some people cannot afford to buy food.*

C after *too* and *enough*, e.g. *It's too complicated to explain. It's not important enough to worry about.*

without *to*

D after **modal auxiliary verbs**, e.g. *All accidents must be reported. An electrical fault could cause a fire.*

E after *let* and *make*, e.g. *I like films that make me laugh. Some parents let their children stay out late.*

---

2 Match each sentence below with one of the uses above by labelling it A, B, C, D or E.

1 .... NASA can be proud of the technology it has developed.

2 .... Cosmic rays possess too much energy for shielding to be effective.

3 .... To get answers to these questions, Daniel Goldin established the NSBRI.

4 .... When astronauts had few tasks, it made them feel stressed.

5 .... Monitoring devices will allow astronauts to take refuge from solar radiation.

Language Fact

By far the most common verb followed by an *-ing* form in academic writing is '*be used for*'. Other common verbs used in this way include: *keep, start, stop, involve.*
The most common verb followed by a *to*-clause in academic writing is *seem*. Other common verbs used in this way include: *try, tend, fail, appear.*

---

3 Complete the following sentences with suitable forms of verbs chosen from the box below.

Motion sickness afflicts more than two-thirds of astronauts upon 1 .... orbit. Though everyone recovers after a while, body systems continue 2 .... 3 .... too much fluid, the body begins 4 .... it, including calcium, electrolytes and blood plasma. The production of blood cells decreases, 5 .... astronauts slightly anaemic. Spinal discs expand, and so does the astronaut, who may 6 .... five centimetres and 7 .... backache.

Russian cosmonauts returned from long flights unable to stand without 8 .... Americans back from months-long flights also paid the price, 9 .... losses in weight, muscle mass and bone density. NASA geared up 10 .... how – even if – humans would 11 .... a mission to Mars

Jeffrey Sutton has treated the head trauma, wounds, kidney stones and heart rhythm irregularities that one could 12 .... on the way to Mars. 13 .... with infection, Sutton plans a factory 14 .... drugs, even new ones.

The NSBRI team found that the diagnostic device they had developed can 15 .... as part of a standard test 16 .... patients at risk from heart rhythm irregularities.

survive	faint	sense	reach
see	use	identify	cope
suffer	make	render	excrete
suffer	change	gain	encounter

Exercise 29 (Unit 15)

Word partners

1 Say what the following adjectives refer to or are connected with, e.g. *aural = the sense of hearing.*
   1 optical   6 psychiatric
   2 solar   7 psychological
   3 astronomical   8 dental
   4 biological   9 orthopaedic
   5 cardiac   10 pharmaceutical

2 Match each adjective from exercise 1 with one or more of the following nouns.

   arrest   clock   eclipse   hospital   illness
   illusion   industry   instrument   panel
   power   profiling   surgeon   telescope
   treatment   warfare

3 Match each definition below with a two-word expression from exercise 2.
   1 The use of various techniques to influence the mind in war, business, sport, etc. intended to make opponents lose confidence
   2 An image of something that is not really there, such as an imaginary oasis in the middle of the desert
   3 A piece of equipment, usually placed on a roof, which collects and uses energy from the sun.
   4 The system in plants and animals that controls when they sleep, eat, etc.
   5 The medical term for 'heart attack'
   6 The result of converting sunlight into electricity
   7 A piece of equipment designed to aid vision, e.g. binoculars, microscope
   8 System of investigating an offender's behaviour, motives and background as a way of guiding an investigation
   9 The moment when the moon passes between the Sun and the Earth so that the Sun is fully or partially covered

Exercise 30 (Unit 16)

Expressing probability

Use language from the following tables to discuss the probability of the events below.

Introducing a personal opinion

I think/don't think …
I believe …
In my opinion/view …

Introducing a more impersonal opinion

It seems/appears …
There seems to be …
They/people say …

Adjectives: *possible/probable/likely*

It is	quite	**possible**	
It is	quite/very/highly	**probable/likely**	that X will happen.
It is	rather/very/highly	**unlikely**	
X is	rather/very/highly	**likely/unlikely**	to happen.

Adverbs: *certainly/definitely/probably/possibly*

I will	most	**certainly/definitely**	do X.
X will	very	**possibly/probably**	happen.

Nouns: *possibility/chance/prospect; probability/likelihood*

There is a	remote/slight strong	**possibility/chance/prospect**	
There is a	strong/90%	**probability**	of X happening. that X will happen.
There	is (very) little isn't much	**possibility/chance/prospect likelihood**	
The	**possibility/chance prospect/likelihood**	of X happening	is remote/small/slight.

Questions

What is the	**possibility/chance prospect/likelihood**	of X happening? that X will happen?

Other expressions

- *In all probability, Leeds United will win the cup.* (very probable)
- *There's every possibility that the economy will improve before long.* (very probable)
- *It's more than likely that there'll be a general election next year.* (very probable)
- *There's little or no chance of finding any more survivors.* (very unlikely)

1 In your opinion, what is the likelihood of the following events happening in the next twenty years? Give reasons for your answers.

1 A woman will become president of the USA.
2 A cure for cancer will be found.
3 A British football team will win the World Cup.
4 Global warming will be reversed.
5 No one will read books any more.
6 Every home will be connected to the Internet.
7 Spanish will become the official language of the USA.
8 A non-polluting 'green' car will be developed.

2 Choose one or more of the following topics and make sentences about possible future events in your life.

e.g. *I think it's quite likely that I'll go to live in the USA.*

There's a remote possibility that I'll win a scholarship to Harvard.

1 The IELTS test	4 Your next holiday
2 Study plans	5 Your family
3 Career plans	6 Your home

For more information on modal verbs see p. 234, ex. 34

Exercise 31 (Unit 17)

British vs American vocabulary

Give the British equivalent of the following. There is a list of jumbled answers below.

1 auto(mobile)	8 parking lot
2 back-up	9 railroad
3 beltway	10 subway
4 expressway	11 traffic circle
5 freeway	12 trailer
6 gasoline/gas	13 mass transit
7 license plate	14 underpass

> *petrol   underground (railway)*
> *public transport   caravan   railway*
> *number plate   car   subway*
> *roundabout   motorway (in city)   tailback*
> *motorway   ring road   car park*

Exercise 32 (Unit 17)

Topic vocabulary: cars and traffic

1 Classify the following words as A, B or C according to whether they are connected with:

A traffic problems
B ways of avoiding traffic problems
C car crime

bottleneck	collision	road rage
breakdown	congestion	roadworks
bypass	hit-and-run	speed bump
car sharing	joyriding	speed trap
carjacking	park and ride	speeding

2 Complete the following sentences with the correct words from exercise 1.

1 an occasion when a vehicle stops working
2 an accident in which two or more vehicles hit each other
3 a narrow raised area put across a road to force traffic to slow down
4 a road that goes round a town rather than through it
5 the crime of stealing a car and driving it in a fast and dangerous way
6 violent and angry behaviour by one driver towards another driver
7 an arrangement by which people travel together to work in one car and share the cost
8 a system where you leave your car outside town and take a special bus into the centre

Exercise 33 (Unit 17)

Talking about research 2

1 Divide the following expressions into two groups, A or B, according to meaning. Check meanings if necessary.

A showing that something is true
B showing that something is untrue

contradict	invalidate	reveal
demolish	prove	show
demonstrate	refute	support
disprove		

2 Complete the following sentences with suitable words from the list in exercise 1.

1 People believed that the sun went round the Earth until the theory was ....in the 16thC.

2 Unfortunately, problems with the research methods .... the findings.

3 A recent survey .... a 95% level of customer satisfaction.

4 There was no evidence to .... the claims made for the new slimming pill.

5 Unfortunately, research findings have been inconsistent. In fact, the results of a recent study completely .... those of an earlier one.

233

Exercise 34 (Unit 19)

Modal verbs

The main modal verbs are: *must, should, can, could, will, would, may* and *might*. Modal verbs are used with main verbs to express ideas such as ability, probability or obligation.

*We **can** underline the points we are making by raising our eyebrows.* (ability)
*The economy **may** improve by the end of the year.* (probability)
*The world **must** find an alternative to fossil fuels.* (obligation)

The modal verbs *can, could, may* and *might* are particularly useful in academic writing as a way of expressing a cautious opinion.
*The phony smile **may** occur too early.* (not 'occurs')
*Studying the face and voice **could** improve lie detection.* (not 'will' or 'would')

FORM

Modal verbs are followed by the infinitive without *to*, e.g. *You must work hard.*
Modal verbs differ from main verbs because they:

- do not take *-s* on the third person, e.g. *He should listen to advice.*
- form questions without *do*, e.g. *Can you hear me?*
- have no past form or infinitive. Other forms are used instead, e.g. *Will you be able to attend?* NOT *Will you ~~can~~ attend?*

	Present	Past	Future
ability	can *do*	could *do* / was able to *do*	will be able to *do*
probability	can, could, may, might, must *do*	can, could, may, might, must + *have done*	can, could, may, might, must *do*
obligation	must	had to *do*	will have to *do*
advice	should	should *have gone*	should *go*

Some of the following sentences contain a mistake. Find the errors and correct them.

1 The malaria test kit should provide results within 20 minutes.
2 She might became an Olympic swimmer but she chose an acting career instead.
3 We must to try to consume as little of the world's resources as possible.
4 There is concern that off-shore windfarms could be disrupt the marine ecosystem.
5 Evidence suggests that 800,000 years ago people were able to control fire to cook food.
6 How we can be sure that black holes really exist?
7 Most people will must wait years before superfast internet access is available.
8 Dinosaurs may have been smaller than previously thought.
9 In France, women cannot vote until 1944.
10 The government should have held a referendum on the issue.

For more information on the role of modal verbs see *Academic Style 5*, page 96.

> **Language Fact**
> 10–15% of all verb phrases in academic writing contain modal verbs. The majority of these express possibility and the most common modal verbs are *may, can* and *might*, e.g. *The cost of fuel may rise even further.*

Writing practice bank

Task 1: Comparing data

EXAMPLE ANSWER

Read the example answers to question 7c on page 42 and answer the questions below.

Paragraph 1. With a population of 13.6 million, Shanghai is only slightly (larger) than Los Angeles while it has similar figures for noise levels, the supply of basic services and the percentage of children in secondary school. However, on two very important counts, Shanghai scores significantly higher than LA. In the first place, it is a much safer city to live in, with a murder rate which is only one fifth that of LA. In addition, the air quality is much better, so it is a healthier city to live in. The only disadvantage, according to the figures, is that there is a higher level of traffic congestion in Shanghai in the rush hour.

Paragraph 2. Of the five cities, Tokyo appears to have the best environment overall. Although it is by far the largest of the five, with a population of 27.2 million, it is also the safest city to live in, with a murder rate of only 1.4 per 100,000. In addition, it has the least traffic congestion, the lowest levels of ambient noise and the highest percentage of children in secondary school. The provision of basic services is excellent, and the quality of its air is relatively good.

FOCUS QUESTIONS

1   It's a good idea to express information from a graph or table in your own words if possible. Which phrases are used to refer to the following information:
    1   Homes with water/electricity'
    2   'Murders per 100,000 people'
    3   'Traffic/km per hour in rush hour'
    4   'Clean air (score out of ten)'

2   It's also important to link ideas together well. Mark the main linking expressions in the two paragraphs by underlining them twice. The first two examples have been done for you.

3   Circle any comparative or superlative adjectives. Underline adverbs which are used to qualify these adjectives. The first example has been done for you.

Task 2: Presenting solutions to a problem

EXAMPLE ANSWER

Read the example answer for the exam topic on page 44, then answer the questions.

Almost half the world's population now live in urban areas and, as cities grow even larger, conditions for city dwellers are likely to get worse. Two of the most crucial problems, it can be argued, are housing and waste disposal.

Of these, housing is undoubtedly the most serious. People need clean, safe accommodation in which to live and raise their families. However, as populations rise, some people are forced to move to unsuitable housing which may lack such basic services as clean water and electricity, while others may actually become homeless. Any civilized society should try to prevent this situation. It is therefore essential for the authorities in major cities to take responsibility for the wellbeing of their poorest citizens and make the provision of secure, affordable housing a priority in their planning and budgeting.

Waste disposal may seem a more trivial problem but uncollected rubbish is not only potentially dangerous but can also cause serious diseases. In the past, waste disposal was cheap and easy, as much rubbish was simply dumped in a convenient place. Today, however, there are numerous problems, including increased transport costs, which make waste disposal expensive, and a shortage of suitable space for depositing waste. The obvious answer is for communities to create less rubbish in the first place. Manufacturers must be persuaded to reduce the amount of packaging they produce, and people need to recycle their household waste efficiently.

In conclusion, it is clear that these are complex problems which will not be solved easily. However, unless we take steps to tackle them now they will represent even more serious challenges in future. (*269 words*)

FOCUS QUESTIONS

1 Why is it helpful to divide a text like this into paragraphs?
2 *Paragraph 1* provides an introduction to the topic and mentions two key problems. What is the function of the other paragraphs?
3 Find examples of **topic** and **qualifying statements** in *paragraphs 2* and *3*.
4 How many sentences are there in each paragraph?
5 How many times is the pronoun '*I*' used?
6 Find a phrase in *paragraph 1* which avoids saying '*I think*'.
7 Underline all the main linking expressions.
8 Find phrases in *paragraphs 2* and *3* which introduce proposed solutions.

Exercise 3 (Unit 6)

Task 1: presenting and comparing data

UNDERSTANDING THE DATA

1 Study the graphs below and answer the questions.

Participation rates in popular leisure activities, by sex (England)

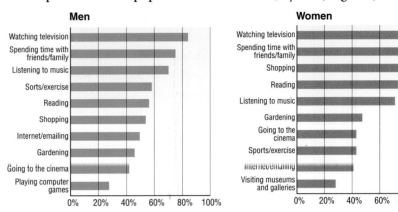

1 What is the main difference between the two graphs? *Listening to music, reading, sport/exercise, shopping, gardening, internet/emailing, going cinema*
2 Which country does the data come from? *England*
3 What do the figures on the bottom line indicate?
4 What are the two most popular activities for both sexes? *WT and spending time with F and F*
5 Which group is more likely to spend time reading, men or (women)?
6 Are there any activities which only appear on one of the graphs? *playing game journey*

GUIDED PRACTICE

2 Study the exam task and then complete the model answer by writing NO *MORE THAN THREE WORDS* in each space.

> *The graphs below give information on participation by men and women in various leisure activities. Summarise the information by selecting and reporting the main features, and make comparisons where relevant.*

The two graphs **1** *compare* the percentages of men and women who take part in certain leisure activities in **2** *England* . From the figures, we can see that watching TV is the **3** *most popular* leisure activity for **4** *more than* 8 in 10 men and women. Spending time with friends and family is the **5** *second* most common leisure activity for both men **6** *(75%)* and women (82%).

However, there are also some differences between the **7** *2 graphs* . Men are more likely than women to **8** *take part in* sport and exercise (58% compared with 43%) while women are more likely to spend their free time **9** *shopping* , with three quarters doing so, compared with around **10** *54%* of men. Similarly, women were more likely to engage in cultural activities **11** *such as* reading (73%), compared with men (56%).

12 *In conclusion* , it seems there is general consistency between the sexes in their choice of leisure activities, despite some differences in individual rankings.

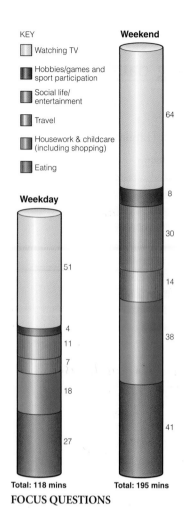

KEY
■ Watching TV
■ Hobbies/games and sport participation
■ Social life/ entertainment
■ Travel
■ Housework & childcare (including shopping)
■ Eating

Weekend

64
8
30
14
38
41

Weekday
51
4
11
7
?
18
27

Total: 118 mins   Total: 195 mins

FOCUS QUESTIONS

EXAM TIP: Try to rephrase information in the heading using your own words.

EXAM TIP: Choose only the most significant or interesting features to write about.

Exercise 4 (Unit 6)

Task 1: Presenting and comparing data

The bar graphs on the left represent: **Minutes per day spent by adult couples in shared activities (UK)**. Study the data and model answer before answering the questions below.

The bar graphs show the number of minutes per day which adult couples in the UK spend in shared activities, both on weekdays and at the weekend. A comparison of the two graphs **shows** that **overall** couples spend significantly more time together at weekends (over three hours a day), than they do on weekdays (about two hours).

Studying the graphs **in more detail, we can see** that the most common shared activity for both periods is watching TV, which accounts for 51 minutes on weekdays and 64 minutes at weekends. The next most common shared activity is eating. Couples spend 27 minutes eating on weekdays and 41 minutes, about 50% longer, at weekends. The difference is even greater with the remaining activities, where couples are involved for at least twice as long at weekends as they are on weekdays.

In conclusion, it is clear that that weekends provide greater opportunities for couples to relax and enjoy each other's company than weekdays do. (*162 words*)

1 The introductory sentence is based on the heading for the bar graphs.
   a) What extra words have been added to the heading?
   b) What extra information is included and where does this come from?
2 What aspect does the writer focus on in the first paragraph? What word indicates this?
3 What aspect does the writer focus on in the second paragraph? Which phrase indicates this?
4 How many activities are included in each graph? How many are named in the example answer? What phrase is used to refer to the rest?
5 Underline all the comparative expressions.
6 What phrase is used to introduce the final sentence?
7 What three different ways are used to talk about what can be seen in the graph?

Task 2: Structuring an argument (evidence-led)

EXAM TASK

Read the following exam topic and then follow the steps below to prepare an answer. Before you start, you may want to look back at the guidance on pages 63–65.

Write about the following topic:

> *Should children be encouraged to be competitive in sports and other activities? Or is it be better for them to learn the benefits of co-operating with other people?*
>
> *Discuss both these views and give your own answer.*

Give reasons for your answer and include any relevant examples from your own knowledge or experience.

Write at least 250 words.

REMINDERS

1   Analyse the topic: highlight the key points you need to consider. Think through the issues by asking yourself questions such as:

   - How can children be encouraged to be either competitive or co-operative?
   - In which activities are children likely to be competitive? In which co-operative?
   - What are the benefits (if any) of being competitive in adult life?
   - What are the benefits (if any) of co-operating with other people in adult life?

2   Decide on your **overall response** and make notes of all the **supporting evidence** you can think of, including personal experience.

3   Make a **paragraph plan** for an evidence-led argument like the one on page 65.

4   If you want to write the essay in full, try to use a range of language to **express reasons** and to **link ideas** (See page 64).

Task 1: Describing information from a table

GUIDED PRACTICE

Study the table below, including the heading and footnotes, and write your summary.

UNDERSTANDING THE DATA

Before you begin, answer these questions.

1 What does the table show?
2 What has been the overall trend in the number of visits to the UK?
3 How much has this increased over the period?
4 Which is the most common reason for visiting the UK: business or leisure?
5 Where do most visitors to the UK come from: N. America or W. Europe?
6 How has the leisure sector changed over the period?
7 How has the business sector changed over the period?
8 Are both sectors still growing?

You should spend about 20 minutes on this task.

The table below shows the number of visits to the UK by overseas residents between 1975 and 1998.

Summarise the information by selecting and reporting the main features, and make comparisons where relevant.

Write at least 150 words.

Visits to the UK by overseas residents	1975	1987	1996	1997	1998
Number of visits (millions) of which	9.5	15.6	25.2	25.5	25.7
Total business	1.8	3.6	6.1	6.3	6.9
Total leisure [1]	7.7	12.0	19.1	19.2	18.9
Total by North American residents	1.9	3.4	3.7	4.1	4.6
Total by residents of Western Europe [2]	5.9	9.3	16.8	16.7	16.6
Total other residents	1.7	2.9	4.7	4.7	4.6

1 Holiday visits to friends and relatives and miscellaneous visits
2 EU and Western European countries

Source: *UK in figures 2000, National Statistics*

Task 2: Presenting and justifying an opinion (evidence-led approach)

EXAMPLE ANSWER

Read the example answer for the exam topic on page 00, then answer the questions.

The UK government reportedly spends almost £500 million a year on supporting the cultural and artistic life of the country. This is undoubtedly a very large sum and the question inevitably arises as to whether the money is well spent.

Some people object to this expenditure, arguing that it is unfair to devote so much tax payers' money to things which only appeal to a minority of people. They believe these attractions should be self-funding, in other words, museums and galleries should set an entrance fee which covers their costs, while theatres and concert halls should also charge a realistic amount for tickets. The public money thus saved could then be spent on more important matters such as improving health care or providing better educational facilities.

However, there is a counter-argument which says that culture and the arts are not a trivial matter but a very important part of a nation's identity. Those who support this view contend that the arts have an important educational role by representing the traditions and heritage of a people. In their opinion, access to museums, galleries and artistic events should be freely available to all, rich or poor. Furthermore, they would argue that there is an important economic aspect to consider in that culture and the arts play a key role in tourism, and are therefore responsible for a significant amount of employment.

On balance, it seems to me that although governments have many demands on their resources, they do have a responsibility to support a range of cultural and artistic activities and to make these available to all their citizens. (*269 words*)

FOCUS QUESTIONS

1 What is the function of each paragraph in this **evidence-led** approach?
2 What language is used to introduce the two opposing views?
3 How is the conclusion introduced and what is the writer's final opinion?
4 How is the following information from the exam task expressed in the answer?
 a) museums and galleries, visual and performing arts (*paragraph 1*)
 b) minority interests (*paragraph 2*)
5 What examples of "more important things' are suggested?
6 What do the following refer to:
 a) This (*paragraph 1*) b) They (*paragraph 2*) c) their (*paragraph 2*)
 d) their (*paragraph 3*)
7 Find adverbs in *paragraph 1* that mean:
 a) definitely b) which cannot be avoided c) according to what some people say
8 Underline the main linking expressions in paragraphs 2–4.

Task 1: Describing a process

EXAMPLE ANSWER

Study the diagram on page 104 and the following model answer, then answer the questions below.

THE CARBON CYCLE

The carbon cycle is a complex series of processes by which carbon is repeatedly passed through the Earth's organisms, the soil, the atmosphere and the oceans.

Plants are a good starting point when studying the carbon cycle. They take in carbon, in the form of carbon dioxide, from the air through their leaves. Animals then feed on plants, absorbing carbon dioxide, which they later release into the atmosphere by breathing. When plants and animals die, they decompose and the carbon in their tissues is subsequently absorbed into the ground, where it can be used again by new plants and organisms. Over millions of years, fossil fuels such as coal, oil or natural gas can also be formed. Eventually these fossil fuels are burnt as a source of energy and, during this process, carbon dioxide is given off. In this way, the same carbon atom can continue to move through many organisms in a never-ending cycle.
(*155 words*)

FOCUS QUESTIONS

1 What is the purpose of the first sentence?
2 Circle all the expressions which mark stages in the process.
3 Why is the word 'First' not used in this description?
4 What is the main tense used in the description? Why?
5 Underline all the examples of the passive voice. Why is this used?
6 Which phrase introduces the concluding sentence?

GUIDED PRACTICE

Exercise 9 (Unit 10)

Task 1: Describing a process

Study the exam task on page 104 then complete the following model answer by writing *NO MORE THAN THREE WORDS* in each space.

PENCIL MAKING

Pencils 1 .... leads and wooden cases, which are combined together in the manufacturing process.

2 .... the production of pencil leads, ground graphite is first 3 .... with clay and water to make a dough. 4 .... the dough is ready, it is passed through 5 .... and emerges as a long thin graphite rod. This rod 6 .... into pencil-length pieces, which are allowed to dry. 7 .... drying, the leads are placed 8 .... and heated to 9 .... of 800 degrees Celsius.

Meanwhile, the pencil cases are prepared. 10 .... is sawn into wide slats and a number of grooves are cut lengthwise into each one. 11 .... a layer of glue is applied and 12 .... is placed in each groove. Another slat is **then** placed 13 .... , making a sandwich. **Finally,** the slats 14 .... into individual pencils, **before** being sent through a shaping machine 15 .... a smooth finish. The pencils now only require sharpening to be ready for use. (*164 words*)

Task 1: Describing a process

Read the following exam question and study the diagram. Follow the *Task Approach* on page 102 to prepare your summary.

Useful language

absorb	*emission(s)*	*lead to*	*radiate*	*(be) reflect(ed)*
release	*result in*	*subsequently*	*(be) trap(ped)*	

EXAM TASK

You should spend about 20 minutes on this task.

> *The following diagram shows how greenhouse gases trap energy from the Sun.*
>
> *Summarise the information by selecting and reporting the main features, and make comparisons where relevant.*

Write at least 150 words.

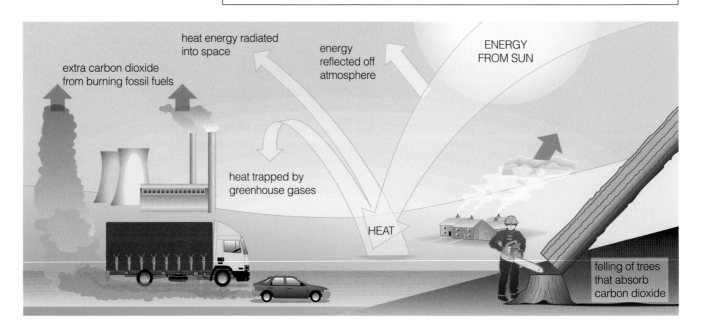

EXAM TASK

Task 2: Presenting and justifying an opinion

Read the following exam topic and then follow the steps below to prepare an answer.

> You should spend about 40 minutes on this task.
>
> Write about the following topic:
>
> > *Too much attention is given to headline- grabbing disasters like earthquakes and floods. Governments should concentrate their resources on educating people about the risks they face nearer to home, which can cost far more lives.*
> >
> > *To what extent do you agree or disagree with this opinion?*
>
> Give reasons for your answer and include any relevant examples from your own knowledge or experience.
>
> Write at least 250 words.

REMINDERS

1   **Analyse the topic:** highlight the key points you need to consider. Think through the topic by asking yourself questions such as:
    - What are 'headline-grabbing disasters'? What other examples can you think of?
    - How and why can the attention given to such disasters be 'too much'?
    - What methods can the government use for 'educating people'?
    - What are some risks 'nearer to home' that 'cost far more lives'?
2   Decide on your **overall response:** Do you mainly agree or disagree, and why?
3   Make notes of all the aspects of the topic you can think of, using a **mindplan**.
4   Organise your ideas in a **paragraph plan** for an evidence-led argument (see page 65) Review the example answer in Writing practice exercise 7 if necessary.
5   Write your essay, using a range of language to **express reasons** and to **link ideas** (See page 64).

Exercise 12 (Unit 12)

Task 2: Structuring an argument (thesis-led)

Read this example answer for the exam topic on page 122, then answer the questions.

Testing is a feature of most education systems but in many countries children are undergoing more tests and examinations during their school career than ever before. These are often imposed by education authorities in an attempt to raise standards. However, the results of this policy are quite often the opposite of what was intended.

A key problem with most tests is that teachers are required to follow a specific syllabus. This means that they are not free to develop a course to suit their students' particular needs, or to introduce different, more relevant, topics. In this way, good teachers are prevented from using their skills and experience to benefit their students as fully as possible.

Another important issue is that tests are stressful. They introduce pressure and anxiety into children's education at a time when learning should be an exciting and enjoyable experience. Excessive testing in the early years may therefore be counterproductive and actually discourage some children from continuing their studies.

A third point is that tests are not equally fair to all candidates. Those with particular skills, such as the ability to memorise facts or write essays in a limited time, are likely to perform well. Conversely, students without these skills may achieve disappointing results, no matter how hard they study or how well they know their subject.

In conclusion, while it is clear that some testing needs to take place in our school system, it seems to me for all the reasons mentioned above, that too great an emphasis on exams too early, is not only unhelpful but also potentially harmful for young learners. (*266 words*)

FOCUS QUESTIONS

1   How does the first paragraph, differ from the introduction in an *evidence-led* approach?
2   When would a *thesis-led* approach like this be more appropriate than an *evidence-led* approach?
3   What is the function of the middle paragraphs? What language is used to introduce each one?
4   What do the following refer to?
    a) These (*paragraph 1*)   b) this policy (*paragraph 1*)   c) This (*paragraph 2*)
    d) they (*paragraph 2*)   e) Those (*paragraph 4*)
5   Underline other main linking expressions.
6   What words or phrases are used
    a) to mean 'having the opposite result to the one intended' (*paragraph 3*)
    b) to introduce an opposite example (*paragraph 4*)
    c) to mean 'do badly in an exam' (*paragraph 4*)
    d) to summarise all the earlier arguments? (*paragraph 5*)

GUIDED PRACTICE

Exercise 13 (Unit 12)

Task 1: Describing data

Study the exam task on page 125 then complete the following model answer by writing *NO MORE THAN THREE WORDS* in each space.

The graph shows the percentages of boys and girls who were successful in their school leaving exams in the period from 2003 to 2004, by subject, Overall, pupils of both sexes **1** .... best in English, Mathematics, and science subjects, **2** .... Biology, Chemistry, and Physics. Results for boys and girls were roughly **3** .... in English, Mathematics and Sciences. In other subjects, **4** .... , there were some significant **5** .... Girls achieved by far their **6** .... in English, with a pass rate of **7** .... , which was **8** .... than the boys. The difference was even **9** .... in French, where **10** .... more girls achieved high grades. **11** .... subject where boys' results were better than girls was **12** .... where they achieved a pass rate of **13** .... , which was 10% higher than **14** .... for girls. In general, **15** .... that during the period in question girls performed better in most subjects in school leaving exams than boys. (*150 words*)

Exercise 14 (Unit 14)

Task 2: Presenting and justifying an opinion

EXAM PRACTICE

> You should spend about 40 minutes on this task.
>
> Write about the following topic:
>
> > *According to a recent study, the more time people use the Internet, the less time they spend with real human beings. Should we worry about the effect this is having on social interaction or should we see the Internet as a way of opening up new communication possibilities worldwide?*
> >
> > *Discuss both these views and give your opinion.*
>
> Give reasons for your answer and include any relevant examples from your own knowledge and experience.
>
> Write at least 250 words.

REMINDERS

- **Analyse the topic:** highlight the key points and think carefully about what you understand by each one.
- Decide on your **overall response:** Do you mainly agree or disagree, and why?
- Make notes of all the aspects of the topic you can think of, using a **mindplan.**
- Choose an appropriate **approach** *evidence-led* (see page 65) or *thesis-led* (see page 122) and organise your ideas in a **paragraph plan.** Review the model answers in exercises 7 and/or 12 if necessary.
- Write your essay, taking care to **give reasons** and **link ideas logically.**

Exercise 15 (Unit 16)

Task 2: Presenting and justifying an opinion

EXAMPLE ANSWER

Read this example answer for the exam topic on page 165 then answer the questions.

The last hundred years have seen rapid and dramatic developments in many areas, including medicine, transport, manufacturing and communications. Over that period our lives have changed in ways that our parents and grandparents could only have dreamed of, but the question we should ask is whether the world is a better place to live in as a result.

There have clearly been many benefits. Advances in medical science have brought cures for once fatal diseases and this has significantly extended the lifespan we can expect. Information technology has allowed us to contact friends or colleagues worldwide at the click of a mouse. We can now gather information, manage our bank account or shop without having to step outside our home. In addition, labour-saving devices such as washing machines and microwave ovens have made everyday tasks much easier.

However, the fact that life has improved in so many ways doesn't mean that all the developments have been positive. For example, the emphasis on acquiring the latest technology has made people increasingly materialistic. We also tend to lead more isolated lives than our parents did, with less concern for other people. The resulting breakdown of traditional social ties can leave the elderly and other vulnerable people without the support they need. Among other serious problems we face are the drug culture, and the ever-present threat of terrorism.

To sum up, we have made great progress over the last hundred years but there are still many important issues to tackle. This may well be a better time to live than any previous age but hopefully the future will be better still. (*268 words*)

FOCUS QUESTIONS

1. What approach does the essay follow: evidence-led or thesis led? How do you know?
2. What is the function of the middle paragraphs?
3. How is the conclusion introduced? What alternative phrase could have been used?
4. What is the writer's response to the topic statement?
5. Find four ways of mentioning examples, one in each of the first two paragraphs, and two in the third.
6. What words or phrases are used to:
   a) refer to 'the last hundred years' (*paragraph 1*)
   b) refer to the way a computer is controlled (*paragraph 2*)
   c) refer to machines that make it easier to do a particular task (*paragraph 2*)
   d) point out a possible false conclusion? (*paragraph 3*)

Task 1: Presenting and comparing data

GUIDED PRACTICE

The results of a survey are shown below. Equal numbers of men and women were asked the four questions listed on the left.

The letters A–E represent:

A Male driver under 25 years old

B Female driver under 25 years old

C Middle-aged male driver

D Female driver more than 35 years old

E Older driver (55＋)

male % female %	Ⓐ	Ⓑ	Ⓒ	Ⓓ	Ⓔ
Who is the safest driver pictured?	2% / 3%	6% / 11%	53% / 16%	33% / 62%	6% ✓ / 8%
Who is the most dangerous driver?	71% ✓ / 67%	10% / 5%	5% / 6%	1% / 0%	13% / 22%
Who is most likely to drink and drive?	70% / 68%	0% / 3%	23% ✓ / 22%	0% / 0%	7% / 7%

Are speeding penalties too strict?

YES 14% / 19%   **NO** 67% / 81%

Source: *AA Members Magazine*

UNDERSTANDING THE DATA

1 Study the table and answer these key questions.

1 What are the correct answers to questions 1–3? How do you know?
2 Which answers were given by men? How do you know?
3 Which driver did women think was safest?
4 Which driver did men think was safest?
5 Which question was correctly answered by both sexes?
6 Were men and women generally in favour of speeding penalties or not?

INTERPRETING THE DATA

Complete the example answer by writing *NO MORE THAN THREE WORDS* or *A NUMBER* in each space.

The results of a recent survey demonstrate that most people are
1 .... of the realities of gender driving habits and accident patterns.
Respondents of both sexes correctly 2 .... young males as the most
dangerous drivers. However, they were incorrect in judging older drivers as the
3 .... most dangerous, since this group is actually
4 .... on the road.

Interestingly, when asked about road safety, the respondents demonstrated a bias
towards their own 5 .... 6 .... of the men questioned felt
that middle-aged men would be the safest drivers on the road, while
7 .... of women thought middle-aged women were safer. Both groups
were 8 .... in thinking that young male drivers were the most likely to
drink and drive, 9 .... it is the middle-aged male driver who is most
likely to offend.

The survey also found that a large majority of men and women were
10 .... of the present level of penalties for speeding, with
11 .... women in particular agreeing. By contrast, less than
12 .... of either group felt that speeding penalties were too strict.

Exercise 17 (Unit 18)

Task 1: Comparing data

Study the bar graphs on page 000, then complete the model answer below, using *NO MORE THAN TWO WORDS* for each answer.

The graphs give information about methods of travel and **1** .... for **2** .... European countries, as well as the **3** .... figure for the European Union as a whole.

From the information, we can see that car use is highest in **4** .... at about 12,500 kilometres per person per year, and lowest in Spain and Germany. The Danish also make far greater use of alternative transport than people in other countries, travelling over **5** .... a year by bus, tram, metro or bike, which is almost **6** .... the EU average. By **7** .... , the British and French travel **8** .... a third of that distance by public transport and bike. When it comes to commuting times, British drivers **9** .... about 48 minutes each day travelling to work, which is **10** .... any other country. In Denmark and Italy, on the **11** .... , where many more people use public transport, commuting times are significantly **12** .... (*155 words*)

Exercise 18 (Unit 20)

Task 2: Presenting and justifying an opinion

Read the following exam topic and then follow the steps below to prepare an answer. Before you start you may want to look back at the guidance on pages 63–65.

> You should spend about 40 minutes on this task.
>
> Write about the following topic:
>
> > *The use of CCTV (close circuit television) cameras in streets, stations, shops and other public places has increased rapidly in recent years.*
> >
> > *Although we are told that these cameras help in the fight against crime, some people are opposed to their use. They believe that everyone has a right to privacy.*
> >
> > *What are your views?*
>
> Give reasons for your answer and include any relevant examples from your own knowledge or experience.
>
> Write at least 250 words.

REMINDERS

- Highlight the **key points** in the question. Think carefully about each one.
- Decide on your **overall response** and think about any **personal experience** you can use to illustrate your view.
- Make notes of all aspects of the topic you can think of, using a **mindplan**.
- Choose an appropriate **approach** *evidence-led* or *thesis-led* and organise your ideas in a **paragraph plan**. Review the model answers in exercises 7 and/or 12 if necessary
- End with a clear **conclusion**.

Exercise 19 (Unit 20)

Task 1: Describing objects

GUIDED PRACTICE

Look at the diagrams on page 205 and complete the following description. Write *NO MORE THAN THREE WORDS* in each space.

All the cameras shown have the same basic structure, consisting of a body and a lens. The Daguerrotype, 1 .... in 1839, was a large device 2 .... wood. It 3 .... three box-shaped sections with a brass lens 4 .... , and was about 36cm 5 .... Towards the 6 .... 19th century, the Kodak No. 1 was introduced. This rectangular metal box was 7 .... and 8 .... in design, measuring less than 9 .... of the Daguerrotype.

The first modern-looking camera was the Leica 1, which appeared in 1925. The camera body was much 10 .... than 11 .... of the Kodak, and it had a number of 12 .... along the top. Finally, in 2001, a credit-card sized digital camera became 13 .... Although only 14 .... of the size of the original Daguerrotype, it provided a 15 .... of technical features, 16 .... Internet access. Overall, the development of the camera has been one of decreasing 17 .... and increasing sophistication.

Exercise 20 (Unit 20)

Task 1: Describing objects

EXAM TASK

In the following task you have to describe a number of types of bicycle.

> You should spend about 20 minutes on this task.
>
> *The diagrams below show a number of different types of bicycle.*
>
> *Summarise the information by selecting and reporting the main features, and make comparisons where relevant.*
>
> Write at least 150 words.

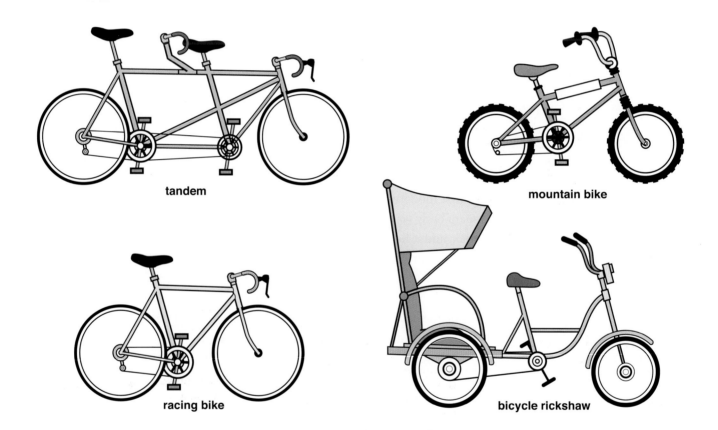

tandem

mountain bike

racing bike

bicycle rickshaw

REMINDERS

- Begin by summarising the common features and end with a suitable concluding sentence.
- Don't describe each type in detail – look for the main similarities and differences between examples
- You are *not* expected to use technical vocabulary. If you don't know the precise word, think of another way of saying it.

Answer keys and additional material

Unit 1

Lead-in
1 C 2 E 3 A 4 D 5 B

Unit 2

Lead-in
1 Healthy eating habits: a), c), d), e), h); Unhealthy eating habits: b), f), g), i), j).

Focus on writing 1
4

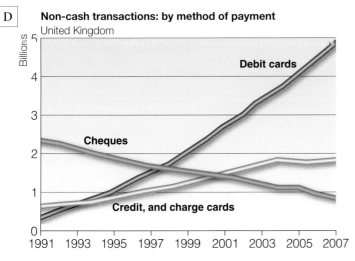

D **Non-cash transactions: by method of payment**
United Kingdom

Unit 3

Lead-in
City facts
1 Tokyo (35.3 million) 2 Rome
3 Singapore 4 Mexico City
5 Bangkok 6 Hong Kong

City plans
A Shanghai, China B Sydney,
Australia C Los Angeles, USA
D Amsterdam, Netherlands

Focus on speaking 1
2 1 year 2 15 3 second 4 twenty

Unit 4

Lead-in
2 **World Quiz**
1 B 2 C 3 C 4 A 5 Iceland,
Norway (Source: *UNs Human
Development Report*) 6 Greece (95%)
7 Japan (82.1 years) 8 South Korea
(2,423 hours per year per person)

Unit 5

Lead-in
1 Five or more 'Yes' responses mean you
live life in the fast lane and need to slow
down.
2 Singapore (1) Madrid (3)
Guanzhou (4) New York (8)
Wellington (15) Cairo (24)
(For complete list of cities see
www.paceoflife.co.uk)

Unit 7

Lead-in
1 men; women
2 Men; women
3 women; men

Focus on speaking 2
Student A

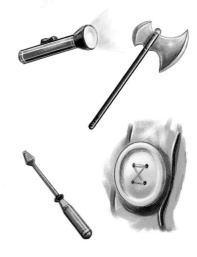

Unit 9

Lead-in

1	taking a bath	average 80 litres
	taking a shower	60 litres for 5 mins
2	washing dishes by hand (in a bowl)	average 5 litres
	using a dishwasher	average 35 litres
3	cooking per day	average 20 litres
	drinking	average 2 litres
4	washing the car	average 450 litres
	watering the garden	average 1,500 litres

Unit 10

Lead-in

Quiz

7–8 You're a thrill seeker and are not afraid of much in life.
5–6 You take limited risks but could probably afford to be a bit more adventurous.
Less than 4 You tend to play it safe but may be in danger of becoming stale.

Focus on speaking 1

3 Hazard characteristics in the following table are graded on a scale of 1 (largest or greatest) to 5 (smallest or least significant).

Overall Rank	Event	Length of event	Area affected	Loss of life	Economic loss	Social effect	Long-term impact
1	Drought	1	1	1	1	1	1
2	Tropical cyclone	2	2	2	2	2	1
3	Flood	2	2	1	1	1	2
4	Earthquake	5	1	2	1	1	2
5	Volcano	4	4	2	2	2	1
6	Tsunami	4	1	2	2	2	3
7	Bush fire	3	3	3	3	3	3
8	Landslide	2	2	4	4	4	5

Source: *Natural Hazards*

Focus on speaking 2

Probability of dying in any one year from various causes	
1 Smoking ten cigarettes a day	One in 200
2 Influenza	One in 5,000
3 Accident on road (driving in Europe)	One in 8,000
4 Playing field sports	One in 25,000
5 Accident at home	One in 26,000
6 Accident at work	One in 43,500
7 Floods (living in Bangladesh)	One in 50,000
8 Earthquake (living in California)	One in 2,000,000
9 = Hit by lightning	One in 10,000,000
9 = Wind storm (living in northern Europe)	One in 10,000,000

Unit 11

Lead-in

Memory Test: Part 1

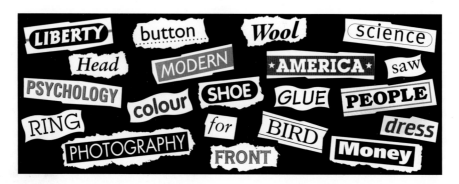

Unit 12

Focus on listening 1

1 True **2** False **3** True **4** False
5 True **6** False

Give yourself two points for each correct answer. Most accomplished listeners will score ten or more. A score under six suggests you don't understand very much about the theory of listening. The chances are you are missing a lot of useful information.

Unit 13

Focus on reading 1

A mobile phone **B** wristwatch
C book **D** fax machine **E** Internet

Unit 15

Lead-in

1 b) (*Sputnik 1*, USSR)
2 The first Moon landing (*Apollo 11*)
3 c)
4 b) Soviet cosmonaut Valeri Polyakov, on the Mir space station 1994/5
5 False (over four times as much, $45 million)
6 True ($31 billion is spent on tobacco products)
7 False (just one tenth of that, 28 tons)
8 True

Unit 17

Lead-in

1 1 e 2 a 3 h 4 f 5 d 6 c
   7 g 8 b
2 1 8,000 2 300 3 100
   4 50 / 8,500 5 7–12

Unit 18

Lead-in

1 (*Total visitors in millions*)
   1 France (79)
   2 Spain (58)
   3 USA (51)

2 (*$ millions*)
   1 USA (74)
   2 Germany (73)
   3 UK (61)

Figures from *The Economist Pocket World in Figures*

Focus on speaking 1

1 Adapted from results of a survey on fairer tourism carried out by VSO (Voluntary Service Overseas)
   1 b) (85%)   2 a) (80%)
   3 f) (79%)   4 e) (75%)
   5 d) (59%)   6 c) (52%)

Focus on writing 2

Example answers
   a) key features/significant trends
   b) facts
   c) 20 minutes
   d) twice as many
   e) introductory statement
   f) general trends
   g) clearest/best
   h) link
   i) picture
   j) compare

Unit 19

Lead-in

1 A fear   B anger   C sadness
   D happiness   E disgust

Unit 20

Focus on listening 2

1 1 A   2 A   3 C   4 Ronald Reagan   5 India (produces close to 1,000 films a year – twice as many as the USA)

Unit 7

Focus on speaking 2
Student B

Unit 11

Focus on speaking

Memory Test: Part 2

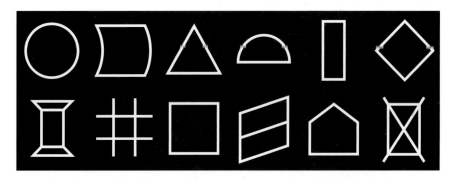

Academic Style

Academic Style 1 *Functions*

1 1 B 2 C 3 A

2 **A** (Example) **B** *Definition*; **main tense**: present simple (e.g. *refers to, functions, allows*); **key language**: *refers to, functions as* **C** *Comparison and contrast*; **main tense**: present simple (e.g. *reports, spends, spend, clean*); **key language**: *By contrast, less than a quarter, Both …* **D** *Describing a process*; **main tenses**: present simple (e.g. *takes place*), present simple passive (e.g. *are heated, is lost, are converted, are broken down*); **key language**: *First, During the … process …*

Academic Style 2 *Formality*

1 The academic English text is shorter and more formal in style. It begins with an impersonal passive construction to avoid the use of the word *people* or the personal pronoun *they*. There are no contractions and the text contains more formal vocabulary.

The spoken English text is longer and more informal in style. It uses the personal pronouns *I* and *they* to avoid passives, and includes more informal vocabulary and contractions. It also begins a sentence with *And* and asks a direct question to the reader.

2 … has made it increasingly difficult to prevent people from photographing subjects they should not record, for example, military equipment. However, now there is a system that can detect any camera phones and emit rays of light to distort any images they take.

3 1 Venus can even be seen …
2 Smoking … was outlawed …
3 A new galaxy … has been found.
4 The tests were repeated …
5 A nasal spray which … is being tested.

4 1 It is thought (by scientists) that …
2 It is now known that …
3 It has been found (by researchers) that …
4 … it used to be thought that …
5 It might/could be argued that …

Academic Style 3 *Nouns and Noun Phrases 1*

1 1 problems 2 trend 3 issues
4 activities 5 type 6 benefits
7 result 8 devices

2 1 fuel which is made from fossils (the remains of animals or plants which have decayed over millions of years) e.g. coal, oil. 2 a place where

people can go to play different kinds of sport. 3 someone employed by a TV station or newspaper to report on business matters. 4 a container in the street where you can put empty bottles so that the glass can be recycled. 5 surgery in which a laser is used to cut or burn the body. 6 a language consisting of hand movements instead of spoken words, used by the deaf.

3 1 information 2 university
3 computer 4 language 5 research
6 laboratory

4 1 rush hour 2 peak season
3 job satisfaction 4 arms trade
5 economy class 6 road rage

Academic Style 4 *Nouns and Noun Phrases 2*

1 coastal areas **of** Senegal the gradual disappearance **of** the mangrove forest (Subject) the quality **of** farmland (Subject) rising concentrations **of** salt a process **of** regeneration (Subject) teams **of** volunteers (Subject) an area **of** about 1,260 hectares. months **of** preparation

2 (*Example answers*)

1 … reasons, points, developments; *Health is one of the most important reasons for investing in good sanitation.*

2 … the course, the research, this policy; *The main aim of the course is to provide a basic understanding of Microeconomics.*

3 … flying, spiders, failure; *The course is designed to help people overcome their fear of flying.*

3 1 the severity of global warming
2 An accurate diagnosis of the disease
3 a dangerous dependence/dependency on oil 4 insurance against loss of income … unemployment 5 the intellectual development of children/children's intellectual development

Academic Style 5 *Hedging*

1 *may, some*. Sentence b), because it sounds more precise and carefully considered.

2 1 appears to be 2 sometimes, certain,
3 helps to, might (one day), some of

3 (*Example answers*)

a) It seems that olive oil may have a similar anti-inflammatory effect to the drug ibuprofen, which could explain why the Mediterranean diet seems to protect against cancer and other diseases.

b) The earth beneath our feet may contain 100 times as many species of bacteria as we thought. According to recent research, one gram of soil can harbour up to a million microbial species.

c) Skeletons recently discovered in Scotland seem to indicate that ancient Britons practised the art of mummification at the same time as the Egyptians and, furthermore, they may have invented the skill for themselves.

d) The floods created by Hurricane Theo are likely to create the perfect breeding ground for mosquitoes, which transmit West Nile virus, and it may be at least a month before we know the scale of the risk to public health. Conversely, it is also possible that the hurricane will have the opposite effect and get rid of the disease altogether.

4 (*Example answers*)

1 It seems that human activities are creating excess greenhouse gases which may lead to serious global warming.

2 It appears that the polar ice caps are melting at an increased rate.

3 It is likely that sea levels will rise as a result of global warming.

Academic Style 6 *Signposting*

1 First, that is, although, nevertheless. Second, therefore

2 **Addition:** + in addition, furthermore, moreover, similarly **Reason/Result:** + due to, as a result, consequently **Giving examples/restating:** + including, in other words, such as **Contrast:** + although, by/in comparison, on the other hand, in spite of (that), while, whereas, yet **Sequence/Listing:** + in the first place, then, eventually, meanwhile finally, **Summary:** + to sum up, overall

3 1 yet 2 therefore 3 because 4 for example 5 and; However

4 1 for example 2 However 3 such as 4 Furthermore 5 but 6 that is to say

Academic Style 7 *Attributive Adjectives*

1 a) empty b) particular/specific c) primary d) initial/final e) minor f) previous/preceding g) complex/complicated/difficult h) positive i) private

2 1 previous   2 positive   3 initial
4 complex/complicated/difficult
5 public   6 particular/specific
3 1 scientific   2 religious   3 rural
4 urban   5 agricultural   6 historical
7 human   8 industrial
4 1 good   2 right   3 important
4 good   5 special   6 important

Academic Style 8 *Nouns and Noun Phrases 3*

1 **a)** Greenhouse gas emissions threaten (to cause) temperature rises.   **b)** The greenhouse gas emissions (subject of the sentence) and temperature rises (object) are described using adjectives: *soaring, dramatic.* A reason for the increase in greenhouse gas emissions is given, using a relative clause (which are) *driven by … . India.*
2 greenhouse + gas; gas + emissions; coal + use; temperature + rises
3 **a)** snakes   **b)** an   **c)** unprecedented   **d)** the   **e)** disappearance
4 **a)** an open-pit coal mine in Colombia   **b)** to be the largest ever to have lived on earth   **c)** back 60m years   **d)** ruled the tropics …
5 **a)** 2 (Headword: bullion)
b) 4 (Headword: company)
c) 3 (Headword: cannon)
d) 1 (Headword: gun)
6 1 **energy companies**; **price reductions** (noun + noun combinations)
2 Natural gas, **believed** to be (past participle clause omitting relative pronoun and verb *to be*); **undesirable** by-products (adjective)
3 a **fast-reacting** electronic thermometer (compound adjective with hyphen); **with** a three digit LED screen (prepositional phrase)
4 **illegal** activities (adjective)

Academic Style 9 *Being Impersonal*

1 My essay; I'm comparing; I'm going to; let's (= let us) start.
2 **a)** report, essay, article   **b)** introduction, list, section, paragraph, conclusion   **c)** figure, graph, table, diagram
3 **a)** (Academic style 2) advised you; (This section) looks at **b)** and **c)**   1 **e)** will argue   2 **c)** shows; **d)** reveals
3 **b)** will be discussed   4 **a)** illustrates
4 (*Suggested answer*)
This essay is a comparison of two methods of producing energy. It will compare energy produced from fossil fuels such as oil, with what is called

renewable energy, that is, energy produced from natural resources. The essay will discuss two aspects of renewable energy production. The first section will focus on wind energy.
5 1 Governments should … 2 Houses … must. …. A house has to … . 3 The best way to … is to … 4 It is essential to …
6 (*Suggested answer*)
Energy is very important in everyday life. Compared with some other countries where it is very cheap, electricity in the UK is very expensive. It is therefore important to try to save as much as possible, by turning on the light only in the room that is being used, and trying to use the washing machine as little as possible, to save electricity

Academic Style 10 *Review*

1 **a)** feature   **b)** purpose   **c)** argument   **d)** process   **e)** main   **f)** information   **g)** impersonal   **h)** probable   **i)** modal   **j)** frequency   **k)** before   **l)** common
2 (*Example answer*)
There are a number of simple steps that office workers can take to help the environment. Firstly, all electrical appliances should be turned off at the end of the day, which will result in a reduction in energy use and costs. Secondly, the use of email can help reduce the amount of waste paper, as well as providing a means of accessing data and storing it safely. Finally using a video conferencing system such as Skype to contact colleagues and hold meetings, is a good way of reducing travel costs. A particular advantage of Skype is that it is entirely free to use.
3 (*Example answer*)
Bad waste practices are costing the UK at least £15bn a year according to a recent estimate. Although 70 per cent of office waste is recyclable, only 7.5 per cent on average reaches a recycling facility. Therefore educating your staff as to what can be recycled will not only help the environment but also save your business money. For example, recycled ink cartridges save natural resources and reduce the amount of toxic waste created. In addition/Furthermore/Moreover they represent substantial savings on the cost of new ink cartridges.
4 **A** is, is (1); find (2); is, are (3); is, generates (4)   **B** cause (1); advantage (4)   **C** major (1); difficult, important (2); impossible (3)
5 1 b)   2 b)   3 c)   4 a)   5 c)

Academic Vocabulary

Academic Vocabulary 1

1 1 c)   2 a)   3 e)   4 d)   5 b)
2 1 N   2 Vb (past participle)   3 N (plural)   4 Adj   5 Vb (past tense)
3 1 idea   2 carried out   3 places   4 earlier   5 showed
4 1 availability   2 maintenance   3 demonstration   4 participation   5 response   6 significance
5 1 in   2 by   3 on   4 in   5 to
6 *Incorrect words*:
1 ship   2 method   3 money
7 *Corrected mistakes*: benefits, research, physical, overall, depression

Academic Vocabulary 2

1 1 the (whole) community (N)   2 site (N)   3 My goal (N)   4 altered (Vb past tense)   5 promote (Vb)   6 trend (N)   7 components (N plural)   8 positive (Adj)   9 specific (Adj)   10 adequate (Adj)
2 1 A longer runway would enable larger planes to land.   2 The company was founded in 1822.   3 There are an estimated 1 million bicycles in Amsterdam. It is/has been estimated that …   4 Thousands of labourers died during the city's construction/the construction of the city.   5 It's an advantage to have overseas work experience/to have worked overseas.
6 There has been a decline in manufacturing output.
3 1 mental   2 physical   3 financial   4 legal   5 visual   6 medical   7 regional   8 minimal   9 global   10 environmental
4 1 suffers from   2 went   3 main   4 plays   5 covers
5 1 available   2 commence   5 maintenance   6 occur   7 purchase

Academic Vocabulary 3

1 1 (*Example*)   2 Adj, g)   3 Adj, f)   4 N, e)   5 N, b)   6 Vb, c)   7 Vb, h)   8 Adv, a)
2 1 inaccurate   2 unavailable   3 unaware   4 incapable   5 abnormal   6 unreliable   7 insecure   8 insignificant
3 1 abnormal   2 insignificant   3 inaccurate   4 unaware   5 unavailable
4 1 analysis, analytical   2 attachment, attached   3 connection, connected   4 emphasis, emphatic   5 interaction, interactive   6 requirement, required   7 stress, stressed/stressful   8 variation/variable/varied/(in)variable

257

5 1 emphasis 2 stressful 3 varied
4 interaction 5 analysis
6 attachment

Academic Vocabulary 4

1 1 A 2 C 3 A 4 C 5 B

2 1 summarise 2 finalise 3 symbolise
4 categorise 5 minimise
6 prioritise

3 1 Your password should <u>consist of</u> …
2 Some drivers <u>are</u> (completely) <u>unaware of</u> the rules …
3 Scientists have <u>made an analysis of</u> …
4 Students are expected to <u>participate fully in</u> discussions.
5 … said there was <u>no alternative to</u> a market economy.
6 Pollution has had <u>a significant impact on</u> many …

4 1 financial 2 consumer 3 global
4 credit 5 environmental

5 1 financial institutions 2 Consumer demand 3 environmental issues/ problems 4 credit cards 5 global view

Academic Vocabulary 5

1 1 resource 2 source(s) 3 economic
4 economical 5 prime 6 initial

2 1 prime cause 2 economical
3 Initial 4 natural resource
5 economic 6 source

3 1 achievement 2 consumption/ consumer 3 contribution/contributor
4 estimation/estimate 5 expansion
6 location 7 regulation/regulator
8 survival/survivor

4 A achieve, consume, expand, survive.
B estimate, regulate C contribute, achievement, consumption, consumer, expansion, survival, survivor

5 1 a decline <u>in</u> … 2 to participate
<u>in</u> … 3 <u>play</u> an important
role … 4 <u>environmental</u>
issues 5 <u>enabled the business to</u>
expand 6 <u>incapable of dealing with</u>
… 7 <u>financial</u> 8 alternative <u>to going</u>

Academic Vocabulary 6

1 1 B 2 A 3 A 4 B 5 B 6 A
7 C

2 1 from 2 as 3 between 4 in
5 as 6 for

3 1 <u>Running</u> your own business often <u>involves working</u> long hours / <u>If you run</u> your own business, it often …
2 <u>Despite the poor economic climate,</u> the company …
3 Many students <u>rely on</u> their parents

<u>for</u> financial support / … <u>rely on</u> financial support from their parents.
4 A <u>normal</u> working week (for most people) is 40 hours.
5 Many … <u>in this location.</u>
6 The translation <u>is not (completely) accurate.</u> Part/some of the translation is not accurate. Not all the translation <u>is accurate.</u>

4 A require (oO) B normal (Oo)
C construction (oOo)

5 1 purchased 2 occurred 3 response
4 impact 5 require 6 consumers

Academic Vocabulary 7

1 1 e) (Vb) 2 d) (Npl) 3 f) (Adv)
4 b) (Npl) 5 a) (N) 6 c) (Adj)

2 1 process 2 tasks 3 issues
4 equipment 5 incidents 6 items
7 medium 8 device

3 1 make 2 give 3 do 4 give
5 do 6 make 7 make 8 give
9 make 10 give

4 1 make an adjustment/alteration to
2 gave … demonstration of 3 do … research 4 gave … indication of
5 made … contribution to 6 gives priority to

5 2 appropriate 3 assistance
5 consistent 6 environmental
7 mechanism 10 specific

Academic Vocabulary 8

1 1 A 2 B 3 B 4 A 5 A 6 B

2 1 consistent 2 visual; visible
3 aspect

3 1 **in**accessible 2 **in**appropriate
3 **in**consistent 4 **il**legal
5 **im**precise 6 **un**specified
7 **un**stable 8 **in**valid

4 1 illegal 2 inappropriate 3 invalid
4 inconsistent 5 unstable

5 1 is a device <u>for recharging</u>; a device <u>which/that recharges</u> …
2 should <u>communicate (regularly) with</u> …
3 <u>make a slight</u> adjustment <u>to</u> …
4 … will be used <u>for/used to carry out/ conduct</u> an investigation <u>into</u> …
5 The psychological … of astronauts is <u>a major concern</u> (for experts)
6 <u>has</u> the potential <u>to</u> save …

6 1 stressful 2 contribution
3 emphasise 4 interaction
5 energetic 6 expand

Academic Vocabulary 9

1 1 A 2 B 3 A 4 A 5 B 6 A
7 B 8 B

2 1 have 2 make 3 give 4 make
5 have 6 do 7 reach 8 reach
9 make

3 1 achievement(s) 2 Creative
3 commitment 4 communicative
5 identification 6 perceive
7 interpretation 8 investment(s)

4 A statistics (oOo) B perception
(oOo) C significant (oOoo)

5 1 <u>There is an error in</u> … 2 <u>was founded in</u> 1900. 3 experience <del>in</del> overseas 4 test <u>consists of</u> 5 which <del>is</del> <u>involves</u> 6 Despite <del>of</del> the high cost …

Academic Vocabulary 10

1 1 c) 2 b) 3 e) 4 d) 5 f) 6 a)

2 1 features 2 exploited 3 enhance
4 precedes 5 equivalent 6 emerge

3 1 economic 2 principle 3 factor
4 structure 5 visible 6 constant

4 1 inaccessible 2 conclusion
3 emphatic 4 expansion
5 prioritise 6 responsive
7 survival 8 variations

5 1 insignificant 2 <u>are/give/provide</u> a good indication 3 <u>under</u> construction
4 <u>analyse</u> 5 <u>abnormal</u> 6 <u>involves</u> studying 7 benefit <u>from</u> 8 <u>have the</u> potential <u>to become</u> 9 <u>regulations</u>
10 <u>an estimated</u> <del>of</del> 600 million

Reflective Learning

Reflective Learning 1

1 (*Suggested answers*)
Good learning habits: 3, 4 (*see Reflective Learning 4*, p.147), 6, 8 (*see Reflective Learning 2*, p.67), 10 (*see Reflective Learning 5*, p.187). Less helpful habits:

1 Mistakes are an opportunity for learning. You can't make progress without experimenting.

2 It's important to have realistic idea of your own strengths and weaknesses and be able to set your own learning goals.

5 Guessing meaning from context is a valuable real life skill. The ability to tolerate uncertainty is important in academic study.

7 The overall mark is of limited value. Your teacher's comments represent really valuable personal feedback.

9 Everyone has different strengths and weaknesses. By co-operating with fellow students, you can both increase your skills and knowledge.

Reflective Learning 3

1 (*Suggested answers*)
1 C 2 B 3 C 4 A B

2 **1 Pronunciation**: sounds are shown using the International Phonetic Alphabet (IPA); the main stress in a word is shown using a mark before the stressed syllable; **Part of speech** (*n* = noun); **Grammar information** ([u] = uncountable).

2 learning process

3 (*Suggested answers*)

A (also called a 'spidergram') A diagram like this is a good way of organising and learning a range of topic vocabulary.

B A word card allows you to make a record of a word together with key information about it. Giving a brief example of the word in context makes it easier to remember the meaning and use. It's also useful to note the pronunciation, so you know how to say it, and its common word partners (collocations) so you know which words it combines with.

Reflective Learning 4

1 (*Suggested answers*)

1 B Errors are an unavoidable part of the learning process. They tell you that you have forgotten or misunderstood a language point and that you need to look at that area again.

2 If teachers tried to correct every mistake in spoken English it could take up most of the lesson, which would be discouraging for some students and boring for others. Similarly, correcting every mistake in written English, could mean that the work was covered with corrections. Accuracy is only one of the criteria used in assessing spoken and written English in the IELTS exam. Others include Fluency and Coherence, Pronunciation and Lexical Range (Speaking), and Content, Organisation and Vocabulary (Writing)

3 Errors matter when they cause a problem in communication. This can occur with serious errors of grammar, vocabulary or pronunciation.

2 **1** was; in   **2** has; the government   **3** Unfortunately; drug which   **4** have; over the last   **5** its; to   **6** people's; carelessness

3 **1** One of the major; …teachers is (to agree with 'one of the major difficulties')

2 people who believe; encouragement
3 However, completely unnecessary
4 It's; at an early age   **5** the worst; misbehave.

Reflective Learning 5

2 **1** 20 minutes   **2** 20 minutes
3 40 minutes   **4** 10 minutes
5 1 minute   **6** 1–2 minutes

Critical Thinking

Critical Thinking 1

1 (*Example answers*)
1 methods of communication
2 materials (e.g. used for making clothes)   **3** signs and symbols used in writing   **4** types of TV programmes
5 types of fuel   **6** (geometrical) shapes   **7** linking expressions/ conjunctions   **8** parts of a book

2 (*Example answers*)
1 voicemail (spoken, not written)
2 nylon (synthetic, not natural)
3 plus sign (mathematical symbol, not punctuation mark)   **4** soap opera (fiction, not fact)   **5** wood (renewable resource, not fossil fuel)
6 cubic (three-dimensional, not two-dimensional)   **7** and (expresses addition, not concession)   **8** index (usually comes at the end, not the beginning)

4 (*Example answer*)
Every activity will benefit from some degree of critical thinking. Those which call for the most active mental engagement, however, are probably 1, 2, 4, 5, 6, 8.

Critical Thinking 2

1 **1** Argument (evidence-led). Thesis statement = *The development … essential.* (Notice the use of the signalling word *therefore*.)

2 No thesis statement, so not an argument. Example thesis statement: *We need to support the development of wind farms.*

3 No thesis statement, so not an argument. Example thesis statement: *We need to encourage people to increase the proportion of fruit and vegetables in their diet.*

4 Argument (thesis-led): Thesis statement: *We need to protect the world's forests.*

5 A series of thesis statements but no evidence, so not an argument. Example evidence: Cars cause serious

congestion in many cities of the world; they cause air pollution, which can affect people's health; they use up our limited supply of fossil fuels; they produce carbon dioxide, which increases global warming, etc.

Critical Thinking 4

1 **1** hopefully   **2** surprisingly   **3** clearly
4 significantly   **5** a predictably

2 (*Example answers*)
1 it is possible that …   **2** it can be difficult to …   **3** it is ridiculous to …
4 that it was unlikely (that) …   **5** it is disappointing that …

3 (*Example answers*)
1 a **fairly/relatively** recent/ **quite** a recent   **2** **slightly/somewhat** delayed
3 **Only/Just /Barely** 45 per cent   **4** was **only** partially successful   **5** **Just** over a fifth

4 (*Example answers*)
1 contributed **significantly** to
2 **strongly/totally** opposed to
3 **highly/extremely** effective   **4** not **completely/entirely** clear   **5** **totally/ completely** contradicts

Critical Thinking 5

1 **1** Some people believe that …
2 (Nelson 2004)   **3** … according to Bill Gates
(Nelson 2004) is not appropriate for an IELTS task because it is a specifically academic convention. The details in brackets normally refer to a research paper or book, full details of which are given in a bibliography at the end of the piece of writing.

2 (*Example answers*)
1 As Gandhi said, …/Gandhi says that …   **2** According to …/As reported in …   **3** Newton's third Law of Motion states (that) …   **4** Some people think (that) …   **5** From what I've read, …/ Studies have shown (that) …

3 **1** claims C   **2** argues B   **3** reveals A

4 **A** find, prove, show   **B** believe, point out, report, say, state

5 (*Example answers*)
1 say/believe/claim (depending on your attitude to their ideas)   **2** have found/ shown that   **3** claim (that)   **4** says/ points out/argues that   **5** had proved/ shown/found
See also *Key language bank* exercises 12 and 33 (pages 219 and 233)

Key language bank

Exercise 1 (Unit 1)

1 1 d 2 c 3 e 4 h 5 a 6 g
   7 f 8 b

2 1 c 2 f 3 b 4 a 5 g 6 h
   7 d 8 e

Exercise 2 (Unit 2)

1 present perfect simple 2 past perfect
simple 3 future simple 4 past simple
5 present progressive 6 present
simple 7 past progressive 8 present
perfect progressive

Exercise 3 (Unit 2)

dramatic A gradual B limited B
marginal B marked A rapid A
sharp A significant A slight B
steady B steep A substantial A

Exercise 4 (Unit 2)

1 1 present perfect 2 past
   3 future 4 present 5 past
   perfect 6 past
   7 present perfect 8 past

2 1 has specialised / been specialising
   2 had lost 3 will see 4 receive
   5 did not exist 6 was jogging
   7 show 8 ceased 9 are doing
   10 is becoming/has become

Exercise 5 (Unit 3)

1 1 object 2 subject 3 the verb *be*
   4 the past participle 5 emphasis
   6 performs/does

2 A are located B is situated, were
   born C is devoted to to
   D is known

3 1 was first used 2 were produced
   3 were (being) sold 4 are required
   5 have been / are being destroyed
   6 be returned 7 (be) fed 8 used
   9 is eaten 10 is packaged

Exercise 6 (Unit 3)

1 further north, furthest north, etc., e.g.
   *What's the furthest north you've
   travelled?*

2 the furthest north, south, etc.;
   northernmost

3 Use *in* to describe the position of a
   place within a larger area. Use *to* to
   describe the position of a place which
   is outside another area.

4 Use capitals when the geographical
   word is part of the name, but not at
   the beginning of other nouns,
   adjectives or adverbs.

5 (Example answers) 1 in the
   (south-)west 2 in the north
   3 to the north-east 4 to the south(-
   east)

5 in the western part of the country
6 to the south-west 7 to the north-
   west 8 the northernmost point

Exercise 8 (Unit 4)

1 1 consonant 2 vowel 3 *further,
   furthest* or *farther, farthest* 4 *more*
   5 *-y* 6 *-er* 7 more than two
   syllables
   8 *more* and *most* 9 *better, best*
   10 *worse, worst*

2 1 largest 2 the most southerly
   3 longer than 4 highest
   5 most important 6 bigger
   7 heaviest 8 the slowest
   9 the wettest 10 the driest
   11 the most widely spoken 12 less
   13 more efficiently 14 greater
   15 fewer 16 shorter
   17 less stressful 18 more commonly
   19 the highest 20 fastest

Exercise 9 (Unit 5)

1 1 against 2 self 3 with/together
   4 against 5 opposite or negative
   6 outside/beyond 7 extreme
   8 opposite or negative 9 between
   10 bad(ly) 11 wrong(ly) 12 too
   much 13 before 14 again
   15 too little

2 1 An antisocial person does not enjoy
      other people's company; antisocial
      behaviour is behaviour that shows
      no concern for other people.
   2 a device which flies a plane without
      the need for a human pilot.
   3 to reduce or prevent the bad effect of
      something
   4 to stop someone taking part in an
      activity usually because they have
      broken a rule.
   5 relating to things that exist outside
      the Earth
   6 extremely fast increase in prices
      (which normally damages a
      country's economy)
   7 lack of attention/concentration
   8 depending on, or necessary to, each
      other
   9 a fault in the way a machine or part
      of the body works
   10 an idea which people believe even
      though it is wrong or untrue
   11 making something seem more
      important or serious that it really is
   12 to form an opinion about something
      before you know all the facts.
   13 to change the way a system or
      organisation is organised.
   14 not providing an organisation with
      enough money to do what is
      required

3 1 disqualified 2 overstatement
   3 counteract 4 malfunction
   5 restructure 6 antisocial
   7 prejudge 8 inattention
   9 misconception 10 interdependent

4 1 -ship 2 -ve 3 -hood 4 -able
   5 -iate 6 -ise 7 -ment 8 -ity
   9 -al 10 -ify

Exercise 10 (Unit 6)

1 the nation = the UK; These figures = a
   cost … of about £7 billion; much
   higher (than £7 billion); Its = stress;
   more profound (than it already is)

   what stress experts have long
   suspected = bosses suffer less …
   (forward reference); their = the
   bosses'; they = junior managers; their
   = the junior managers'; A similar
   situation (to that of the junior
   managers)

   The control factor = what is explained
   in the next sentence; those = the
   people; their = of those; That = what
   is explained in the previous sentence

2 My research into workaholism shows
   that the workaholic whose physical
   and emotional health suffers from
   working long hours was someone who
   wanted to be unavailable emotionally.
   They would find a way of being so
   even if they weren't in paid
   employment, perhaps by taking up an
   obsessive hobby. But people who work
   long hours because they love what
   they are doing are physically and
   mentally uplifted by their work.

   For unwilling workaholics, forced to
   stay at their desks for fear of losing
   their jobs, long hours can be a killer.
   For those to whom work is a pleasure,
   being forced into unsought leisure
   time can adversely affect their health.
   Such people, I found, were the ones
   most likely to fall ill on holiday.

3 1 don't 2 don't 3 that/which
   4 can 5 so 6 not / you can't
   7 this (problem) 8 he/she
   9 Another (idea)
   10 they / such/these activities
   11 it 12 ways / methods

4 **1** economy <u>where/in which</u> there; to leave <u>their</u> native land

2 a term <u>which</u> is used / a term used; The term; In <u>that/this</u>; Professor Schumann; stages <u>that/which</u>; <u>his or her/their</u> … assimilation

3 anyone <u>who</u>; <u>which</u> may; <u>Those</u> suffering (from <u>the condition</u>); <u>such</u> feelings as …/feelings such as …

Exercise 11 (Unit 7)

1 **a)** also, as well, furthermore, in addition, moreover

b) although, despite/in spite of, however, on the other hand, whereas/while,

c) as, due to, in view of, since

d) as a result, consequently, for this reason, so, this means that, thus

2 **1** also **2** due to, because of **3** in spite of/despite **4** as a result, consequently **5** while/whereas **6** In addition, furthermore **7** in view of **8** this means that,

Exercise 12 (Unit 7)

1 published **2** shows/reveals/indicates **3** findings **4** According to **5** emerge **6** carried out **7** showed/revealed/indicated **8** showed/revealed/indicated

Exercise 13 (Unit 7)

1 junk mail **2** market research **3** window shopping **4** customer service **5** opinion poll **6** chain store

Exercise 14 (Unit 8)

1 did so **2** this/that **3** those **4** one **5** This/That **6** respectively **7** The former; the latter **8** these/those **9** that

Exercise 15 (Unit 8)

1 **A** Type 2 **B** Type 1 **C** Type 3
2 The *if* clause refers to the past; the main clause refers to the present.
3 a comma; it is not followed by a comma
4 (Example answers)
1 If there hadn't been a hold-up … I wouldn't have been late for work.
2 Unless we take immediate steps, there will be further redundancies.
3 Provided that you cancel a reservation / reservations are cancelled at least … , there will be no cancellation fee(s) / cancellation fees will not be charged.

4 If there had not been ice on the runway, our flight would not have been delayed.
5 Unless I get more overseas experience, it will be difficult for me to further my career.
6 The professor agreed to come on condition that we put him up in a five-star hotel.
7 So/As long as there is a shortage of medical supplies, operations will have to be cancelled.
8 You run the risk of getting lost in the desert unless you go with an experienced guide.
9 If I had a computer, I could get through my workload twice as fast.
10 You won't get a table at the restaurant unless you book in advance.
11 If there hadn't been such a poor harvest this year, we wouldn't be facing the prospect of food shortages.
12 If interest rates hadn't increased, it would be easier for people to buy …

Exercise 16 (Unit 9)

1 **1** ND **2** ND **3** D **4** D
2 **1** which **2** which/that **3** which **4** which/that **5** whose **6** where **7** -- /(which/that) **8** which
3 **1** … pork, <u>which</u> is the country's …. meat, has doubled …. (ND)
2 … museums <u>which</u> charge an entrance fee have fallen. (D)
3 … parks, <u>where</u> fishing … are banned, have become … (ND)
4 … TVs <u>which/that</u> contain …. (D)
5 … Eisenhower, <u>whose</u> nickname …. "Ike", was …(ND)

Exercise 17 (Unit 9)

1 **Usually true**: Typically, As a general rule, By and large, In the normal course of events
Expected outcome: Inevitably, Not surprisingly, Predictably
Unusual/unexpected outcome: Paradoxically, Surprisingly
2 NB Any expression from the same group as the following is acceptable.
1 Not surprisingly **2** As a general rule
3 Surprisingly
4 Paradoxically **5** Inevitably

Exercise 18 (Unit 19)

1 clarity/clearance **2** completion **3** consumer/consumerism/consumption **4** desperation **5** destruction

6 emission **7** expansion **8** extension **9** inhabitant/habitat/habitation **10** opposition **11** proposal **12** provision **13** restoration **14** diversity/diversion/diversification **15** sustainability

Exercise 19 (Unit 10)

2 (Example answers)
The tornado resulted in the destruction of four towns.
Severe damage to six other towns resulted from the tornado.
Eleven thousand people were made/ became homeless as a result of the tornado.
3 **1** A heatwave in New York resulted in a 75 per cent increase in the murder rate.
2 There is a 50 per cent rise in traffic accidents in Geneva as a result of the Fohn wind.
3 The seven per cent drop in economic activity in the UK in 1962–63 resulted from the severe winter.
4 It has been estimated that global warming will cause sea levels to rise 18cm by 2030.
5 Recent coastal flooding may lead to an increase in insurance premiums.
6 Damage of about $16 billion a year results from worldwide flooding.
7 By 2030, warmer winters could cause snow to melt at many ski resorts around the world.
8 Arthritis sufferers' swollen joints can become more painful as a result of changes in atmospheric pressure.

Exercise 20 (Unit 11)

1 long → lengthen, strong → strengthen
2 **1** lengthen **2** shortened **3** widen/broaden **4** strengthen **5** hardened **6** lessens **7** deepened **8** weakened

Exercise 21 (Unit 11)

1 The **2** an **3** the **4** – **5** the **6** the **7** the **8** a **9** the **10** the **11** – **12** a **13** the **14** – **15** The **16** – **17** – **18** – **19** – **20** the **21** the **22** The **23** – **24** – **25** the **26** – **27** the **28** A **29** the **30** the **31** the **32** – **33** – **34** – **35** – **36** – **37** – **38** a **39** – **40** – **41** the **42** a **43** – **44** – **45** – **46** the **47** – **48** the **49** – **50** – **51** a

Exercise 22 (Unit 12)

1 take 2 made 3 take/do 4 give
5 draw make 6 done 7 set 8 plays
9 make 10 has 11 pay 12 took

Exercise 23 (Unit 12)

1 (Example answers)
  1 less likely
  2 more motivated; the faster
  3 more/faster; the more
  4 the more thoroughly; the better /
  more confident
  5 The further; the more similar
  6 The bigger / The better; the more
  detailed / the better

Exercise 24 (Unit 13)

1 Three most common verbs in -ing
  clauses: *being, containing, using*
  Three most common verbs in -ed
  clauses: *based, given, used*
2 1 concerned 2 involving 3 based
  4 containing 5 produced
  6 obtained/produced/used 7 being
  8 caused
  9 using 10 taken

Exercise 25 (Unit 13)

1 ✓ 2 I doubt <u>it</u>.
3 I <u>have any doubts about</u> / I <u>am not
sure</u> how 4 <u>There</u> is no doubt 5 ✓
6 <u>in doubt</u>. 7 ✓ 8 <u>have (some)
doubts about</u>.

Exercise 26 (Unit 14)

1 1 f 2 d 3 c 4 h 5 j 6 e
  7 i 8 a 9 g 10 b
2 1 edition 2 correspondent
  3 readership 4 journalist 5 copy
  6 broadcast 7 coverage
  8 the press

Exercise 27 (Unit 15)

1 1 adaptation 2 adjustment
  3 density 4 discovery
  5 disturbance 6 expansion
  7 investment /investor
  8 isolation 9 loss/loser
  10 recommendation 11 renewal
  12 survival/ survivor
2 1 survival 2 expansion 3 density
  4 adaptation 5 loss 6 discovery
  7 isolation 8 recommendations

Exercise 28 (Unit 15)

1 1 D 2 B 3 E 4 A 5 C
2 1 D 2 C 3 A 4 E 5 B
3 1 reaching 2 to change / changing
  (no significant difference in meaning)
  3 Sensing 4 to excrete / excreting
  (no significant difference in meaning)
  5 rendering 6 gain 7 suffer
  8 fainting 9 suffering 10 to see
  11 survive 12 encounter

13 To cope 14 to make
15 be used 16 to identify

Exercise 29 (Unit 15)

1 1 vision or sight 2 the sun 3 the
  stars 4 living matter such as plants
  and animals 5 the heart 6 (the
  study and treatment of) diseases of
  the mind 7 the mind 8 the teeth
  9 bones, joints and muscles
  10 drugs and medicines
2 1 **optical** illusion, instrument
  2 **solar** eclipse, panel, power
  3 **astronomical** telescope, clock
  4 **biological** clock, warfare
  5 **cardiac arrest**, surgeon
  6 **psychiatric** hospital, illness,
  7 **psychological profiling**, warfare
  8 **dental hospital**, surgeon, treatment
  9 **orthopaedic hospital**, surgeon
  10 **pharmaceutical industry**
3 1 psychological warfare 2 optical
  illusion 3 solar panel 4 biological
  clock 5 cardiac arrest 6 solar
  power 7 optical instrument
  8 psychological profile 9 solar
  eclipse

Exercise 31 (Unit 17)

1 car 2 tailback 3 ring road
4 motorway (in city) 5 motorway
6 petrol 7 number plate 8 car
park 9 railway 10 underground
(railway) 11 roundabout 12 caravan
13 public transport 14 subway

Exercise 32 (Unit 17)

A bottleneck, breakdown, collision,
  congestion, roadworks
B bypass, car sharing, park and ride,
  speed bump, speed trap,
C car jacking, hit-and-run, joyriding,
  road rage, speeding
2 1 breakdown
  2 collision
  3 speed bump
  4 bypass
  5 joyriding
  6 road rage
  7 car sharing
  8 park and ride

Exercise 33 (Unit 17)

1 A demonstrate, prove, reveal, show,
    support
  B contradict, demolish, disprove,
    (have) invalidate(d), refute
2 1 demolished/refuted/disproved
  2 invalidate(d)
  3 showed/revealed/demonstrated
  4 support
  5 contradict/ed

Exercise 34 (Unit 19)

1 ✓ 2 might <u>have become</u> … 3 We
must ~~to~~ try to consume … 4 could ~~be~~
disrupt … 5 ✓ 6 How <u>can we</u> be
sure … 7 will <u>have to</u> wait …
8 ✓ 9 <u>could not/were not able to</u>
10 ✓

Writing practice bank

Exercise 1 (Unit 4)

1 supply of basic services/the provision
of basic services
2 murder rate 3 level of traffic
congestion 4 air quality 5 *Para
1*: while, however, In the first place, In
addition, so also; *Para 2*: Although, also,
In addition and, 6 *Para 1*: <u>slightly</u>
larger, <u>significantly</u> higher, <u>much</u> safer,
<u>much</u> better, healthier, higher; *Para 2*: the
best, <u>by far</u> the largest, the safest, the least,
the lowest, the highest, relatively good

Exercise 2 (Unit 4)

1 It enables the writer to organise his/her
  ideas clearly and makes it easier for the
  reader to follow them.
2 *Para 2* provides further details of the
  first problem and suggests a possible
  solution; *Para 3* provides further details
  of the second problem and suggests
  possible solutions; *Para 4* provides a
  conclusion.
3 *Para 2*: **Topic statements**: People need
  … families; It is therefore essential
  … budgeting; **Qualifying statement**:
  However, as … homeless. *Para 3*: **Topic
  statements**: Waste disposal may …
  problem; the obvious answer … place;
  Qualifying statement: but uncollected
  rubbish … diseases.
4 *Para 1*: 2 sentences; *Para 2*: 5 sentences;
  Para 3: 5 sentences; *Para 4*: 2 sentences.
5 The pronoun "*I*" is not used at all.
6 it can be argued
7 *Para 1*: and, as; *Para 2*: Of these,
  However, which, such … as, while,
  therefore, and; *Para 3*: but, not only …
  but also, as, however, including, which,
  and, and; *Para 4*: which, However,
  unless,
8 It is therefore essential …; The obvious
  answer is …

Exercise 3 (Unit 6)

1 One represents the results for Men, the
  other represents those for Women
  2 England 3 The percentage of
  people who participate in an activity
  4 *Watching television* and *Spending time
  with friends/family* 5 Women (73%)
  (compared with 56% of men)